MORE NOBLE THAN WAR

More Noble Than War

The Story of Football in Israel and Palestine

Nicholas Blincoe

CONSTABLE

CONSTABLE

First published in Great Britain in 2019 by Constable

1 3 5 7 9 10 8 6 4 2

A CIP catalogue record for this book
is available from the British Library.

ISBN: 978-1-47212-437-1 (hardback)
ISBN: 978-1-47212-436-4 (trade paperback)

Typeset in Electra LT Std by SX Composing DTP, Rayleigh, Essex SS6 7EF
Printed and bound in Great Britain by Clays Ltd, Elcograf S.p.A.

Papers used by Constable are from well-managed forests
and other responsible sources.

MIX
Paper from
responsible sources
FSC
www.fsc.org   FSC® C104740

Constable
An imprint of
Little, Brown Book Group
Carmelite House
50 Victoria Embankment
London EC4Y 0DZ

An Hachette UK Company
www.hachette.co.uk

www.littlebrown.co.uk

Dedicated to the Sons of Jaffa Orthodox Football Club

Contents

Part 1

Part 1

Chapter One:

The Palm Court

The Palm Court was a scrappy little football stadium by the rail tracks in Jaffa, overlooked by a few tall date palms, hence the name: a sardonic reference to the grand salons of hotels like the Ritz in London or the Alexandria in Los Angeles, where dance orchestras played the new jazz hits under domed glass ceilings. The playing surface was usually dusty and dry, but the night before the big match, a winter storm blew in from the sea. The weather in Jaffa is almost always unseasonably hot, no matter what the season, but when the weather breaks, the sky turns to slate and the rain comes down hard. The stadium was laid out in what had once been orchards, beneath a long high ridge that had provided shelter for the fruit trees. The ridge was no longer much shelter, as new paved roads created a slick surface for the rainwater. The water cascaded downwards, too fast for the drains to carry to the sea or for the earth to absorb. At dawn, a construction crew began work filling the puddles and repairing the surface with barrowloads of fresh sandy soil. The old orchards were still designated as farmland under Ottoman zoning laws, though the fruit trees had been cleared to leave just those few stray, swaying palms. To the east there was a long row of tin-sided workshops. To the west, a breezeblock clubhouse known as the Maccabi barracks, a reminder of the Maccabi sports club's origins in 1905 as a kind of military boys' brigade.

This was 8 January 1924. Jaffa was the main seaport of Palestine and had been under British control since it was captured from the Ottoman Army of the Levant on 16 November 1917. The home side, Maccabi Tel Aviv, took its name from the new Jewish suburb on the hills above the orchard. The name 'Tel Aviv' combines an archaeological term for a fortified mound, 'Tel', with the Hebrew word for 'spring-time'. It was the building of the suburb that had caused the pitch to flood. The visitors were the all-conquering Hakoah Vienna, the football team of the Austrian city's Jewish sports club. With 5,000 members, Hakoah Vienna was not only the biggest sports club in Austria, but probably the largest in all of Europe. The team arrived with a ninety-strong entourage, comprising athletes and well-wishers. Their short Middle Eastern tour had begun in Egypt with games in Alexandria and Cairo, and would continue against British military sides in Haifa and Jerusalem, but the biggest crowds turned out for this all-Jewish game.

By 8 a.m., 1,000 people were waiting to greet Hakoah off the Egypt train at Tel Aviv's brand new train station. By the afternoon, 10,000 spectators had descended on the Palm Court – and the workmen were still struggling to dry out the ground. The crowd were held back from the pitch by British and Jewish policemen. Many clambered on the roofs of the surrounding barracks and makeshift buildings. The best views came from the single wooden stand, reserved for the local celebrities and dignitaries, including the grandest of all, Sir Herbert Samuel, the first British High Commissioner for Palestine.

The wartime occupation of Palestine had officially ended in 1920 when Britain's allies recognised British imperial rule over the country. Sir Herbert, a Liberal politician from a Liverpool family, was the first Jewish ruler of Palestine since the Roman era, something that had become a point of pride for the British and, indeed, Sir Herbert himself. He cut a dandyish figure at the football match in his tropical dress whites, the long white ostrich feathers on his helmet flapping in the winter breeze.

Before the game kicked off, the crowd was treated to gymnastic displays. Athletes paraded in white to represent youth, purity and the classical age of the first Greek Olympics. The original Maccabi had rebelled against Greek rule in the second century BC (*maccabi* means 'hammer' in Aramaic), so a cynic might feel the Greek allusions were out of place, but the club put on an impressive show. The girls in their long skirts, the men in slacks, performing star jumps and synchronised dips and bends, ending with the famous showstopper: a human menorah. This polished routine had been choreographed by the club secretary, a 24-year-old ex-soldier named Yosef Yekutieli who had served as a gym instructor in the Ottoman army. A photograph of Yosef taken in 1929 shows him in his Maccabi uniform, which resembles the dress whites of a naval officer. He and Sir Herbert would have made a matching pair on that blustery wintery day on the Palm Court. After the gymnastic display, the party from Hakoah Vienna – players, gymnasts, swimmers, wrestlers and officials – paraded beneath their blue and white club banner embroidered with the Magen David symbol. The Maccabi sent out a brass band, and quiet fell as the

Palm Court echoed to the first notes of the British national anthem, 'God Save the King', followed by 'Hatikvah', the song of the Jewish nationalist party, the Zionist Organization (ZO). The entire display was designed to resemble a state event, and Yosef held himself like a state official. His great dream was to lead a team from the Maccabi at the Olympics. He had pinned his hopes of Olympic glory on membership of the International Association of Athletics Federations (IAAF). Unfortunately, six months earlier, Yosef's application to the IAAF had failed because the association did not see how a Jewish sports club could represent the whole population of Palestine. There were 85,000 Jews living across the country, according to the 1922 census, or 11 per cent of Palestine's population. It was only in Jaffa and the surrounding district that the Jewish population had grown to be a real demographic force. The same 1922 census put the population of Jaffa at almost 48,000, of whom 20,000 were Jewish, while a further 15,000 Jews lived in Tel Aviv. The numbers continued to rise as construction work attracted Jewish workers from Hungary, Czechoslovakia, Poland and beyond.

At the kick-off, the teams faced each other in the classic foot-balling line-up: the 'pyramid' formation, comprising five forwards, three midfield players and just two defenders at the rear. The centre of the Maccabi's attacking line was Abie Wilson, a kind of young prince of the community. The 24-year-old athlete was not only a star sportsman, he also came from one of the wealthiest local families. Like almost all of Jaffa's original pre-war Jewish *Yishuv*, or community, Abie was Russian. A Russian sect named *Bnei Moshe*, or the Sons of Moses, had started building a community in Jaffa from the mid-1890s. All of the most important Jewish figures in Jaffa were connected to the sect. Abie's father, Shmuel Natan Vishnitsky, arrived in the port in 1910, after six years in the United States where he had acquired the new family name of Wilson. Shmuel was Jaffa's biggest building contractor, responsible for the line of mansions and apartment blocks above the Palm Court. It was his work crew that had struggled so hard to make the pitch playable. The freshly painted white lines, shimmering on the muddy ground, disappeared soon after Abie Wilson kicked off and the players began chasing the heavy leather ball in their equally heavy boots. The Maccabi kit had blue and white vertical stripes, resembling the strip of Argentina, or perhaps England's Brighton & Hove Albion. Hakoah also wore a blue and white strip, supplied by their manager, Arthur Baar, who owned a sports outfitters in Vienna. As long as no one got too muddy, the players and spectators could distinguish the half-and-half design of the Hakoah strip from the vertical lines of the Maccabi.

The 1920s saw the Viennese and Hungarian football clubs refine the basic pyramid formation, in an innovation that became known as the Danube School. In January 1924, the Danube School was in its infancy but the idea was to pull the centre forward back – an early version of the False 9 – and tempt the opponents to move up to meet the man they regarded as the main strike threat. This left space to their backs, which could be attacked with diagonal crosses. It was a style of play that depended upon a level of trust between teammates. The players needed to know the system, and believe the forwards would run into space to find the ball. In fact, not all the Hakoah players knew each other at all. The striker, Ernő Schwarz, had joined the team only three weeks earlier. But on a slow and water-logged pitch Hakoah did not need to play avant-garde football. They were faster, fitter and more skilful. The Vienna league had turned professional in the 1923–4 season, and Hakoah had the innovative idea of recruiting players from abroad. The state of Austria was not yet six years old, a product of the wartime disintegration of the old Habsburg Empire. Hakoah were not looking any further than the old Habsburg cities to scout talented Jewish players. Yet many German-speaking nationalists in Austria condemned the creation of a multinational team full of Polish, Czech and Hungarian Jews. Despite the disapproval, the Hakoah policy paid off immediately. Men such as Schwarz and the great defender Béla Guttmann, both from Budapest, turned the team into a fearsome side, moving quickly as they made short and accurate passes, and always looking for goals. Hakoah were relentless against Maccabi Tel Aviv, scoring five times while the defensive partnership of Guttmann and the goalkeeper, Sándor Fábián, easily kept out any shot from the Maccabi.

The IAAF's rejection of Yosef's application had been a blow to Yosef's dreams of leading a Jewish team at the Olympics. However, Yosef knew that the Fédération Internationale de Football Association (FIFA) offered another path to Olympic glory. FIFA was still part of the Olympic movement in the 1920s. Watching the Hakoah team demolish the Maccabi was far from demoralising. It proved inspirational. The match was a turning point. From 1924, the Maccabi began to pour resources into football that had previously gone into physical fitness drills and gymnastics.

The 1920s and 1930s were the decades of flappers, of youth and glamour, which celebrated the body beautiful. Hakoah produced many sports stars, such as the wrestler Nikolaus 'Micki' Hirschl and the swimmer Hedy Bienenfeld. The athletes promoted the club in photographic series, while the most successful and attractive worked as professional models: Hedy posed in her swimming costume while promoting cigarettes, as though to prove that fire and water could mix. Hundreds of photographs survive of the young men and women in the club's heyday, professionally posed, all confidently promoting the health and fitness lifestyle. The idea that sports clubs could help celebrate ethnic identity was on the rise across Central and Eastern Europe. The first European sports club based on an ethnic identity was the Czech 'Sokol', founded in Prague in the 1860s to boost Czech nationalism. Inside Vienna, however, not all Jewish sports lovers were comfortable with a Jewish-only club. Many preferred the socialist sporting clubs, or those with a mixed membership like Rapid Vienna or Amateure (which became the present-day Austria Wien FC), both of which included Jews among their founder members. Many of the sports clubs in Austria were adopting racist 'Aryan' clauses into their constitutions, however, which gave an impetus to Jews to join the larger and more successful Hakoah. Many Hakoah members joined for the social life; the dances were legendary and the club had Vienna's best dance orchestra, which was quite an achievement in the city of music.

Yosef noted the effort put into Hakoah's touring schedule: it was relentless. Hakoah aimed to be the world's Jewish team. The club not only wanted to deepen ties of friendship and solidarity among Jews everywhere, but also to represent Jews as their sporting ambassadors. The football team was the first foreign side to play an international in Czechoslovakia, and also travelled to play major European clubs such as Fiorentina and Olympique Marseille. In 1923, a two-leg match against London's West Ham United attracted a crowd of 40,000 in Vienna, where Hakoah earned a creditable draw. The summer return match at Upton Park brought a far greater shock: Hakoah won 5–0 in front of a large crowd that included the fanatical Jewish football fans of London's industrial East End. The West Ham team is said to have been made up largely of reserves. If so, it was foolish to underestimate Hakoah. The victory over West Ham was the first time an English side had ever been beaten on English soil by a foreign team.

Although Abie Wilson was the captain of the Maccabi team, it was something of an honorary position. The Maccabi were run by a player-coach, Shimon 'Lumek' Ratner. Lumek had actually played for Hakoah, though only as a sixteen-year-old junior before the war. He was the Yishuv's best player and, once his side was five goals down, his old friends in Hakoah allowed him to score a consolation goal for the sake of the team and the spectators.

The crowd surrounding the Palm Court brought out a few curious Palestinians, including a small, shrewd man named Issa al-Issa, the editor of the long-running nationalist newspaper, *Falastin*, or 'Palestine'. The sight of the Jewish Yishuv, gathered together in force, waving flags and singing anthems, led Issa to write a fiery editorial in the form of a letter to Sir Herbert. The British had banned both the Yishuv and the Palestinians from flying their flags or singing nationalist songs. The High Commissioner defended Yosef's pre-match entertainment, however, by claiming the songs and banners only represented sports associations. It was a convenient explanation, rather than the truth, as Issa knew.

In a roundabout way, however, the match had a positive effect on *Falastin*'s sports coverage. Issa expanded the number of sports pages, and launched a campaign for a national football league. The same year, his 24-year-old nephew, Daoud al-Issa, helped found a team to represent Jaffa's Christian Orthodox Church. The family were stalwarts of Jaffa's Christian community (*Issa* means 'Jesus' in Arabic). The team founded by Daoud in 1924 survives today as Sons of Jaffa Orthodox FC, still run by descendants of the parish priest of Jaffa during British rule. When Daoud al-Issa took over from his uncle as the editor of *Falastin*, he devoted even more pages to the sports news, and even introduced a dedicated football column.

The 1924 Hakoah visit changed football in the country, but it also had a huge impact on the politics. Everything in Israel and Palestine eventually comes down to politics, of course. As Issa al-Issa saw, football has an almost mystical ability to mobilise a city's population. What he failed to see was how transient this show of unity could be. Football also has the power to split communities, bringing buried antagonisms of class and nationality to the surface.

Exactly a year after their visit to Palestine, Hakoah Vienna returned for a second visit. On a fast dry pitch, they brought their real game – and it was breathtaking. Maccabi Tel Aviv were thrashed 11–2. The Maccabi boys were amateurs, playing the greatest Hakoah team of all. A few months later, Hakoah would win the 1925 Viennese league, becoming the de facto

Austrian champions. Like all great football victories, the goal
that made them champions came late – and was dramatic. The
goalkeeper Sándor Fábián broke his arm in a collision with a
player for the opposition Simmeringer FC. The rules did not
allow for substitutions, so Fábián bound his arm into a sling and
switched places with an outfield player. With Simmeringer
ahead 3–2, Fábián somehow bundled the ball over the line in a
tussle that levelled the scored at three-all. Hakoah had the
trophy. They were riding high, indisputably one of the best
teams in the world. But the sports fans in Jaffa and Tel Aviv
could not simply accept that the Maccabi team was so easily
outclassed. They wondered, instead, why the team had put up
such a poor show. How had they been defeated twice, by such
huge margins, on their own Palm Court?

Sir Herbert's colonial administration brought many Russian
Jews into government as civil servants, building contractors,
commanders in the new police force and town-planners. Yosef
Yekutieli's day job gave him responsibility for compulsory
purchase orders, buying Palestinian-owned land for the British-
funded electrification programme. From electricity, to roads,
to railway stations, the Yishuv was laying down the framework
for present-day Israel. Yet these achievements also fomented
grievances. Newer immigrants thought the Russians were guilty
of inertia and favouritism. The criticism was especially sharp
among football players. The youngest members of Maccabi Tel
Aviv came from the same cities as the Hakoah stars: from Austria
and Hungary, Poland and Czechoslovakia. Football was part of
the lifeblood of young men in these industrial cities. The sport
mattered to them in ways that it could never do to gymnasts and
drill instructors such as Yosef and his pals on the Maccabi's

committees. The anger began to grow over the summer of 1925, as the senior squad of Maccabi Tel Aviv undertook a European tour. The players received payments, amounting to a wage, which effectively professionalised the team. The tour took them to Vienna, where they played and lost against Hakoah yet again, before continuing around Czech and Polish cities. Back in Jaffa and Tel Aviv, many Maccabi members believed the most skilful players were stuck in the junior team, where they were being denied the opportunity of travel, fun, money and perhaps even glory. The junior team responded by resigning en masse and joining the sports association of the socialist party.

The youth team rebellion helped to create one half of Israel's present-day landscape: the Labour Party. The year 1925 was a watershed for the Jewish Yishuv in Palestine. The British government recalled Sir Herbert, and simultaneously imposed austerity measures, which brought the construction sector in Palestine to a standstill. The economy soured, Jewish immigration went into reverse. A year later, in 1926, a 27-year-old industrialist named Menachem Arber founded the Beitar sports association in Tel Aviv, the forerunner of the Likud Party. Arber had been a star football player as a child before the war, and was now the young boss of the family's cement business. He was also from a Russian family, and had known Yosef Yekutieli since childhood. But he rejected Yosef's obsession with the Olympics and international sporting associations. Instead, he wanted to return to what he saw as the original Maccabi mission: a fit, strong fighting force. In the 1930s, Beitar evolved into an underground terrorist cell that played a bit of football on the side. Indirectly, the Hakoah games fed resentments that would define both sport *and* politics in the new state of Israel.

*

Hakoah Vienna FC faded in the later 1920s and 1930s. In its later years, the club's stars were its wrestlers and swimmers. Micki Hirschl picked up two medals for Austria at the Los Angeles Olympics in 1932. Hakoah's champion women swimmers, Judith Deutsch, Ruth Langer and Lucie Goldner, were selected for the 1936 Olympics. When the summer of 1936 arrived, the three women chose to boycott the games, showing a strength of mind that was remarkable in such young women; Ruth Langer was just fourteen. They stood up to the Austrian Sports Federation with blistering letters that referenced the signs banning 'Jews and dogs' that adorned German swimming pools. In 1938, Germany and Austria were united as the homeland of the German people. Lucie Goldner's protests were remembered and she was picked up by the police. Her interrogation left her so badly beaten that she needed a doctor, who patched her up and left the back door open for her to escape. Lucie dyed her hair blonde and took a train to Berlin. On the train, she was recognised by an Austrian airman who gave her a gold Swastika lapel pin, telling her it would help her pass through any checkpoints. Lucie escaped carrying only her trophies, which she left at the Hakoah's sister club in Berlin. At Tempelhof airport she managed to board a flight to London despite having no passport. It was a Saturday, and on any other day the plane would have turned around at London and headed straight back to Berlin. Her timing ensured that she would be in England for the weekend, and when she recounted her story, the passport officials recalled her stand against the Nazis' Berlin Olympics. A sponsor was found to allow her to stay as a refugee.

Lucie married a Czech fighter in London. After the war, she walked across Europe with her child to re-join him, and the family eventually settled in Australia. As an old woman, with one leg amputated after a blood clot, Lucie chose to stop eating. She timed her death to coincide with the 2000 Sydney Olympics so that her mourners could attend the games after her funeral.

In Vienna, in 1938, the Hakoah football team was poised to re-enter the top tier of the Austrian league after years in the lower reaches. Their hopes ended as the new Nazi government closed down the club, seized its property and nationalised the splendid Hakoah building. Hakoah survivors were scattered around the world. Béla Guttmann had played football in the States, but returned to Budapest to take up his first coaching job. He won Hungary's Mitropa Cup in 1938–9 season as the manager of Újpest FC. In 1944, he was swept up with the destruction of the Jews in Hungary, but though his father and sister died in Auschwitz, he escaped from a prison camp. Many other Hakoah members made their way to Palestine, including Arthur Baar, the sports-shop owner. Baar briefly coached the Israeli football team after the creation of the state. Judith Deutsch became the Israeli swimming champion.

The story of the Nazi holocaust is what makes Israel's survival so important, illustrating its value as a haven, an insurance policy, or simply as the only country in the world where it is OK to be Jewish. This is Israel's external value, a worth that could never change. But it's not the story of Israel, at least, not the inside story. The idea of writing about football came about through a growing fascination with teams such as Maccabi Tel Aviv and Jaffa Orthodox, and men such as Yosef Yekutieli and Issa al-Issa. This seemed, to me, a better way to reveal an insider's account of the last century in Palestine and Israel. There may be many other ways to tell it, but the impact of a football match in January 1924 on the hard clay of the Palm Court was swift, dramatic and jaw-dropping.

Chapter Two:

The Young Ambassadors

I became a football fan in 2004 when I was living in Palestine –
though not actually a fan of Palestinian football, which made
no impression on me at all. I enjoyed life in Bethlehem, but it
was a tough year as the Israelis began to build a wall around the
city. There were soldiers on the street, and each day brought new
confiscation orders, which meant friends were losing their
homes, their land or their jobs. I was born in Rochdale, in Lancashire, but I was married to the Palestinian film-maker Leila
Sansour and she wanted to record what was happening to her
home town. I started to follow football because it was a way to
deal with homesickness, or so I told anyone who wondered why I
had suddenly become such a passionate supporter of Manchester
City. A couple of Bethlehem cafés showed satellite games and I
was able to watch the Premier League – so long as there was no
clash with a Barça match (Barcelona is the most loved team in
Palestine, and in Israel, too). Although Bethlehem sits on the
edge of the desert, the winters are cold. The café owners don't
much care for fresh air, so the windows were always tightly

closed, sealing me and the other football fans in a thick fug of shisha smoke. The metallic taste set my teeth on edge, while Lebanese techno drowned out the commentary. I knew so little about the game, I couldn't follow what was happening without the commentary so I often preferred to stay at home and read the live updates on the BBC or *Guardian* websites. Somehow, I had turned football into a literary experience.

I would read anything I could find about the game, not only strategy and team news but also gossip on wives and girlfriends, and transfer deals: the two memorably came together when Helen Dunne negotiated a multimillion-pound Golden Handshake for her husband Richard, Manchester City's captain. I pored over the predictions before the games and week-by-week learned that experts are nearly always wrong. William Goldman's famous dictum, 'No one knows anything', is even more true of football than of the film industry.

Slowly, I did start taking notice of Palestinian football. The players and teams of the West Bank Premier League were becoming more visible, thanks to the sponsorship of the mobile phone company, Jawwal. Photographs of players began to appear in supermarket adverts and on billboards. At the time, my brother-in-law Max was working in the PR department of the rival phone company, Wataniya, and he responded by sponsoring the Palestinian women's national team. The captain, Honey Thaljieh, came from Bethlehem and could be seen singing in the choir at the Nativity Church. For much of the past two years, the army had placed the West Bank under lockdown and the Palestinian football team found it impossible to play internationals. The Palestine Football Association responded by hiring yet another Bethlehem man, Nicola Hadwa, who lived in

Santiago, Chile. Nicola had little football experience, but an enormous Rolodex of friends and contacts. Soon the Palestinian football team was filled with Latin Americans who could get around Israel's travel restrictions. I discovered that the Chilean Premier League side, Santiago's Palestino FC, was created by Bethlehem immigrants in 1916. The names of the footballers on a 1920 Palestino team photograph – Saffie, Lama, Deik – were all familiar to me: these are the surnames of friends and neighbours in Bethlehem. Later, when Manchester City hired the Chilean coach Manuel Pellegrini, I was overjoyed to learn he had also once managed Palestino. I continued to follow Manchester City rather than local football, but at least I was aware I was missing out. I had attained that first, Goldman-esque level of wisdom: I knew that I knew nothing. Eventually I did something about it.

Football arrived in Palestine with the British. English missionaries reached Jerusalem in the 1830s representing a charity named the London Society for the Promotion of Christianity Among the Jews, or more commonly 'The Jews' Society'. This was the dawn of an age of liberalisation in Ottoman politics, known as the 'Auspicious Reordering', which allowed European charities and governments to operate in the Holy Land, after 400 years of pretty much tight closure. The Jews' Society aimed to re-establish the city's Jewish community, not out of altruism but in the hope it would bring the chaos and destruction predicted in the Book of Revelations. The society offered grants to European and Russian Jews who wanted to visit the city, and sponsored Ottoman Jewish families who were prepared to relocate to Palestine. The society built a church, Christ Church, near Jaffa Gate in Jerusalem's Old City. In the 1840s, Christ Church became the seat of Jerusalem's first Protestant Bishop, a German-Jewish convert named Michael Alexander. The Jews' Society grew to become an immensely powerful global institution, among the richest foundations in the world until well into the twentieth century. It has a complicated legacy. The longest-serving Mayor of Bethlehem, Elias Freij, was one of many Christian Palestinians educated at Christ Church school, which at the very least gave him an insight into the minds of English and American evangelicals. The Jews' Society still exists, under the name of the Church Mission Among the Jews, and enjoys the support of those angry Christians who obsess over other people's sex lives. In 2008, the society hosted a world conference in Jerusalem, in partnership with the Church of Uganda and a coalition of anti-gay American Episcopalians, to condemn homosexuality. The church continues to pray that Jewish nationalism will bring about world destruction, a position that successive Israeli administrations have treated with unlikely indulgence.

In the 1880s, an English vicar named George Blyth travelled through Jerusalem on his way back from a posting in India. He was over fifty years old and had been living in India for the best part of twenty years. Once in London, he reported that the Jews' Society was doing a disastrous job, alienating both Christians and Muslims alike in their attempts to convert locals, while spouting predictions of vengeance and destruction. Blyth was a man who believed in soft diplomacy, and the leadership of the Church of England was receptive to his message. In 1887, Blyth was made Jerusalem's Anglican bishop and after a decade of fundraising he started work on a new cathedral, St George's, which he built at the end of Saladin Street, as far from Christ Church as it was possible to get in nineteenth-century Jerusalem. In 1899, Blyth opened a school next to the cathedral. The little campus of buildings and gardens represents a flavour of Victorian England in Jerusalem. Old photographs show the distinctive Norman-style square tower peeping above olive groves. The city soon grew to envelop the grounds and today the school and cathedral are overshadowed by Israel's Ministry of Security, a vast concrete Lubyanka from where Israeli security forces control the city.

On a bright and sunny day in November, I got on a bus in Bethlehem and followed in the footsteps of earlier pilgrims to St George's School, the birthplace of football in Palestine and Israel.

The local bus from Bethlehem to Jerusalem takes fifty minutes to go five miles, winding its way through checkpoints and the settler bypass road to end its route at Damascus Gate. The bus station sits in the heart of the Palestinian side of Jerusalem, where the gate into the Old City connects the shopping district around Saladin Street to the Muslim Quarter. The bus station is lined by a row of backpacker hostels and shwarma joints. Three Israeli police recruits, two men and a woman, were leaning against a wall and giggling as they listened to music on a mobile phone. A Border Police truck patrolled the road. There were army snipers perched in the castellation above Damascus Gate. It was a busy midweek lunchtime and the streets were full, but I didn't see any civilian Jewish Israelis.

As I entered the school yard, I heard the smack of a football against brickwork and my heart simultaneously leaped (football)

and sank (school): a very physical illustration of cognitive
dissonance. Turning the corner, I found three boys playing
wallie. There isn't much to wallie beyond kicking the ball as
hard as you can, while reading the angles and keeping the rally
going. Like the best street games, it is difficult to see where
cooperation ends and the competition begins. The ball
skimmed the uneven surface of the playground, adding a touch
of unpredictability. I dawdled to watch as the yard emptied
around us. It was the end of the lunch hour, but the boys kept
playing, eking out the time between the bell and the next
lesson. Two were wearing school uniforms, while the third was
in a sports strip, which did not confer any clear advantage.

The school's principal, Dolly Namour, was in her first term
as head teacher. She had warned me that things may be a little
disorganised, and when I arrived the secretary didn't have me
on her list. A woman dressed formally with coal-black hair set in
the kind of style that requires an hour under a salon dryer, the
secretary eyed me from her high counter. Running a boys'
school in Jerusalem is stressful. Once the boys were outside the
school yard, you never knew if they were safe, she told me. The
Border Police target groups of youngsters, handing out beatings
and arrests. When I explained why I had come, she knew exactly
what to show me: a photograph of the original 1908–9 football
team, kept in a folder inside a drawer in Dolly's office. The year
is painted in both European and Arabic numerals on a leather
football held by a boy sitting in the centre of the bottom row.
The photograph includes a visiting team of older men, a scratch
team judging by their improvised sports clothes and cricket
caps. A tear across the photograph had been repaired more than
once, leaving overlapping shadows of Sellotape. Nevertheless

I was astonished by the clarity: the miracle of the old box cameras with their outsize glass-plate negatives.

The 1908–9 school team was the first standing team in the whole of Palestine, according to Yosef Yekutieli, who mentioned it in letters he wrote in the 1920s, and in a short history he wrote for a FIFA yearbook in 1932. I knew the team photograph because it reappears, down to the repair, in a work by the Palestinian sports historian Issam Khalidi. I was following in Khalidi's footsteps, greeting a holy relic. The school had no record of the names of the boys in the picture, and even after I cross-referenced with other photographs, most remained unknown to me. They wear dark sweaters and tarbushes – the conical felt hat often called a 'fez'. Two boys, including the one holding the football, wear the Cross of St John stitched on their breast. The crosses suggest that these two boys are Christians and, in turn, that the others aren't. The boy holding the ball has a relaxed and impish smile. He reappears in a photograph dated 1911, sat beside a boy with a pinched and anxious face, named Izzat Tannous, who became a well-known Palestinian politician in the 1920s and 1930s. A picture of the 1913 team contains Tannous again, still looking worried. He was from a family that had converted to Anglicanism, and at this time in his life he could be described as an Anglophile. The English ended up disappointing him, but his love of football never faltered.

Palestine grew in prosperity through the nineteenth century thanks to the Ottoman reforms. It was one of the first places to see package tours from the UK, marketed as both historical and religious experiences. Local Palestinians got into the hotel and import–export business, including a highly lucrative trade in religious ornaments that were sold with certificates of authenticity to prove they were manufactured in the Holy Land. The Chilean diaspora began life in Santiago, with Palestinians selling religious trinkets door-to-door, using this as the platform for other trading businesses. Palestinian communities sprang up across Latin America, but also in cities in Russia, Europe and even Australia. In Palestine, the rising middle class wanted their children to be able to speak the languages of their global trading partners, and by the end of the nineteenth century, Jerusalemites could pick from a number of competing European schools. The students were the children of merchants and industrialists as well as from the hereditary aristocracy of the city, known as 'Notables'. They studied alongside the children of the various consuls, adventurers, missionaries and romantics who were drawn to the Holy Land. Among these schools, St George's immediately stood out because it was a feeder school for the prestigious Victoria College in Alexandria, reputed to be the best school in the Middle East and inevitably known as the Eton of the Orient.

St George's was not the only school to offer a sports programme. The Ezra school, a German-Jewish school offering a secular education, already had a dedicated gym instructor named Abraham Goldschmidt. Unfortunately for the Ezra school, the generation of Jews that had arrived in Jerusalem under the sponsorship of evangelical Christians were extremely conservative. The Ezra school was ex-communicated by the local rabbis, led by the vocal Persian-speaking Bukharan Jews of Uzbekistan, who had been housed in their own splendid city quarter built by Christian charities. The Orthodox rabbis were appalled at the idea of physical exercise, and after their boycott the Ezra school struggled to attract pupils. The school relied on the smaller community of non-religious European Jews, as well as a sect of Yemeni Jews who had made their way to Jerusalem in the 1880s in the expectation that the arrival of the Messiah was imminent. St George's stood out from both the Ezra school and the Catholic De La Salle College because it offered a sports education to students of all faiths. This was deliberate: part of a philosophy that viewed sportsmanship as a way of building friendships across religious and ethnic divides. Football proved a perfect vehicle for this philosophy. It wasn't just a game: it was the country's first spectator sport, and its players were the community's stars, role models and ambassadors.

The turn of the twentieth century was the high point of British power. The empire was the closest thing to an international rule-maker in the days before the United Nations. The British imposed trade rules, acted as global judge and policemen, and offered a common language for business and law. A key part of the British success was a strategic tolerance for local faiths. The British tended to co-opt elites rather than destabilise them, reasoning that revolutionary change only risked undermining the empire. Where evangelicals such as the Jews' Society had blown the trumpet for conversion, the smoother empire men like Blyth favoured ambassadorship. Football was at the heart of his approach, captured in the ideology known as 'Muscular Christianity', which promoted sportsmanship as a means to encourage leadership in a multi-faith and international arena. The boys of St George's School were the elite of Jerusalem and in football they discovered a challenging sport that encouraged goodwill, foreign travel and meeting new people. It made everyone in the team an ambassador, which in turn reflected the boys' ambitions for their role within their country, and in the wider region.

In another age, the sport might have been cricket or rugby, but by the turn of the twentieth century, the teachers who arrived in Jerusalem tended to be football men. It helped that football is easier to play in a land where the soil is hard and compacted, and grass never lasts throughout a whole season. But the decisive reason that football took off in Palestine was its worldwide popularity, and the global infrastructure that had already grown up around it. Before the arrival of football, Palestinians passed evenings entertaining at home or in the city's coffee shops playing card and board games. Even today, it is easy to find smoke-filled cafés where men play complex rummy-style games such as tricks, tarneeb or pinochle, and backgammon, which draws on a long history of games such as shesh besh, mancala and tavle. Field sports are still popular, though it is difficult to go hunting or fishing when the countryside and beaches are under Israeli military control. Despite the long roots of other games and sports, football caught a wave of enthusiasm. It is was the perfect game for an age that had discovered the idea of the 'masses', the great crowds of young men and women who had moved to the cities, who worked long hours, yet had some spending money for entertainment as they strolled and shopped in the evenings. Football arrived at a perfect time for twentieth-century men with an internationalist mind frame and a desire to shape their country.

The rules of Association Football – swiftly abbreviated to 'soccer' – were drawn up in 1863 and became the basis of the international game after 1886 when they were adopted by the grandly named International Football Association Board (IFAB), composed of representatives of the four British 'Home Nations' and no one else. In 1904, six continental football associations met in Paris, along with an official from Real Madrid FC who was happy to represent the whole of Spain. The German association sent a friendly telegram. This meeting produced the Fédération Internationale de Football Association, which started life in a room borrowed from the French Athletic Association. By 1908, FIFA had an English president, the indefatigable Daniel Woolfall. This was the year of the London Olympics and Woolfall made football the centrepiece event, the world's first international football tournament. The 1908 Olympics surely encouraged St George's School to create its first team, soon followed by a team from Rawdat al-Ma'aref, which translates as 'Garden of Knowledge', a school established by Palestinian nationalists to offer a secular curriculum in Arabic.

The team in the photograph inside Dolly Namour's desk drawer travelled to Lebanon and beat the Syrian Protestant College, the school that later became the American University in Beirut. In 1912, the Protestant College team visited Palestine to play St George's and St John's, its sister school in the coastal city of Haifa. The Jerusalem fixture was enthusiastically covered by the *Falastin* newspaper. The photographs show a pitch that slopes alarmingly. The large crowd includes the students of the Alliance Israélite Universelle, which, like De La Salle College, offered a French education. The Alliance school was part of a Middle Eastern chain operated by a French-Jewish charitable foundation to offer a modern education to students regardless of their faith. It had started life in Algeria in the 1860s, which at the time was a French administrative *départment*. Alliance schools soon opened in Morocco and Tangiers and, in the next decade, Baghdad. The Jerusalem and Tehran Alliance schools opened in 1882. The Alliance school and St George's, one

French and one English, were regarded as the best in the city. The al-Husseini family, the most powerful of Jerusalem's aristocratic Notables, split their children between the pair. Jamal al-Husseini, a future politician, was a star player for St George's football team. His younger cousin, the future Grand Mufti of Jerusalem, Amin al-Husseini, watched from the sidelines with his schoolmates from the Alliance.

The graduates of the city's schools soon started their own team. The first adult club was founded in 1910, and existed purely to play visiting foreigners. The team sheet is a roll call of the elite families, both Muslim and Christian: Ballouta, Oda, Dis, Nashashibi and, of course, al-Husseini. The year 1910 was a high point in Palestinian national life. The Ottoman government had embraced democracy and Palestinian cities were not only electing their mayors but, in that year, Palestinians sent elected delegates to the parliament in Constantinople. Yet the Ottoman reforms took place against a backdrop of continual crisis. The empire was on a permanent war-footing from the 1890s onwards, fighting a series of nationalist rebellions across the Balkans. The situation worsened considerably between 1911 and 1913. The empire faced an invasion from the Italians in Libya and a rebellion by a Serbian–Greek alliance in Thrace, immediately followed by a revolt in Bulgaria. The Ottoman army began conscripting Palestinians, and thousands of poor Palestinian farm labourers died in foreign wars. Their absence from the fields brought crop failures and led to a devastating famine. Across the empire, the Ottomans lost a quarter of a million men.

The defeats and famines led to a 1913 military coup in Constantinople. A triumvirate of Turkish nationalists, collectively known as 'The Three Pashas', seized power. The Pashas ended the empire's experiment with multinational democracy and promoted a Turkish-first philosophy. Fears that Palestinians would follow the example of the Balkans and launch their own nationalist revolution led the dictators to clamp down on political parties and nationalist institutions. The *Falastin* newspaper and the Rawdat al-Ma'aref school, two of the most prominent champions of Palestinian autonomy, were shut down.

As Palestine's farmers were fighting Turkish wars in Europe and North Africa, the more prosperous families made use of their international business contacts to send their boys abroad. One of the St George's football players to leave the country was William Said, the father of the Palestinian writer Edward Said. Edward Said never knew much about his father, not even his real birthname. He was born in either 1892 or 1895. If it is the later date he would only have scraped on to the school's 1913 team before the outbreak of the First World War. William and his brother left for the United States, an unusual choice at the time as most Palestinian Christians preferred Latin America (the Said family was Anglican, which influenced the choice). Of course, when the US joined the war, William and his brother were conscripted anyway. They ended up fighting in France. Izzat Tannous and Jamal al-Husseini were both studying medicine at Beirut's Syrian Protestant College in 1914 when the war came to Palestine. The war changed Palestine – at first, it seemed, for the good and footballers such as Tannous and al-Husseini welcomed the arrival of their sporting friends, the British.

Chapter Three:

Gym Jews

The earliest photograph of Yosef Yekutieli, then known as Zusmanovitz, shows a serious-looking boy sat at the feet of his parents with a Torah on his lap. It is 1904, he is seven years old and the family are living in the city of Grodno, straddling the Neman River at the point where Belarus, Lithuania and Poland touch. Yosef was an athletic child but short-sighted, a trait he inherited from his father – along with ears shaped like jug handles. Yosef's father soon left his family to pursue a literary career in Moscow. Yosef and his two older brothers, Israel and Chaviv, grew up under the influence of their grandfather, a rabbi named Eliezer Yehuda.

Before 1904, there was still little Jewish migration to Palestine. Those who visited tended to favour cities with a biblical pedigree, such as Jerusalem and Hebron, or else the Galilee where exalted rabbis of the late Roman and early Islamic era are buried. The tombs of these rabbis – the authors of the earliest version of the Talmud – became pilgrimage sites thanks to the Russian eighteenth-century Jewish revival movement known as *Hasidim*.

The visitors and pilgrims were often poor. Many were elderly men who wished to die in the Holy Land; others were students who would return to their home country to work as rabbis. It is possible that as many as thirty-five thousand Jews passed through Palestine from the 1840s to 1900, but the number that stayed to raise families was far lower. They came on travel grants from Christian charities, or with the help of Jewish benefactors such as the English industrialist Moses Montefiore and the French financier Baron de Rothschild. Montefiore essentially created Hebron's small Jewish community by sponsoring Ottoman Sephardic Jews who were escaping a wave of Christian violence on the island of Rhodes. Montefiore also bailed out an American evangelical project in Jaffa, known as the American Colony, that had been set up to teach farming techniques to Jewish settlers. Baron de Rothschild bought farmland in the north near the Lebanese–Syrian border as well as to the south of Jaffa, where he established a vineyard at Rishon LeZion. The vineyard sponsored Jaffa's first Jewish sports club, the Rishon LeZion Gymnastics Club; founded by a Jaffa doctor named Leo Cohen around 1904. The winery, Carmel, continued to supply trophies for tournaments into the 1930s.

Jaffa's old town sits on a rocky promontory. The grid of limestone streets above the harbour has changed barely at all in the past century, yet it takes an effort to imagine what Jaffa looked like at the turn of the century. Jaffa was the port of Palestine, served by six steamer lines, French, Austrian, Russian, Anglo-Egyptian, Genoese and Venetian. Freight ships brought in heavy industrial machinery, luxury goods and even livestock, winched from the depths of the ships' holds. In return, Jaffa shipped Palestinian products back to Europe, Odessa and

Constantinople. The warehouses held countless paletts of the local Jaffa oranges, each individually hand-wrapped in tissue paper; crates of religious souvenirs from the workshops in Bethlehem; and sacks of potash and quicklime dug up from the shores of the Dead Sea. Passenger steamers and luxury cruise liners brought in pilgrims, tourists and migrants, while porters would swarm over the dockside ready to take visitors to guesthouses, or to the railway station for onwards travel to Jerusalem and beyond. The Jaffa–Jerusalem train began operations in 1890, shuttling back and forth on a single track, part of a spur from the great Hejaz railway. The Jaffa train offered a gateway to all the great Ottoman Arab cities: Damascus, Baghdad, Medina, Basra and Jeddah. Before the railway, there were barely 5,000 people living in Jaffa. By the turn of the twentieth century, the port city held around 19,000, of whom 2,000 were Jewish. The vast majority of these arrivals were from the Bnei Moshe sect, an eccentric religious movement that rejected the millennia-old authority of the Talmud. As a consequence, the Jews in Jaffa had little in common with the religious Jews elsewhere in Palestine. It was 1904 before Bnei Moshe's elders found a sufficiently sympathetic rabbi and hired the Russian Rabbi Avraham Kook.

The Russian population of Jaffa grew rapidly from 1904 as their home cities in Russia saw a wave of anti-Jewish violence. Most Russian Jews lived in an area named the Pale of Settlement, a vast region cutting a swathe through the empire's recently acquired Catholic borderlands: Ukraine, parts of Poland, Belarus and the three Baltic countries. The Pale of Settlement was the result of a toxic ethnic nationalism that led Tsar Nicholas II's government to move entire Jewish communities into Catholic lands, thereby creating zones of ethnic homogeneity in the areas inhabited by Russian Orthodox Christians. The government hoped to strengthen a Russian ethnic identity around the national church, while simultaneously weakening the influence of the Catholic church in its new provinces. The Jews not only experienced the destabilising shock of this early ethnic cleansing, but also brooding hostility and sporadic violence from the Catholic locals.

The first pogrom, however, was not in Catholic territory. The spark came in Kishinev in Moldova in 1903. Kishinev was a one-time Ottoman city that had become the industrial and financial powerhouse of the new Russian acquisition named Bessarabia. Kishinev had grown rapidly from almost zero in the early nineteenth century to well over a hundred and twenty thousand by the turn of the twentieth. The city was well-served by the nearby port at Odessa, which put it in easy reach of markets across the Black Sea and the eastern Mediterranean on the far side of the Bosphorus straits. The growing city attracted Jewish and Christian Russians in almost equal numbers. Kishinev was the home city of Dr Leo Cohen, later founder of the Jaffa sports club. In 1903, the anti-Jewish riots saw forty-nine Jews murdered and many hundreds injured. Leo Cohen joined an armed patrol in Jewish areas, and when he later created his sports club in Palestine he was as interested in Jewish self-defence as much as sports. The Moldova massacre led to a three-year wave of anti-Jewish violence across Russia, and the deaths of 3,000 Jews. This was racism at its most barbaric. As perverse as it now seems, the murders were linked to a demand for representative democracy. Many Russian democrats saw the ideas of liberalism and ethnic purity as interconnected: in order for a democratic nation to shape its own future, it first had to have some deeper soul: to first be a tribe or a family. The linking of democracy with ethnic nationalism had a profound effect on the version of political nationalism favoured by Russian immigrants to Palestine . . . and arguably still does.

The Zusmanovitzes were among 35,000 Russian Jews to sail to Palestine between the outbreak of the pogroms and the First World War, doubling the Jewish population of the whole country. The most popular city for new arrivals was Jaffa, the most dynamic and exciting city in Palestine. The Jewish population reached 20,000 by 1914. In the same period, the Arab population of Jaffa doubled, making it the country's biggest city. The Russians built rapidly and cheaply, rejecting Palestine's traditional stone in favour of mass-produced breezeblocks, from a factory owned by a local industrialist named David Dov, the head of the family that would later take the name Arber. Bnei Moshe's elders helped new arrivals such as the Zusmanovitzes to find their feet, offering loans, raising investment funds to back new businesses and selling them property. The elders also forged connections with the Jewish nationalist Zionist Organization led by Theodor Herzl, a journalist-activist based in Paris. Jaffa sent delegates to the ZO's biannual conference, usually held in Basel. Despite these links, however, the largely Russian Yishuv in Jaffa and the ZO remained separate. These were two streams of Jewish nationalism, developing along parallel tracks. Their isolation from each other would become complete with the outbreak of the First World War.

The Russians of Jaffa not only operated independently of Herzl's party, they kept apart from the Jews elsewhere in Palestine. As their wealth and size started to overshadow Jerusalem, they began to deride their rivals as 'Germans', because so many favoured the Yiddish language. They called Jerusalem the 'Old Yishuv'. Jaffa was the New Yishuv, a more forward-looking city. It was not just a cultural difference. Traditional rabbinical Judaism looks to the collection of wisdom, commentaries and folk tales of the Talmud, which were assembled in the Roman and early Islamic period first in Palestine and later in Baghdad. In the rabbinical tradition, the Talmud takes precedence over the Torah, the Jewish Bible. The Russians reversed this hierarchy, making the Bible the pre-eminent holy book. The leaders of the community often took the honorific title 'rabbi' even though they had little or no Talmudic training. Nevertheless, they believed they were doing God's work in returning to the Holy Land. They recognised their similarity to Western Christians and borrowed the Victorian evangelicals' innovation that the borders of Palestine were identical to those of the mythical 'Land of Israel' mentioned in the Bible. The city of Jaffa was retro-engineered as a sacred city, promised to the Jews, though it barely figures in the Bible, receiving only the briefest of mentions as 'Joppa', a city belonging to a non-Jewish people.

Evangelical Christians believe that our personal relationship with God is corrupted by the institutions and hierarchies of the established church. Bnei Moshe shared this suspicion of established religion. They believed they needed no external help to interpret the meaning of the Bible. They got on well with their neighbours at the American Colony, but they were even closer to a sect of Russian dissenting Christians known as Subbotniks, or Sabbatarians, who formed a substantial community within the New Yishuv. Before the Russian pogroms led to the explosion in immigration, the Subbotniks amounted to as many as one in five Russians in the country.

The Subbotniks were Christians who tried to live according to the precepts of the Old Testament, keeping the sabbath on Friday and following other self-interpreted Jewish practices. In Russia, the Subbotniks were reviled and condemned as apostates, suffering even greater official persecution than Jews. Once they arrived in Palestine, the Subbotniks knew there was no way back home and this made their commitment to life in Palestine total, and brutish. In the later days of the Ottoman Empire, rural farms in Palestine were plagued by gangs of livestock thieves, often described as Bedouins but including renegade farmhands who were avoiding the draft into the Ottoman army. The landowners combatted the rustlers by hiring armed Palestinian guards. The Subbotniks founded their own security company and touted for work by threatening any Russians who refused to sack the Palestinians and employ them. They took the name *Hashomer*, meaning watchmen. The Subbotniks' company forged a close relationship with a senior figure in Bnei Moshe, a landowner and real-estate agent named Yehezkel Sukowolski. In 1905, Sukowolski personally installed a young Subbotnik ex-soldier named Zvi Orloff as the head of the Jaffa gym club founded by Dr Cohen.

Zvi Orloff was one of six brothers and sisters who arrived in Palestine as adults, alongside their parents. Orloff was the last to reach Jaffa, as he was fighting in the 1904–5 Japanese–Russian war. When he met Sukowolski, he was working as an overseer on Sukowolski's farm in the nearby Jewish colony of Rehovot. Sukowolski was impressed by Orloff's physicality, military training and handling of local Palestinian labour. Sukowolski's teenage son, Moshe, was a leading light of the gymnastics club and at the time Sukowolski was looking for a new instructor for the club. Orloff assured Sukowolski he was the right man for the job. The idea of training youth in military-style callisthenic drills was growing in popularity across Europe, associated with the Czech Sokol movement and other ethnic clubs. The drills were adopted by Jewish nationalists under the term 'Muscular Judaism'.

Orloff was not the first person to bring callisthenics to Palestine. Abraham Goldschmidt of Jerusalem's Ezra school offered classes at his own sports club. After taking over the Jaffa club, Orloff asked for a grant to study German and Swedish callisthenics in Europe. (At the same time, his sister Chana Orloff was sent to Paris to study to become a school sewing mistress; she rebelled and switched to painting. She remained in exile in Paris, even during the Second World War, where she moved in the same circles as Picasso and the stars of the Parisian avant garde.) Orloff returned to Jaffa to declare that Swedish callisthenics were more suited to the needs of the New Yishuv than Goldschmidt's German version, as the Swedish exercises did not require heavy equipment and so were both flexible and economical. Rejecting the German system also served as another contrast between the New Yishuv and Jerusalem.

The Zusmanovitz family emigrated from Grodno in 1908, taking the train to Odessa followed by the regular steamer to Jaffa. Yosef's grandfather Rabbi Eliezer had been appointed as head of a religious junior school in Jaffa named Tachkemoni, named after a poem of moral instruction by a medieval Kabbalist. Yosef took to his new life by the sea. He was a popular boy, with a life that revolved around beach games and Orloff's gym club. Yosef met lifelong friends, including his two closest, Yehuda Dvorecki and David Todersovitz. Yehuda and David were both born in Jaffa, but their families also came from the Grodno region. Yosef took to the new sport of callisthenics, and I think I know why. I was also one of those active kids with bottle-bottom glasses, who found ball games difficult to the point of being demeaning, while excelling at gymnastics and drill routines (in my case, back in the Bruce Lee-obsessed 1970s, the sport was karate). Yosef was a natural at callisthenics, and his mastery of the sport shaped his life, both as an army instructor and later as an official within the Maccabi.

The New Yishuv was a project shared by the Bnei Moshe and the Subbotniks, with the aim of creating a living, Bible-based culture. Orloff staged a festival each year at the Sukowolski farm in Rehovot, and the first was witnessed by Yosef shortly after his arrival in the country in 1908. If Yosef was mesmerised by the festival, the correspondent from *Falastin* was utterly mystified. He described horsemen riding into the arena in lurid oriental clothes that looked like fancy dress: 'so you would have thought they were Arabian Knights'. The knights came from the Subbotnik security force, the Hashomer, and their costumes were modelled on the Ottoman army's Circassian cavalry. The programme included horse races, athletics, shooting and wrestling. The central event was a display of callisthenics by hundreds of children. Club members such as Moshe Sukowolski, Yehuda and David performed precision drills, ending with the human menorah, which Orloff designed personally to replace the more mundane human pyramid. In essence, the Rehovot games were a military tattoo, from the Hashomer cavalry charges and swordplay, to the synchronised displays of the gym students. Only at the final games of 1912 does football make an appearance for the first time, introduced by a new instructor at the club named Emanuel Gur Aryeh, who had embraced soccer while living in France. Yosef dates the arrival of football in the Yishuv to these games of 1912, but the event receives only a cursory mention in the Yishuv press as 'various other games such as football'. Its low status in the Yishuv contrasts with the love of the game among Palestinians in Jerusalem, where soccer was already a popular spectator sport.

I received a beautiful photograph from Yosef's daughter, Edna Kohen, taken in 1914. Yosef and his two best friends are modelling box-fresh football kits for the catalogue of the sports shop run by the Todersovitzes. The boys stand on a rumpled Turkish carpet against a painted backdrop. Yosef is not wearing his bottle-bottom glasses and is caught with a rare smile as he poaches the football from between David's feet. Yehuda plays the part of the referee, lifting a whistle to his lips. The wing collar on Yehuda's shirt is rather formal attire for a referee even in 1914. David is wearing his everyday black socks, which are held up with a comical pair of suspenders: he must have forgotten to bring a pair of football socks to the shoot. David was the natural leader of the three friends. He had lost his father when he was ten years old, around the time he and Yosef met. He lived with an aunt, while his spiritual and moral welfare had been placed in the hands of Yehezkel Sukowolski. David grew to be a streetwise kid, even something of a loudmouth. The Todersovitzes had been tanners before they branched out into leather goods and opened their sports store. In a photograph that Edna Kohen dates to 1913, the three boys are together again, tight friends, all wearing their sabbath best. Yehuda holds a straw boater on his lap, and Yosef wears a smart tarbush.

A rare photograph captures two teams before a game. The boys are posed in four rows in a roughly plastered room. Mediterranean light streams through an early example of a mass-produced steel-framed window. These are the 'barracks' built by the club at their Palm Court, beside the American Colony (now described as a German Colony, as German Christians had taken over the lease and built a church and guesthouse). The photograph was preserved by one of the players, Moshe Yatowitz, who stands in the second row with his thick hair almost-but-not-quite flattened into a side parting. Yatowitz, by then known as Maurice Yatt, rediscovered the picture in 1969 and made a note of all the names that he was able to remember. A label on the photograph dates the picture to 1913 but Yatt's memory may deceive him. Neither Yosef nor Yehuda are in the picture, which suggests it was taken after war was declared, when Yosef joined the Ottoman army and Yehuda found himself stuck in Russia and then Egypt. On the other hand, Emanuel Gur Aryeh returned to France to enlist in the army, and he is there sitting centre left and wearing a jaunty moustache. His brother Rehuven, centre right, is similarly moustached. Perhaps Yosef and Yehuda were simply not good enough to make the team, but another argument for a later date is that David looks two years older than in Edna Kohen's picture. He is sat cross-legged on the far left of the first row, a darkly handsome tough kid with broad shoulders, as cocky as ever.

The two teams in the Yatt picture wear similar shirts with three-inch vertical stripes, almost but not quite identical. Eleven of the boys, including David, have close-fitting collars. The other eleven wear open collars with points, and also have cadet stripes on the turnover of their socks. The football kit is likely to have been bought off-the-peg, and could very well be the Brighton & Hove Albion strip. The picture was probably taken to commemorate a match between two Jewish sides, though David is wearing a different strip to two boys from Jaffa, Menachem Dov and Asher Goldberg. Menachem sits beside David, a slightly younger child. It was the Dovs' cement factory that donated the building material for the clubhouse.

Unlike the early Palestinian teams, the boys of Orloff's club did not see football as an exercise in diplomacy: a way to reach out and make new friends. Where the English-educated schoolboys of Jerusalem looked outwards, the Russian Yishuv turned inward, only playing games among themselves. Yatt's photograph is a testament to this: the two teams wear almost identical strips. The New Yishuv built by landowners and industrialists such as the Sukowolskis and Dovs was a garrison community: close-knit, suspicious and protective. The Ottomans actively encouraged faith groups to live within defined city quarters. This was a practical measure at a time when civil law was administered by religious authorities, from marriage law to births and deaths. The Yishuv took this separation further, wishing to live entirely separately, first by building schools and clubs that excluded non-Jews, and later the entirely separate Jewish city of Tel Aviv. They were ready to fight to protect their private space. In their memoirs, both Yosef and David recall beach football games against the local Palestinians in Jaffa, but David also quickly segues into accounts of the club's street fights with the locals. On David's account, the boys of Orloff's club were always fighting, whether against local Arab boys or further afield against 'Germans' – meaning, of course, Yiddish-speaking Jews in Jerusalem.

Orloff can be seen at the centre of the Yatt picture, a thirty-six-year-old man with a bold, almost hostile stare and a neat military moustache. His sister Chana kept a family photograph album containing other pictures of her brother. One from 1919 shows him working at a desk in a military uniform with the same fixed stare and clipped moustache he wears in the football photograph. He is always so severe in pictures that it is a shock to find a picture of him as an eighty-year-old, looking relaxed and enjoying a joke. The photographs of the commander in his military dress, however, are not a pose. He saw himself, always, as a leader of a cadet force. One reason the club took up football late was that Orloff actively frowned upon any activities that did not directly promote fitness and discipline. The club only took up football under pressure from its younger members, impressed by the 1908 and 1912 Olympics, and at the instigation of the Frenchman Emanuel Gur Aryeh and his brother.

The Subbotniks largely disappeared within two generations as they married into the wider Jewish community. Their legacy, however, casts a shadow over Israel, revealed in a series of investigations into the massacres of Palestinian civilians. Again and again, those responsible share a Subbotnik heritage. Ariel Sharon was indicted for the Qibya massacre of 1953, and for the 1982 massacres at Sabra and Shatila refugee camps in Lebanon. General Raful Eitan was held co-responsible with Sharon for the 1982 Lebanese massacre. Police Commander Alik Ron was one of those held responsible for the October 2000 massacre in Sakhnin in the Galilee. The Subbotniks were brought up to believe they had no home except Palestine. With their backs to the wall they embraced the most ruthless tactics as a first response, the pre-emptive strike. The first significant outbreak of violence led by Orloff was not against Palestinians, however, but against Jews. The attacks were carried out by his two most senior lieutenants, Moshe Yukowolski and Isaac Silberman. The hostilities are remembered under the grand name of the 'War of the Languages'. The Russians' aim was to take over all the rival Jewish institutions in Palestine, predominantly schools, but also Goldschmidt's sports club, which had recently joined an Ottoman association named 'Maccabi'. Orloff's capture of the club led him to adopt the Maccabi as his own club's name.

Chapter Four:

The War of the Languages

In 1910, Baruch Yekutiel Zusmanovitz – Yosef's father – abandoned his literary ambitions in Moscow and returned to his family. He found a job as a Hebrew teacher at the Tachkemoni junior school run by his father, Rabbi Eliezer. The Tachkemoni was a religious school, and Hebrew lessons ensured the Yishuv's children would grow up with a knowledge of the Jewish scripture. The school was only a beginning point, however. The Yishuv hoped to revive Hebrew as the language of everyday life. This project required more Hebrew teachers. The problem was, Hebrew teachers tended to be religious scholars, and recruiting Jewish scholars was impossible as long as Bnei Moshe stood so far outside of rabbinical Judaism. The Yishuv's first rabbi, Avraham Kook, brought about a reciprocation with the rabbis, thanks to an ingenious theological judgement. He argued that just as the Torah comes to life when it is read aloud, so the ancestral lands of the Jews are a kind of forgotten book that will return to life if they are appropriated and spoken of in a Jewish way, meaning in Hebrew. The judgement ran counter to the views of the Orthodox community in Jerusalem where the rabbis believed Hebrew was too sacred for everyday use. Kook continued to be emollient, agreeing that anyone using Hebrew in a profane way was committing a sin. But by reviving an authentic Jewish way of life, these sinners were all the more in need of rabbis to lead them back to righteousness. It was not an argument that found favour in Jerusalem, but it slowly gained traction with the Jewish diaspora, especially in Britain and America. Kook had found a way of endorsing the Christian-style back-to-the-Bible theology of Bnei Moshe and the Subbotniks, while helping them reconnect with the Talmudic tradition they had abandoned (or, indeed, never knew). Kook had laid the groundwork for a new strand of Judaism that came to be known as *Dati Leumi*, or 'National Religious', the most popular form of the faith in modern-day Israel.

Rabbi Kook's judgement allowed the New Yishuv to start recruiting teachers, a matter of urgency as a Jewish high school had been built and was standing empty. Bnei Moshe had won a grant from the French Alliance Israélite Universelle to open a secular French language school. The school was built in 1903, but immediately the elders reneged on their deal and insisted the school teach in Hebrew alone. The French responded by pulling the funding. The Alliance aimed to provide children of all faiths with the best possible education. Teaching in Hebrew would not only alienate Jaffa's Muslim and Christian children, it would fail the Jewish students. As yet, there were no Hebrew textbooks, nor even any Hebrew words in most modern scientific and technical subjects. Hebrew existed only to preserve liturgy and scripture: it was a language frozen in time. The Alliance insisted that Hebrew could never be adapted to a modern curriculum but when they realised Bnei Moshe would never back down, they agreed to split the school property, effectively donating a school building to the Yishuv. In 1904, the year Avraham Kook arrived in Jaffa, the building was turned into two schools, one for girls, named the Neve Zedek, and one for boys. It opened in 1905 under the name Gymnasia Herzliya in honour of Theodor Herzl, who had recently died, quite unexpectedly, at just forty-four years of age. Zvi Orloff was the new school's sports master as well the sports club's director.

The War of the Languages was ignited in 1911, the year after Yosef Zusmanovitz moved up from the Tachkemoni to the Gymnasia. The war followed the same pattern that had proved so effective against the French. This time the opponent was the Ezra foundation, which was planning a new German college in Haifa. The foundation was informed it must teach in Hebrew, and reacted as the French had done, declaring it was crazy to use a dead language in a modern engineering college. Hebrew text-books were being feverishly produced at night by local teachers (Orloff was particularly prolific, publishing his own pamphlet-sized books on physical education), but it was an amateurish operation compared to Germany's vast and dynamic academic publishing industry. In 1911, it seemed obvious to almost everyone that German was a far better language of instruction in science and technical subjects than Hebrew. But the Yishuv soon had a major defector from the Ezra school: David Yellin, a senior teacher from one of the first families to be brought to Jerusalem by the Jews' Society in the 1840s. Yellin was not a native German nor a Yiddish speaker. He was not even wholly European; on one side, his family was related to the Sassoons, the great Jewish trading family of Baghdad. Yellin was a professional schoolmaster who had taught at the French Alliance before moving to the Ezra school. The local rabbis' decision to ex-communicate the Ezra school because of Goldschmidt's exercise classes threatened to ruin Yellin's career. However, Yellin did not join forces with Jaffa's Russian community purely out of careerism. He had a personal connection. Yellin was married to Yehezkel Sukowolski's sister, which made him the uncle-in-law of Moshe Sukowolski. Nineteen-year-old Moshe was a key agitator when the dispute over the new Haifa college turned violent. Moshe led the boycotting and picketing of the Ezra school, and, in a choreographed move, Yellin resigned to open his own Hebrew-language teacher training college, known hereafter as the David Yellin College.

Yosef's brother Chaviv Zusmanovitz was at the Ezra school in Jerusalem when the War of the Languages broke out. He was at the forefront of all the action, helping to organise the strikes that closed the college. Moshe Sukowolski's boys from Orloff's club acted as flying pickets, arriving on the train. They did not simply blockade the school, however. David Todersovitz and his friends formed 'language patrols' and roamed the city in gangs threatening anyone they heard speaking Yiddish or German with the command: 'Jew, speak Hebrew.' The language patrols could be armed: Orloff had raised fifty pounds from Bnei Moshe to buy rifles, which he supplied to Isaac Silberman. His loyal lieutenant headed a team responsible for break-ins and vandalism in Ezra schools. With all the firepower in the hands of the Russians, it was a foregone conclusion that they would win out against the Germans.

The Germans gave way, just as the French had done. The Technical College in Haifa opened as a Hebrew-language school, employing Russian-born instructors. In Jerusalem, the

David Yellin College eclipsed the old Ezra school. The War of the Languages had been as much about a Sukowolski family take-over of the Ezra outfit as a Russian–German sectarian skirmish. Yosef Zusmanovitz had his own personal connection to the family; his oldest brother, Israel, had married Yehezkel Sukowolski's daughter. When Yosef graduated from the Herzliya school in 1913 he followed his brother Chaviv to David Yellin's college.

The War of the Languages gave the New Yishuv a reach and authority far beyond their Jaffa base. They were turning into a national force, which gave Orloff and Moshe Sukowolski the chance to assume the leadership of Jewish sports in Palestine. Goldschmidt's original Jerusalem club also had close ties to the Hashomer, through another Subbotnik named Alexander Zaid, who was prominent in both. Unlike Jaffa's club, the Jerusalem club was overtly political. Its members, a mix of Germans, Russians and Yemenis, leaned towards the fledging Jewish Workers Party, and disdained Russian bosses and factory owners such as the Sukowolskis. The Jerusalem club was already a member of a Constantinople-based Jewish federation named 'Maccabi'. Orloff and Moshe Sukowolski performed a kind of reverse take-over by forming their own Maccabi Union and posing as the umbrella organisation of all the country's Jewish sports clubs. In 1912, they renamed their club Maccabi Tel Aviv, and formed new clubs named Maccabi Petah Tikvah, and Maccabi Rishon LeZion. They listed Goldschmidt's club as 'Maccabi Jerusalem'. The two men had to move quickly because the year 1912 saw an international meeting of Jewish sports clubs in Berlin. Orloff and Moshe Sukowolski attended the convention as the Palestinian representatives.

The period defined as the War of the Languages saw the Russians renounce their existing family names in favour of newly coined Hebrew surnames. The change was not simply cosmetic. The Russians were applying for Ottoman citizenship and these new names appeared on their Ottoman passports. There were practical reasons for the change. Only Ottoman citizens could own property in Palestine, which made it impossible for foreign foundations and speculators to invest in land and rental properties. Yehezkel Sukowolski became Yehezkel Danin, his son Moshe Danin. The new nationality allowed the Danins to legally control a large land fund, which was run on behalf of foreign investors, notably Baron de Rothschild. Prior to becoming an Ottoman citizen, Danin had been forced to find other ruses, including buying property in the name of the Yellins, his in-laws, who had been Ottoman citizens for a generation. Much of the land that would become Tel Aviv was held in David Yellin's name. Danin's holdings ultimately became the basis of the Jewish National Fund, a national corporation that today owns 90 per cent of the land in Israel.

Yosef Zusmanovitz became Yosef Yekutieli, taking his father's middle name. Menachem Dov's family became the Arbers. David Todersovitz became David Tidhar. Their friend Yehuda Dvorecki became Yehuda Hezroni. Zvi Orloff became Zvi Nishri. His lieutenant Isaac Silberman took the name Meir Caspi. Adopting citizenship meant that boys such as David and Yosef were liable for conscription but few seem to have regarded this as a problem. Where their Palestinian counterparts had found excuses to travel abroad (or simply hid in the hills), the Russian boys volunteered for officer training: 120 boys from the Gymnasia Herzliya went on to officer training in Constantinople.

When war broke out, Ottoman citizenship brought an extra layer of security because Russians risked deportation as enemy aliens. Yehuda Hezroni was unlucky. He had been visiting family in Russia when the Ottoman navy brought the empire into the war, so he found himself banned, as an enemy national, from re-entering Palestine. He ended up living in British-occupied Cairo. The Egyptian capital hosted a sizeable outpost, with a community of 6,000 from the Yishuv. Yosef Yekutieli followed his brother Chaviv into the army where he was employed as a gym instructor at the Ottoman army barracks in Nablus. David Tidhar chose to avoid military service, taking a job as a lumberjack, a reserved occupation, which allowed him to avoid the draft. Moshe Danin became a quartermaster, supplying food to Ottoman troops in Palestine. Menachem Arber was perhaps the most fortunate: he was stationed in Jaffa where, according to David Tidhar, he became a football instructor.

Chapter Five:

British Promises

The best-known old boys of St George's football team, Izzat Tannous and Jamal al-Husseini, became famous as politicians rather than as footballers. In 1914, when war broke out, they were both aspiring doctors at Beirut's Syrian Protestant College, the future American University.

As early as July 1914, the British were anticipating a war against Germany. The height of summer saw the Royal Navy shadow a German battlecruiser, the SMS *Goeben*, around the Mediterranean. The German ship was lost, re-found at port in Italy, and then pursued to the Ottoman capital of Constantinople. As war was declared, the Royal Navy ships waited in the Bosphorus straits, confident the *Goeben* was at their mercy. The Ottoman port was neutral territory but the British could sink the *Goeben* the moment it took to sea. To their amazement, however, the lookouts saw the enemy sailors appear on deck and switch their sailor caps for tarbushes, then hoist and salute the Ottoman flag. The *Goeben* had been officially renamed the *Yavuz Sultan Selim*, and the German sailors had taken Ottoman nationality. As the Ottoman national anthem carried over the water, the German sailors stood to attention, before breaking off to wave at the British ships, taunting them that there was nothing they could now do.

The Turkish dictators kept the Ottoman Empire officially neutral until October 1914, when the new *Yavuz Sultan Selim* shelled Russia's Black Sea coast. It was a pre-emptive strike, in its way comparable to Pearl Harbor, and it brought the Ottomans into the war on Germany's side. In retrospect, this was a disastrous decision, and the ship's German commanding officer, Admiral Wilhelm Souchon, may have acted unilaterally. Yet the attack had a compelling logic. The Ottoman Empire had been at war since the 1890s, and continued to face enemies on all sides: the Greeks, Serbians, Russians, as well as Italy and the Austro-Hungarian Empire. The greatest threats all came from European powers, and by standing alongside the Germans, the Pashas hoped to neutralise, squeeze or simply scare off their foes. After a generation of damaging wars, they had every reason to believe a partnership with Germany would buy stability on their borders.

The Ottoman forces in the Levant, the 4th Army, was head-quartered in Damascus under the command of Djemal Pasha, one of the three Turkish dictators. Djemal led a crackdown on the Arabic literature clubs that functioned as proxy organisations for local nationalists. The clubs were particularly active in the universities. Djemal immediately placed the Protestant College under military law and in 1915 the army hanged four medical students suspected of being members of a secret political society named al-Fatat (*Jam'iyat al-'Arabiya al-Fatat*, the Young Arab Society), which was led by Palestinians. Jamal al-Husseini was a member of his family's rival nationalist society, al-Muntada al-Adabi (the Arab Literary Society). As the crackdown intensified, al-Husseini abandoned his studies in Beirut and fled to Jerusalem. Once at home, he was immediately conscripted into the Ottoman army along with his younger cousin Amin. Izzat Tannous remained at the university, where he finished his medical studies.

In early 1915, Maccabi Tel Aviv played a football match against the Ottoman soldiers in the local barracks. The game was a fundraiser for the Ottoman war effort, organised by the head of the Tel Aviv building committee, Meir Dizengoff. A year earlier, the Ottoman army had lost two aeroplanes in test flights over Palestine, one in the high country of the Galilee and the other in Jaffa's bay. Dizengoff made a flamboyant declaration that the Jewish community would buy the army a new plane and Jaffa's Ottoman governor wasted no time in reminding him of his promise. In an indication of football's status as the sport of international friendship, Dizengoff suggested a football match between the Maccabi boys and the local garrison.

Most of the stories of the early days of football in the Yishuv come from David Tidhar, an energetic storyteller of wild schemes and street brawls. A flavour of his unreliability comes from his account of this wartime football match. According to David, he and Menachem Arber were the organisers. In his story, the two teenagers (aged eighteen and seventeen) first had to teach the game to the Turks, including one Mustafa Kemal, who became better known as Atatürk, the father of the Turkish Republic. The lesson was so successful that Kemal went on to score the final goal in a face-saving 2–2 draw. The problem with David's story is that in 1915 the thirty-something Mustafa Kemal was based in Bulgaria where he was the Ottoman military attaché. That same year, Kemal was promoted to field commander at Gallipoli, the battle that turned the tide on the attempted Allied invasion of Anatolia and Constantinople. In addition, Kemal was a native of Salonica (now Thessaloniki), where football had been a popular sport since the turn of the century.

Many of David's stories fall apart on examination. For instance, he claims to have run a Jewish death squad during the war, murdering Palestinian 'spies' who had infiltrated Jewish farms. There is no other record of these murders. The isolated Jewish farms in the north of Palestine were regarded as unsafe because they were on the border between British and Turkish lines. The farms were owned by Baron de Rothschild and as concern for the Baron's property grew, a member of Goldschmidt's sports club named Zvi Nadav joined a party of Subbotniks to scout the land. Rather than Palestinian spies, Nadav discovered the properties were being squatted by Armenian refugees, providing an early eyewitness account of the results of the Armenian holocaust. These were refugees who had survived the massacres and ethnic cleansing in Anatolia, as well as the forced death march, which saw Armenian survivors driven hundreds of miles into the Syrian Desert. Nadav discovered starving and terrified survivors, so desperate that they were prostituting their children to Ottoman soldiers for food.

David Tidhar wrote his accounts of the war years in the 1960s, at a time when he felt the contribution of his generation to the Jewish state had been forgotten. His stories of spy rings are implausible, yet he may have been responsible for the first political murder in Palestine: he wrote a plausible account of the ambush of a real-estate officer employed by the Turkish governor of Jaffa. At the time, the death was blamed on bandits,

54

which in wartime would mean commandoes or *fedayeen* from the Arab insurgency.

Given his tendency towards exaggeration and self-aggrandisement, David's account of Yosef Yekutieli's war should be treated with caution. He claims that Yosef caught the eye of Djemal Pasha, the Ottoman dictator, and was plucked from the Nablus barracks and appointed as a translator for the army's elite unit, the Yildirim ('Thunderbolt') Army Group. The Ottomans needed translators to communicate with their German-speaking allies, and Yosef knew some German. It is less plausible, as David claims, that Yosef was sent to the Macedonian front as the personal translator of the Ottoman General Abdulkerim Pasha. He may, however, have been part of the team liaising between Abdulkerim's staff and the kk 502, an Austro-Hungarian army force based in the Balkans. Abdulkerim subsequently went on to suppress a rebellion by Armenians in Anatolia, one of the events that preceded the Armenian genocide.

The British had been massing in Cairo since 1914. They were boosted by the decision of the Sharif of Mecca to join the Allies in 1916. The Sharif's son, Prince Feisal, ran *fedayeen* operations in Palestine, helped by the underground al-Fatat club, which had evolved into a formidable intelligence operation under the leadership of a Palestinian double agent, Izzat Darwaza, whose civilian job was director of the Syrian Post Office.

The Allied invasion came late in 1917. In the run-up, both Palestinian and Jewish conscripts began to defect or go AWOL, in the belief that the British would support their national aims. The British encouraged defections by making promises to all sides. Yosef, however, remained loyal to the Ottomans until the end.

In October 1917, on the eve of the invasion, Djemal Pasha
was demoted and replaced by the German Field Marshal Erich
von Falkenhayn. Falkenhayn set about organising the final
defence of Palestine. The need for translators between Ottoman
and German forces saw both Yosef and his brother Chaviv in
Falkenhayn's forces. In November, combined British, ANZAC,
Indian and Sharif pan-Arab forces invaded Palestine. They
captured the desert city of Beersheba and pushed north to take
Bethlehem and Jerusalem before the end of the year.

Once in control of Jerusalem, the British installed a Cairo-
based intelligence officer named Ronald Storrs as the governor
of Jerusalem. It was only as Storrs was taking office that someone
pointed out he needed to be a military officer to command an
army of occupation. Storrs was hurriedly made a colonel,
leading the ex-spy to joke that he was the first military governor
of the city since Pontius Pilate.

It would be six months before the final battle between Allied
and German–Ottoman forces. During this long, wary pause,
the British augmented their forces by signing up local fighters,
both Jewish and Palestinian. The British allayed local qualms
over switching sides by employing well-respected recruiters. On
the Palestinian side, the British used Amin al-Husseini, who had
gone AWOL from his artillery command in Anatolia. To target
the Yishuv, the British employed a journalist-activist from
Odessa named Vladimir Jabotinsky, who had joined the British
Army in England. Menachem Arber and Abie Wilson were
among the Maccabi boys who Jabotinsky persuaded to swap
Ottoman for British uniforms. The recruits might have ended
up fighting against their erstwhile teammates, the Yekutielis, but
the British avoided this problem by side-lining the Yishuv

recruits, sending them to Tel El Kebir in Egypt for training. To their intense frustration, they missed the war.

When the final battle came, Palestinian forces fought along-side Indian, ANZAC and British forces. Two existing battalions, the British 38th and the Canadian 39th, were predominantly Jewish, and were informally referred to as 'Jewish Battalions'. The 38th Battalion was commanded by an evangelical Irish Christian named John Patterson who would become one of the most significant leaders of the right-wing Beitar party in the 1930s and 1940s. The 38th and 39th took part in the final battle of September 1918, which the British named the Battle of Megiddo, or Armageddon. This was the kind of grandiose reference to the Bible that fired the imagination of men such as John Patterson, and biblical references would become a hall-mark of British rule. The Turks, in contrast, named the battle the Rout of Nablus.

After the war, Izzat Tannous and Jamal al-Husseini easily moved into jobs with the British army of occupation. They believed they were laying the groundwork for an independent Palestinian state. Menachem Arber returned from Egypt with other Yishuv recruits and was put on border patrols in northern Palestine, where they guarded Baron de Rothschild's deserted farming outposts. This was now the border with French Syria, thanks to a deal drawn up in Paris between French and British diplomats: Picot and Sykes. Any captured Ottoman soldiers, such as the Yekutielis, were regarded as enemy aliens and imprisoned in camps far away from Palestine.

Chapter Six:

A Different Country

Yosef Yekutieli received the Iron Crescent from the Ottomans as a veteran of the battles for Gaza in 1917. He was captured on the surrender of the Ottoman forces in 1918 and remained a prisoner of war until 1920. When he finally made it back to Palestine after six years in uniform, he found a very different country.

The Governor of Jerusalem, Ronald Storrs, was a vicar's son. He gazed on Palestine through the lens of Victorian Christianity, believing the Bible was closer to history than myth. His view chimed with Jewish nationalists, of course, but also with Christian archaeologists who flooded the country, determined to prove their biblical theories were correct. Storrs contributed to this 'biblification' of the landscape by reviving Roman-era Latin names such as Judea and Samaria (replacing the Ottoman-era terms for these districts: Jerusalem and Nablus). He made idiosyncratic decisions about the urban architecture, demolishing a recently erected Ottoman clock tower in Jerusalem because it lacked authenticity, but also removing the shepherds' livestock market in Bethlehem that dated back to the era of Christ, and demolishing the core of Bethlehem's old city to build a new fruit and vegetable market.

Storrs's actions show how far the evangelical interpretation of the Bible had penetrated the Christian mainstream. Yet the pendulum had not entirely tilted away from the Muscular Christian tradition. Storrs lauded sportsmanship and recalled his days on the school football pitch as the most idyllic time of his life. In 1920 he laid the foundation stone for the Jerusalem Sports Club, which would open the next year as a club for the city's upper crust, regardless of faith. Like Bishop Blyth before him, Storrs believed that sport fostered mutual respect between elites. This made him a natural ally of figures such as al-Husseini and Tannous, who had been educated in the public school system and were now working with the British military. But Storrs was wary of turning football into a popular spectator sport. His work as a spy chief in Cairo taught him the power of football to create modern, tribe-like allegiances from the new urban masses, and to draw sectarian battle lines. An Egyptian nationalist named Saad Zaghloul had founded Cairo's Al Ahly football club as a wing of his nationalist party. The fans had in turn built a force of tough streetfighters. In November 1918, Al Ahly football supporters seized Cairo, igniting an eight-month rebellion against the British.

Storrs did not want to see the same thing happen in Palestine. His new sports club would sponsor tennis tournaments and chess matches for individual players, as well as genteel receptions and dances. But the club's football tournament was restricted to military sides. By retaining control of the leagues, Storrs hoped to keep a lid on football's potential to encourage violence.

Nevertheless, violence soon came, ignited by the boys of Maccabi Tel Aviv and Zvi Orloff, now known as Zvi Nishri.

Nishri was no longer as close to the leading lights of the Maccabi as he had been before the war. In 1912, shortly after he and Moshe Sukowolski returned from the international sports conference, the Sukowolskis fell out with the Hashomer. It was an argument between the bosses and the workers over pay. The dispute spelled the end of the annual sports festival held at the farm in Rehovot, and crystallised the sympathies of the Subbotniks for socialism. The party Poale Zion, the forerunner of the Labour Party, had been founded by a Russian named Michael Halpern (also known as Halperin), a friend and mentor of the Subbotnik Alexander Zaid. The party was beginning to establish a role as the anti-elite party, representing those marginalised by the leaders of the Yishuv in Jaffa, as well as the incoming workers from the cities of the old Habsburg Empire. The Hashomer decided to back the socialists, which affected Zvi Nishri's standing with the Maccabi sports club. He was out of a job.

Nishri found a new role with the scout movement in Tel Aviv. Chana Orloff's 1919 picture of her brother in a military-style uniform reflects his post-Maccabi position as a scout master. This was a kind of lateral move rather than an expulsion from the club. There was no great difference between the new scouts and the old Maccabi. Nishri was inspired by the Czech-nationalist Sokol clubs, which in turn had inspired the scouts of the German Youth Movement and the Hungarian nationalist Levente clubs. All of these youth organisations were simultaneously sports and scouts groups, and their chief focus was performing military drills. Nishri moved seamlessly from the

Maccabi to his new role as a scout master, continuing to run his callisthenics drills. These took place before work on Jaffa's beach, attracting hundreds of youths and alarming the British. Their fears were justified at the start of April 1920, as Nishri's boys travelled to Jerusalem looking for a fight.

The occasion was the great annual Palestinian holiday, the feast of Nebi Musa (the Prophet Moses). In Palestinian mythology, Moses is said to have been buried near Nablus. Events began with a pilgrimage to Moses' tomb and a feast after Friday prayers on 2 April. This kicked off a two-day-long procession to Jerusalem. Palestinians from across the country marched holding embroidered banners decorated with the symbols of their cities. In 1920, the feast was sponsored by the al-Husseini family. Along the course of the march, a series of political speeches was delivered by Amin and other members of the family's party, the Arab Literary Society. The tone of the speeches was nationalistic, but also anti-immigration and anti-Jewish. The Palestinians had finally seen the text of the Balfour Declaration of 1917, in which the British promised to help establish a Jewish homeland in Palestine. The mood was angry and defiant and the British expected trouble. They chose to police the festival using Indian Muslim military police, hoping that this would show sensitivity. Indeed, the first few days of the procession passed off peacefully. There was no expectation of trouble on the Sunday, the day chosen by Tel Aviv's youths to confront the marchers. It was only six years since the language patrols, when club members had handed out beatings to Jews who did not speak Hebrew. Now the same youths and their younger brothers had returned, claiming that they were there to protect the city's Jews. Contemporary accounts of the riots, including an intelligence report from the French consul gathered by direct interviews, state the first violence came from the young Jewish boys. Palestinian banners were torn down, and shots were fired by Jewish gunmen from a balcony close to Jaffa Gate. Following the shootings, the military police closed the gates to the city. Predictions that the Jewish population of Jerusalem were in danger came true, as Palestinian rioters locked inside the city destroyed shops and desecrated synagogues. There were five Jewish deaths and four Palestinian. The Jewish victims were Jerusalemites with no interest in the politics of Jewish nationalism.

In the aftermath of the riot, the British Army recruiter Vladimir Jabotinsky tried to take the blame – or the credit – for leading the rioters. He seems to have been overstating his role. It is true that Jabotinsky had the respect of the boys he had recruited into the British Army, including Menachem Arber. In so far as the rioters represented a fighting force, however, this came from the discipline and drills instilled by Zvi Nishri over two decades. Nishri had run the Maccabi, he was the sports master at Tel Aviv's boys' school, and he was now the city's scout leader. The claim that Jabotinsky commanded the rioters only took hold after Jabotinsky voluntarily turned himself in to the police. He also took responsibility for the shooting at Jaffa Gate, but the guns were supplied by the Jerusalem-based Zvi Nadav, aided by Jeremiah Halpern, the nineteen-year-old son of the founder of Poale Zion, Michael Halpern. Like many young men in the post-war period, Jeremiah was on a political journey from socialism, via nationalism, to Italian-style fascism.

The myth of Jabotinsky's command during the Nebi Musa riots is intended to support the idea that Jabotinsky led

Palestine's first Jewish defence force: the Haganah. In truth, the Haganah defence force (the forerunner of Israel's army) was formally created in the summer of 1920 in a deal between the Hashomer and the Jewish trade union, Histadrut. In the years to come, the main aim of the paramilitaries was to pressurise Jewish bosses into sacking Palestinian workers and employing Jewish immigrants.

The Nebi Musa riots came at a difficult time for the British. It had become clear that the Anglo-French agreement to carve up the Middle East could not survive without international approval. In the weeks after the riots, the British were scheduled to present a new plan for Palestine at a conference at San Remo in Italy, attended by their allies: the US, French, Italian and Japanese. (There were no representatives from either Prince Feisal, commander of the Sharif's army, nor from Egypt, which was now independent thanks to the streetfighters of Al Ahly football club.) The British plan laid out a new, civil administration that would run Palestine. This marked a legal change: Palestine was no longer under a 'hostile military occupation'. It would be governed as part of the British Empire, and recognised as British territory by her allies. British passports were issued, Royal Mail post offices sprang up across Palestine, and Palestine was soon filled with all the paraphernalia of the British-run world.

The shortish legal document approved at San Remo put a little meat on the 1917 Balfour Declaration. The document states, 'The administration may arrange with the Jewish Agency . . . to construct or operate on fair equitable terms, any public works, services and utilities.' This was the first mention of the Jewish Agency, an institution that owes its creation to this document. The San Remo motion became international law in the eyes of Britain and her allies on 20 April 1920. The British recruited the Jewish Agency from the ZO Jewish nationalist party. The British head of the ZO, Chaim Weizmann, drew upon the predominantly Russian families of the Yishuv to fill out the new administration. The partnership between the ZO, the landowners, financiers and industrialists of Tel Aviv, and the British administration, remained in place throughout the 1920s, and exerted huge influence ever afterwards, even as the demographics in the Yishuv changed to favour non-Russian workers.

The San Remo agreement finally allowed Yosef and Chaviv Yekutieli to be demobbed and return from imprisonment abroad. Chaviv went back to his old profession as a teacher. Yosef found work with the Jewish Agency's land department, buying up land for government projects. He had connections to the Danins, through his other brother Israel's wife, and soon married Yehudit Weiss, the 24-year-old daughter of Akiva Arieh Weiss, one of the founders of Tel Aviv.

Reviving the Maccabi was a side job for Yosef, yet he seized it with relish. The acting head of the club was Meir Caspi (formerly Isaac Silberman), Nishri's lieutenant, but Yosef was moving up quickly. The future of the Maccabi under British rule would depend upon the club abandoning its old paramilitary pretensions, and becoming a conventional athletics association like the official sports bodies of the Olympic-member countries. Since childhood, Yosef had dreamed of Olympic glory and he soon proved to be the right man to move the club into the new age.

Chapter Seven:

Boy Scouts

On 5 May 1921, an angry mob of Palestinian farmhands were bombed by RAF planes as they marched on the farms of Petah Tikvah. This was the culmination of a week of riots that had begun five days earlier on May Day 1921, with a parade by the Jewish Communist Party in Jaffa. The background was the campaign by the Histadrut union to force employers to hire Jewish labour exclusively. The Communists challenged the sectarian politics: they wanted to see the Palestinians and Yishuv unite against British imperialism. The Communist march began in Jaffa's beach-front district of al-Manshiyya, which was then the commercial heart of Jaffa. The Communists handed out leaflets in Hebrew and Arabic, and chanted anti-British slogans. They were met by armed men from the Histadrut. The ensuing street fights soon drew in the local Palestinians, and a Palestinian mob attacked a ZO hostel set up to accommodate the influx of Austrian, Hungarian and Polish workers. Most of the forty-seven Jewish fatalities occurred in that single attack on the hostel.

The British were in the process of establishing a multifaith civilian police force, but swiftly discovered the new recruits were unreliable. The pay was too low to attract volunteers from the Yishuv. The Jewish Agency raised money to augment the salaries of Jewish recruits. David Tidhar and other Maccabi boys such as Asher Goldberg (now known as Asher Ben David) signed up, and were immediately placed on officer training courses. Unfortunately, during the week of the 1921 riots, the British found the new policemen simply sided with their communities, adding to the violence.

The riots spread to the countryside. Here, the Jewish owners of farms and fruit orchards resented the pressure to sack skilled Palestinian workers. They complained that Jewish immigrants from industrial cities did not understand agricultural work and would down tools on the stroke of five o'clock, even if the harvest was still in the fields. Nevertheless, Palestinian farmhands were being thrown out of work, which meant they were in danger of losing their homes, too. Under the old Ottoman feudal-style system, rural workers were tied to specific farms, being essentially bought and sold with the land.

The Palestinian agricultural workers were bombed by the RAF on 5 May under order from Sir Herbert Samuel. The same day, a young man named Avshalom Gissin was also killed trying to ambush the Palestinians. Gissin was a Maccabi boy and a graduate of the Gymnasia Herzliya in Jaffa, though his family lived in the farming district of Petah Tikvah thirteen miles away. As a sixteen-year-old, Gissin had helped Zvi Nishri found Maccabi Petah Tikvah sports club. After high school, Gissin went to military college in Constantinople, fought for the Ottoman army and was imprisoned by the British. When he returned with other ex-soldiers in 1920, he followed the Yekutieli brothers in trying to re-establish the Maccabi clubs. Chaviv Yekutieli focused on Rishon LeZion, where he had found employment as a schoolteacher, and Yosef was trying to establish a sports club in Jerusalem. Gissin returned to Petah Tikvah. His plan on 5 May was to lead an attack on the farmhands by hiding in an olive orchard at the roadside. The attack somehow went awry, and Gissin was killed alongside another three Maccabi boys. In memory of Gissin, Maccabi Petah Tikvah FC took the name Avshalom Petah Tikvah. The name remained for a generation.

Calm was finally restored with troops brought in from Egypt, while gunships were moored off the coast, and a new gendarmerie was brought in from Ireland, packed with members of the 'Black and Tans' Protestant security force. The 1921 riots led to the flight of the Jewish population from Jaffa to Tel Aviv, which stood on the heights above al-Manshiyya, and was soon recognised as an independent municipality. Tel Aviv was policed by a Jewish force, and Jaffa by a British-led force. The separation took several years, however, because Tel Aviv as yet had no shopping district and no commercial area.

The British were attempting to run a multifaith country while siding with the Yishuv, the most sectarian community. The Jerusalem-based Arab elite continued to hope they could sway the British. They had been educated in facsimiles of English public schools, and many had completed their education at Oxford and Cambridge. They had fought alongside the British in the First World War. Surely, they thought, they spoke the same language as the British and could persuade them to see sense? Jamal al-Husseini and Izzat Tannous led a delegation to London, believing their war record would win them a fair hearing, but they were treated with contempt by Sir Winston Churchill, the new Colonial Secretary, who told them that a Jewish homeland was a government priority, and would be established in Palestine. It was Churchill who sent in officers from his pet force, the Black and Tans, to maintain order in Palestine.

The editor of *Falastin*, Issa al-Issa, reported a similar response from Sir Herbert Samuel. Issa was only allowed to return from exile in 1920, despite having supported the Allies throughout the war. The Pashas had imprisoned him first in Damascus, before transferring him to Konya, a city deep in Anatolia. Issa escaped and in 1918 reached Syria, where he joined Prince Feisal's staff. He was overjoyed that Palestine was in the hands of Feisal's British allies: he believed Palestine was on the verge of independence. But when he tried to return to Jaffa he discovered his name was on a list of political undesirables. This was his first introduction to the Balfour Declaration. Issa was a small man, and though implacable when opposed he was also courteous, and could find ways of rolling with the punches. He began editing the newspaper of Feisal's administration in Syria, devoting a large portion of every issue to Palestine's independence. On the side, he gave Arabic classes to a British intelligence officer, W. F. 'Michael' Stirling. The two men grew close, and when Stirling was appointed Governor of Jaffa, Issa's exile was lifted. In 1920, Issa returned to Jaffa and reopened his newspaper, but was warned not to publish anything seditious. Despite the injunction, he began translating statements and speeches by the Yishuv leaders. He was soon called to Jerusalem to explain himself to Governor Herbert Samuel. In Issa's account of the meeting, Sir Herbert complained, 'If you weren't publishing these things, we wouldn't have the tension that exists in the country.' Issa demanded to know if Sir Herbert was speaking as the representative of the British or as a Zionist leader. According to Issa, he declared that he was both. This version might be coloured, but it conveys the spirit of the times. Sir Herbert saw his role as a dual one: his government was a partnership between the British and the ZO party, and as the British governor he would be the midwife of a Jewish homeland.

The one Palestinian initiative that won British approval was the national scouting movement. Almost all of the next wave of Palestinian football clubs grew out of the scouts.

Scouting took off in Palestine before the war, but the troops were ad hoc affairs, set up by social clubs attached to mosques and churches. The British were wary of scout movements. They knew how easily uniformed youths could turn into a sectarian force, given the rise in blackshirt and paramilitary groups attached to nationalist organisations in Central Europe. To counter the inward-looking nationalism of these groups, the British encouraged scout associations to sign up to the International Conference of the Boy Scout Movement, the society founded in 1922 out of Lord Baden-Powell's British scouting movement. The International Conference was supposed to promote friendship through virile woodcraft and international meet-ups, which Lord Baden-Powell termed 'jamborees'. This was Baden-Powell's own spin on Muscular Christianity. The British supported a single national scout body, as long as it joined the conference. The

Palestinians agreed, Muslim and Christian alike. Only Nishri refused to play nice.

In 1921, Lord Baden-Powell himself visited Palestine for a major jamboree. The scouts paraded in front of the imperial dignitaries, including Sir Herbert in his whites and ostrich feathers. The spirit of these jamborees continues today. One of the most startling sights in Palestine is seeing the pipe bands descend on Bethlehem's Manger Square at Christmas, hearing the caterwauling swirl of bagpipes echo off the stone streets, and seeing the scout leaders twirl and juggle the troops' banners. The great legacy of these days is the network of social clubs, which created the sports associations and football teams.

The creation of a national scouting movement under British sponsorship was a first defeat for the Yishuv. They had refused to join the British scouts and watched from the sidelines as its leaders travelled the world and soaked up the pomp that flows from international recognition. The scouts held international jamborees every four years. Palestine was represented at three events in the 1920s: 1920 (London), 1924 (Denmark) and 1929 (Liverpool). Nishri tried to bypass Palestine's national organisation by putting in an application to join the world movement alone but was rebuffed. As long as a national Palestinian organisation existed, the conference would not recognise a Jews-only body. The Yishuv's scouts continued to apply for recognition for the next thirty years, without success. Their movement was only finally accepted in 1949, after the establishment of the state of Israel.

By 1923, Yosef Yekutieli was the secretary of the Maccabi Union in Palestine. He witnessed the failure of Nishri's scouts to gain international recognition. Yet he was slow to draw the appropriate lesson. He put in his own application to join the world athletics body, the IAAF. It was only when this also proved a failure that he turned his attention to football, inspired by the visit of Hakoah Vienna and the possibility that FIFA might be more easily manipulated than the IAAF.

Chapter Eight:

Sir Alfred Mond

The Maccabi's application to FIFA benefited from the backing of a retired British politician, Sir Alfred Mond, a football enthusiast, one-time cabinet member and gifted business leader. Yosef Yekutieli first met Sir Alfred in March 1921, six weeks before the May Day riots. The occasion was another of the Maccabi's famous gymnastic displays, this one organised by Meir Caspi. The ex-streetfighter was now a respectable banker, working for the Anglo-Palestine bank, the official bank of the Yishuv (on the establishment of Israel, Caspi's bank became Bank Leumi, the National Bank of Israel). Caspi's guests of honour that day included Sir Alfred and his older brother Robert Mond, an archaeologist, as well as Sir Herbert Samuel and Sir Rufus Isaacs, the new Viceroy of India, who had broken his journey to Delhi to see the Jewish homeland for himself. Sir Herbert, Sir Alfred and Sir Rufus were good friends. They were all members of the Liberal Party, and served together as the three Jewish cabinet ministers in David Lloyd George's government. Sir Rufus and Sir Alfred were even in-laws since the marriage of their children. During the war, Sir Alfred had run one of the biggest ministries: the Ministry of Works. He was now out of politics and focusing his attention on the family business, the United Alkali Company, making him the world's largest trader in potash, a source of industrial alkali. This gave him a commercial interest in the Dead Sea, one of the largest natural sources of potash. Sir Alfred's support for the newly established Palestine Potash Company immediately turned the company into one of Palestine's most valuable companies. Robert Mond had been working on digs in Egypt's Valley of the Kings but since the revolution in Cairo had moved to Palestine and switched the focus of his fund to biblical archaeology.

The audience that day also included Chaim Weizmann, the academic and ZO party leader who had moved from Manchester to take up the role of head of the new Jewish Agency. Under the terms of the San Remo agreement, Weizmann would run the country in partnership with Sir Herbert. Weizmann was accompanied by his lieutenant, Nahum Sokolow, a journalist and activist, and the man who had coined the name Tel Aviv as the Hebrew translation of Theodor Herzl's utopian novel, *The Old New Land.*

The final member of the party was Walter Rothschild, an aristocratic amateur zoologist. The Balfour Declaration, the first draft of which was written by Sir Herbert and Chaim Weizmann, had taken the form of a letter to Walter Rothschild, in his capacity as a senior member of the British branch of the ZO party. The Yishuv in Tel Aviv were anxious to cement relations with such powerful sponsors. The visit led to the creation of the Palestine Electric Company, founded by Sir Alfred, Sir Rufus and Sir Herbert. Yosef was tasked with buying land to build Palestine's national grid. The electrification of the country did more than anything to institutionalise the borders between Jewish and Palestinian communities, because the pylons and the power lines demarcated the districts. Housing developments built for new Jewish immigrants to the Yishuv were connected to the grid, while older Palestinian neighbourhoods were completely bypassed.

Sir Alfred Mond's visit to Palestine in 1921 hit him hard. He loved sports and he took Yosef and the Maccabi under his wing, becoming president of the international Maccabi World Union, as the conference of world Jewish sports clubs was known after 1921. Until his visit to Palestine, Sir Alfred apparently thought little about being Jewish. His parents were Germans who in 1862 had moved to Lancashire, England, where they set up their globally expanding chemical company. The couple retained a deep love of German culture, reflected in their large collection of art works and original manuscripts by seminal figures such as Goethe. Both his mother and father were Jewish, but neither were religious. Alfred was educated in England, proving to be a talented chemist. He married a non-Jewish Protestant of German heritage.

When he came to think about his Jewish identity, Sir Alfred seems to have been influenced by Weizmann and Rothschild, two men who shared his scientific background. Weizmann was also a chemist, a professor at Manchester University, which made him a near neighbour of the Monds in Lancashire. Weizmann theorised that being Jewish was, first and foremost, a communal way of life; it was something that people did, before it was codified in laws and prayer books. He felt that the religion of exile was a shadowy memory, even a perversion, of this more original way of life, lived on Jewish home soil. Rothschild shared Weizmann's theory, adding a few embellishments thanks to his work as a naturalist. Though only an amateur, he had built up the most important collection of birds and butterflies in the world. He employed German zoologists to author theoretical papers to which he appended his name. The vast majority of this work addressed the notion of race in the natural world. Rothschild defined 'race' as a synonym of 'subspecies'. In zoology, a subspecies depends entirely on geography (as, for instance, the markings on the wings of a subspecies of a butterfly reflect the flora of a particular place). While Rothschild's political pronouncements are rare, it is notable that his scientific work predominantly focuses on the argument that difference can only be preserved by environmental factors, and by the strict separation of communities. To put it bluntly, race depends upon place. In his view, the category of 'Jewishness' was part of the natural world, and if it was to survive then it had to be returned to its natural environment . . . in Palestine.

These hopes were encouraged by archaeologists such as Robert Mond. The discovery of ancient cities such as Nineveh, which contained an entire Babylonian library, seemed to offer hope that texts would be discovered to support the stories found in the Bible. Robert Mond funded much of the archaeology in Palestine. The museum he built on a hill facing Herod's Gate is a remarkable and beautiful building, decorated with stone carvings by the artist Eric Gill. The museum is fronted by a hexagonal tower intended to recall the 'Tower of the Flock' mentioned in the Bible, the watchtower built to oversee the tribes of Israel.

This group of wealthy and privileged men reflected the strange post-war world of the 1920s. The First World War brought destruction on an unimaginable scale. The terror didn't end with the war. The pneumonia epidemic that followed in its wake, the holocaust that brought the flood of Armenian refugees into Palestine, and the revolution in Russia, all seemed to carry terrible warnings about the Modern Age. A generation turned away from modernity and found solace in a romantic yearning for ancient history. The circle of British Jewish dignitaries knew little of the Talmud and the arcane laws treasured by the rabbis. But they desperately yearned for the romance of the ancient world, with its stories of pharaohs, Romans and Israelites. In Herzl's phrase, humanity seemed to stand on the brink of an old-new world.

Even though Mond failed to put any flesh on the Bible's myths, his museum reflects the old-new building style of the 1920s. It is the art deco style of New York skyscrapers and movie theatres, the cathedrals of their day, part science fiction, part Valley of the Kings. The world's greatest film star Valentino was celebrated as *The Sheikh* in 1921, and America was falling in love with its new beach cities of Palm Beach and Miami. In Israel, the old-new Pharaonic style can be found everywhere from the grand Rothschild Boulevard (named after the French Baron, not Walter) to the little alley in Tel Aviv named Simta Plonit ('Alley What's Its Name') off King George Street, which has cement replicas of Cleopatra's needle at its entrance. You did not have to be religious to believe in the revival of a Jewish land, you just needed access to concrete and labourers.

Sir Alfred encouraged the Maccabi to take football seriously. As MP for Swansea he followed local football and in 1923 established the Mond Cup, which would give him a great deal of influence in the Welsh Football Association and in the governing body of the Home Nations. He seems to have attended the Hakoah Vienna game of 1923 at Upton Park, which saw West Ham United defeated 0–5. He was soon asking Yosef to create a Maccabi touring side to promote Jewish nationalism around the world. When the IAAF refused Yosef's membership application in 1923, Sir Alfred pushed football as an alternative route to international recognition and the Olympics.

Pursuing football also made sense as the sport continued to grow in popularity in Jaffa and Tel Aviv. Between 1919 and 1924, 45,000 Jewish immigrants arrived in Jaffa, doubling the population of Jaffa/Tel Aviv, and bringing the overall Jewish population of Palestine to around 130,000 (the total population, according to the 1922 census, was a little over 750,000). Half of these new immigrants came from Poland, another old-new country that had been resurrected in the aftermath of the First World War by clawing territory back from Russia, Germany and Austria-Hungary. The project fuelled xenophobic nationalism, which led in turn to a rise in hostility towards the Jews.

The Jews who left Poland for Palestine tended to side with the socialist party, Ahdut HaAvoda (Labour Unity), which soon merged with another party to become Mapai (*Mifleget Poalei Eretz Yisrael* or Workers' Party of the Land of Israel). Their arrival boosted the party leader, David Ben Gurion, and the associated Histadrut labour union. They also created a revolution in the quality of Palestinian football. The footballers mostly came from Poland's southern cities of the Austro-Hungarian empire. Lwów (Lviv) had four teams, while Krakow had two, all formed between 1903 and 1909. Shimon 'Lumek' Ratner was born in Krakow in 1898, moved to Vienna at sixteen, and reached Jaffa in 1920. Another Polish footballer, Yohanan

Sukenik, arrived in Jaffa in 1923 from Łódź, a one-time Russian city that contained both Polish and German speakers. As the Maccabi football squad grew, the club added a junior side named Maccabi Nordia, in memory of Max Nordau, the journalist-activist who had coined the term 'Muscular Judaism'. It was this junior side that would shortly break away from the Maccabi to join David Ben Gurion's socialist party.

Chapter Nine:

The New Leagues

One of the first editions of *Falastin* after it was allowed to begin re-publication in 1921 was news of Ronald Storrs's Jerusalem Sports Club:

> Last Saturday was the inauguration of the cornerstone of the Sports Club in Jerusalem. The Palestine Weekly mentioned that Mr. Storrs, the Governor of Jerusalem, insisted on the participation of everyone regardless of his religion or beliefs. The Weekly added that the partisan athletic clubs in Egypt were a factor in the turmoil there, so this mistake must not be repeated in Palestine.

Storrs's club did not actually open until 1922, and it was another two years before it created what became the first national football league. The army had been running a military league since 1920. Storrs's new league pitched military teams against government employees, competing for the new Palestine Cup. The founding teams included the RAF team Flying Amman, which was actually based outside of Palestine in

Transjordan; the Jerusalem Police Force; and the South Lancashire Regiment (6th Battalion), who had won the earlier military-only cup in 1922. The 1923 military league was won by RAF Ramle, the squadron responsible for bombing the Palestinians on the road to Petah Tikvah. RAF Ramle went on to win the Palestine Cup for four years straight: 1924–7. Although Storrs's club operated a de facto national league, it had no teams from the actual civilian population of Palestine, and the only Palestinian or Yishuv competitors were those working for the government or the police. Storrs was not going to take a risk by creating teams with 'partisan' supporters.

If Storrs ran the only national league, small local leagues were springing up across the country. A junior league in Jerusalem saw teams from both Palestinian and Jewish communities play together throughout the 1920s. The Palestinian nationalist Garden of Knowledge school, Rawdat al-Ma'aref, was permitted to reopen in 1921 and joined the junior al-Zahra league. Al-Zahra is the Palestinian name for Herod's Gate, which is known as the Gate of Flowers in Hebrew, *Sha'ar HaPrakim*. The league cup was the Flowers Cup, which suggests the sponsors were Jewish, as were many of the teams including a Jewish high school, Ofir; Jerusalem Nordia, the Maccabi youth team recently established by Yosef Yekutieli; and the youth group of the local Histadrut union. The rivalry between the Maccabi and Histadrut meant that both of these teams claimed descent from the pre-war Goldschmidt sports club. The al-Zahra league was reported in the city's Jewish newspaper, which seems to be the only source of information on a league that included both communities, playing together. Despite the violence of the 1920 riots, Jerusalem was far more integrated in the 1920s than the cities of Jaffa and Tel Aviv, reflecting the underlying ideological differences between the Russian Yishuv and other Jewish communities in Palestine.

Jerusalem's mayor, Raghib al-Nashashibi, sponsored a knock-out competition known as the Nashashibi Cup throughout most of the 1920s. The Nashashibis were the chief rivals to the al-Husseinis, and as the politics developed throughout the decade, the al-Husseinis became associated with a conservative and patrician politics that had nationwide appeal, especially outside the triangle of Jerusalem, Jaffa and Haifa. The Nashashibis, in contrast, were more urban, more liberal and modernising. Football inevitably became the sport of the cosmopolitan cities.

Maccabi Tel Aviv created a senior team with Lumek Ratner as the player-coach and in 1923 the club launched its own tournament, the Magen Shimson, or Shield of Samson. The first two championships were taken by Maccabi Nes Tziona, the team of a small farming community that according to the 1922 census had a Jewish population of just 300. The years 1923 and 1924 saw Nes Tziona grow rapidly thanks to the new electrification programme that hooked Nes Tziona, Rehovot and Rishon LeZion to the national electric grid. The adjacent Palestinian population centres of Lydda and Ramle were left off the grid. The tournament was sponsored by a senior officer of the Jewish Agency, Colonel Frederick Kisch, a British officer born in India. Kisch was recruited from military intelligence in 1919 by Chaim Weizmann. He headed up the Jewish Agency's political division, making him, in effect, the Yishuv's spymaster. The Colonel was a keen football fan, and besides sponsoring the Magen Shimson, he organised games between the Maccabi and British military teams. The aim was to strengthen bonds between the Yishuv and the military. This was often hard work. At least one 1924 game had to be abandoned because of violence, with a Maccabi player stating, 'this wild game ended before it was due, and although we lost we showed the British we are not giving any quarter and we gave them what they deserved'.

Other ad hoc leagues and informal games became common across the country as the new social clubs and their scout troops embraced the sport. The Armenian refugees created their own social clubs, with the Jerusalem Homenetmen emerging as the most formidable Armenian team of the 1920s and 1930s. Jaffa got a second team in 1926, the Islamic Sports Club, which fielded both Christian and Muslim players. In Haifa, old boys from the Christian Salesian school started their own team, which also fielded Muslim players, while another Haifa side took the name Haifa White Star, a popular name for teams as far apart as Peru and Belgium. At least twenty other Palestinian teams emerged through the 1920s, from the scouts attached to social clubs or from dedicated sports clubs such as the Gaza Sports Club, the Nablus Arab Club, the Jerusalem Sports Club and the Sports Club of El-Carmel (Haifa). The network of Arab Orthodox Christian clubs, created by Issa al-Issa in 1923, launched a series of football teams through the 1920s, with Jaffa Orthodox the first in 1924; Jerusalem Orthodox in 1926; and Lydda and Akka both in 1927. Team photographs show well-equipped football players from Haifa, Jerusalem and Jaffa. The teams travelled to play each other, and also conducted friendly matches against British military teams.

Despite the explosion of Palestinians teams, the reports in the *Falastin* convey a sense of inadequacy. The pomp of the

January 1924 visit of Hakoah Vienna unnerved al-Issa: it seemed to show that Maccabi Tel Aviv was a powerful organisation, enjoying international links. The quality of the match registered less than the anthems, parades and Jewish nationalist flags. The fanfare was repeated when Hakoah returned in January 1925. The Maccabi's flags and parades were even brought out for a 1925 visit by a team of Egyptian scouts. When the Maccabi teams played army sides, the British national anthem was invariably followed by 'Hatikvah'. These confident expressions of nationalism blinded the *Falastin* reporters to the actual skill of the Yishuv footballers. In Jerusalem, the Rawdat al-Ma'aref school hired a dedicated sports master, an Egyptian named Hussein Husni, who went on to become *Falastin's* sports correspondent. Husni preached his own 'scientific' approach to sports, a throwback to the callisthenics of the pre-war years, and frequently suggested that the Palestinian game lagged behind the more advanced British and European Jews.

If this was true, it was not necessarily because the Palestinians were less fit, however, but because the game had changed. The tough, hacking and swashbuckling football of the pre-war years had been superseded by a new passing game, which demanded that players develop some basic positional sense. The match reports in both Hebrew and Arab press began to put a new emphasis on the wing players in an attacking midfield. The sense from reading these reports is that the journalists from both communities are teaching themselves about modern football even as they write their reports. The learning curve was helped by watching and playing competent British military sides. The Yishuv teams may have had a head start, thanks to European immigrants such as Lumek and Sukenik, but Husni was probably mistaken to believe the Yishuv teams were so much better. The Palestinian sides were also playing British Army teams and giving good accounts of themselves. The irony is that Husni's columns advocated physical fitness drills, just as the Yishuv was beginning to abandon the old ideas of Zvi Nishri and his regimented dips and bends. Footballers were learning that soccer needs more than simple physical fitness: it is a team game of strategy at heart.

When Falastin reported on football in the Yishuv, the focus was less on the quality of the matches than the strength and unity of the Jewish nationalists. The sense of unity, however, was deceptive. In 1925, the image cracked entirely. That year, Sir Alfred Mond became the President of the Maccabi World Congress at the second conference in Vienna. Sir Alfred paid for Maccabi Tel Aviv to travel to Vienna to play a third match against Hakoah Vienna. This was a highlight of the Maccabi World Congress, but it continued the Tel Aviv losing streak: the team lost 5–1. After Vienna, the Maccabi team went on to tour Czech and Polish cities to play local Jewish teams. Sir Alfred and Yosef Yekutieli hoped to turn Maccabi Tel Aviv into a touring side to promote the Jewish homeland, but the tour sowed division in Tel Aviv. Ben Gurion's Ahdut HaAvoda socialist party and the Histadrut union had been unhappy to see the international Jewish sports association take the name of their rival, the Maccabi, in 1921, and were now angered by the portrayal of Maccabi Tel Aviv as the representatives of Yishuv sporting life and the leading club of Jews around the world. The socialists had their own sports club, named Hapoel (or, 'the Workers'), and the club sent delegates to Vienna to attend the 1925 Maccabi World Congress, but resigned almost immediately afterwards. For good measure, they condemned the membership as bourgeois stooges.

The Maccabi were riding high, supported by the Jewish Agency, and close to the British administration and the military. The conflict between the socialist Hapoel and the Maccabi reflected a struggle for the leadership of the Yishuv. The Maccabi held all the cards, except for the most important one: the shifting demographics that worked in the socialist party's favour.

The European tour also angered the junior footballers left behind in Tel Aviv. Sir Alfred had paid for the tour. The rules on amateurism allowed for some wiggle room: footballers could be paid to tour if their wages were described as compensation for any money they might have earned if they had stayed at home. This effectively allowed players to earn their living as footballers. The Maccabi youth team, Maccabi Nordia, already felt their best players were being blocked from moving up to the first team. Now they were being denied the opportunity to earn money from football. Moreover, the fixtures on the Maccabi tour were played in the European cities where these younger players were born, and where they still had friends and family that might turn out to watch them play. In 1926, the entire Maccabi Nordia team resigned to create a new team, named Allenby Tel Aviv. The next year, 1927, the team signed up with Hapoel to become the flagship socialist side of the Yishuv.

In March 2018, I was staying in an Airbnb apartment near Carmel Market on Allenby, the street that gave the Allenby boys their name. The football historian Jonathan Wilson had put me in touch with the sports journalist Ouriel Daskal and we met at the Minzar Bar in Carmel Market, where I ordered pork dumplings and seafood noodles at Ouriel's prompting, a very Tel Aviv dish as it was so very un-Kosher. I asked Ouriel if he knew where the Allenby boys had lived, and he raised his hand towards the restaurant windows, with a gesture somewhere between waving and pointing.

'Right along there.'

Later, I took a walk, scouting the area for any sign or monument to the renegade footballers. I didn't find anything, though there is a 1920s concrete substation opposite the Minzar Bar, for aficionados of early electrification programmes. Walking down the steep hill of Carmel Market at night, when the street-cleaners were washing away the detritus of the fruit market, I got a sense of the city's geography: how paving the hills had affected the lower-lying areas. The cleaners used powerful hoses, sending foul-smelling torrents down the slope, bobbing with rotten tomatoes, squashed peppers and disintegrating cartons. The foot of the hill, now a bus terminus, was once the Jaffa district called al-Manshiyya. The Allenby boys played their football on the outskirts of al-Manshiyya on a pitch leased from the Abu Laban family, the farmers who had invented the Jaffa Orange brand.

Allenby Street runs north off the high, wide Rothschild Boulevard, at an intersection close to the Great Synagogue, which was the highest point in the original settlement, known as *Ahuzat Bayit* or Homestead before it adopted the name Tel Aviv around 1912. Allenby follows a curved ridge that begins to descend towards the shoreline at Carmel Market. The Airbnb apartment was picked out for me by two old friends, Tamar Keenan, the theatre actor, and her husband, film-maker Eitan Anner, because it was close to their apartment. In the evenings,

I would watch films with Eitan, who was looking after the kids because Tamar was on tour in a play opposite the popular comedian, Samuel Vilozny. The play, called *We Are the Champions*, was about another Hapoel soccer team: Hapoel Haifa FC. Vilozny was playing the team's mascot, a mascot that only knew bad luck. Hapoel Haifa is supposed to be the team for perennial losers in Israel, but an odd thing had happened. Ever since the play opened, the team had gone on a winning streak. They were in the midst of a blinding season: it looked as though Tamar was bringing them luck.

The Allenby boys are often said to be the first Hapoel football team. This is not universally accepted. Chiefly, it is not accepted by fans of Hapoel Haifa. The exact timeline is vague for the reason that all dates in Israeli history are vague: everyone backdates their claims to strengthen the sense of a long pedigree. It seems a group of Haifa dockworkers had formed a team before 1924, the year the Hapoel sports association was created. This made them the first 'workers' team in the sense that they were a team of workers and trade unionists. The Allenby boys, however, were the first team to formally sign to the Hapoel sports association.

The dispute, as minor as it is, shows how important the Allenby boys were to Ben Gurion's party. They were instantly made the flagship side, in part to get one over on the Russian old guard, but even more importantly to mark a generational shift in power. The team was young and dynamic and working class, everything the socialists hoped to represent. The Allenby boys' defection came against a deepening economic crisis. A new Tory government in Britain had reverted to the gold standard, an insane step, the Brexit of its day. The pound was suddenly overpriced, and untradeable on the open market.

Investors turned away, and the government responded by imposing austerity at home and across the empire. In Palestine, all the grand projects conjured up by the Jewish Agency and approved by Sir Herbert Samuel were cancelled, including electric trams in the cities and the electrification of the Jerusalem–Jaffa railway. Sir Herbert himself was replaced. Unemployment rose. The year 1925 saw negative Jewish immigration to Palestine for the first time since the war. The country also faced an agriculture crisis, as a poor citrus harvest came on top of rising wages and falling productivity, a direct result of the Histadrut/Haganah intimidation of landowners, forcing them to sack the Palestinian farm labourers.

Sir Alfred Mond's plan to create a touring team to represent Jews everywhere had only created animosity and ignited divisions. The Maccabi and Hapoel refused even to recognise each other. It took another year, and a personal visit from Sir Alfred, before the teams agreed to speak.

Chapter Ten:

The Fake Application

In 1926, Yosef Yekutieli applied for membership of FIFA as the Palestine Football Association. The officials in Paris rejected the application but Yosef was encouraged to try again. He faced the old problem, that the Maccabi represented Jewish players alone, but also a new one: there were no qualified referees in the Yishuv. Without home-grown referees it was impossible to run tournaments and leagues to FIFA's standards. The Maccabi's own tournament relied on friendly officials from the British Army and colonial civil service. Yosef saw that he could solve both of his problems by creating a Palestine Football Association that incorporated British military and government teams. If he had English players in the league, it was possible to claim that the new FA was not a sectarian organisation, even if it was run out of the Maccabi headquarters. The break with the socialist Hapoel organisation in 1927 was a setback, but Yosef continued to work towards a rapprochement with the help of Sir Arthur Mond. Only the Palestinians remained a problem. If FIFA demanded that a national football association represented all sections of Palestinian society, Yosef needed to at least create the impression that Palestinians were involved.

Unwitting help came from the Palestinian sportsman Ibrahim Salim Nusseibeh. Nusseibeh was a tennis champion at Storrs's Jerusalem Sports Club, and an enthusiastic footballer who played on the left wing. More significantly, he was an approved referee, a qualification he may have picked up in Egypt while studying at the Victoria College, or during his time at university in England. He was the only non-British referee in the entire country. In 1927, he founded a new team, known as the Jerusalem Arab Sports Club, and informally as al-Araby. This soon became a leading club in the country, but when Nusseibeh called the inaugural meeting, he had not yet signed the lease on his club's new premises. The first meeting took place under the shade of a tree inside Herod's Gate. One winter day on a shopping trip to Jerusalem, I was inspired by Robert Mond's Palestine Archaeology Museum to attempt my own urban archaeology and identify Nusseibeh's tree. Since the early 1980s, the houses around al-Zahra gate have been targeted by Jewish settlers, and the only tree of the right age is inside a playground reserved for their children. The tree is obscured behind a high metal barrier, but as I jumped up and down to catch a glimpse of the tree, I thought I could see a bench beneath it. When he addressed the meeting, Nusseibeh asked the founding members of al-Araby to take an oath that the club would admit any member regardless of faith, and never discriminate between religions. The seat where he made this plea is now reserved for the exclusive use of one faith.

Al-Araby signed up to the al-Zahra league, no longer a junior division by 1927. The teams included the YMCA team, which was waiting to move into the half-constructed million-dollar

YMCA building that stands opposite the King David Hotel. Another team was drawn from employees of Shell Oil, which was run by an Anglo-Jewish family of Iraqi descent, the Samuels (no relation to Herbert Samuel). The al-Zahra League of 1927 continued to reflect life in the multicultural city as it looked after ten years of British rule. Football was still a game of elites, of gentlemen sportsmen, and amateurs who worked for global corporations. The Nusseibehs were 'Notables' from the city's aristocracy. The family traced their roots to a female chieftain of the late Roman era, and the family arrived in Jerusalem at the time of the Islamic conquest. The Nusseibehs are the traditional custodians of the keys of the Church of the Holy Sepulchre, acting as a neutral party between the antagonistic mix of the church's Christian tenants. In the 1920s, the Nusseibehs filled a similar placatory role in the political realm, having married into both the al-Husseini family and their rivals, the Nashashibis. The British had rewarded Amin al-Husseini for his wartime role as a recruiter by making him Grand Mufti, over the protests of every other family in Jerusalem. The Mufti is a Roman-era title that translates as Magistrate. The British handed the impetuous young Amin (only twenty-four when he was appointed) enormous and wide-ranging authority as head of the Supreme Muslim Council, which was in charge of Muslim community affairs in Palestine and was responsible for dispensing marriage licences and notarising civil law documents. The role enabled Amin to reach out to the rural villages and tribal communities as an arbiter and judge in a way that no other leader could match. This gave Amin real political power and, as a consequence, the al-Husseini faction, known as the *Majlisiya* or 'Council Supporters', was regarded as the party of power. The non-Husseini grouping centred on the Nashashibis became known as the *Mu'aridun*, the 'Opposition'. Amin was never religious until he became Mufti, but once in position he began to dress in traditional robes, which he topped off with a tarbush wrapped in a long silk sash, the traditional uniform of a Muslim imam. The al-Husseinis represented a politics of tradition and religious morality. As the 1920s progressed, Amin's views increasingly became both anti-British and authoritarian.

The Nusseibehs had married into the al-Husseini family, but they were closely associated with the Opposition, the party of business and compromise with the British. The Opposition was also the anti-Yishuv party, however, because its strongholds were those with the largest Jewish populations. Where Amin grew more hardline against the British, the Opposition was more placatory, but implacable in their demands for immigration controls. The names of the members of Ibrahim Nusseibeh's al-Araby Sports Club are a roll call of these Opposition families, including Fawzi al-Nashashibi, as club secretary, and others from the al-Jawzi family, who were literary intellectuals and progressives. With families such as Jaffa's al-Issas also associated with football, it cemented its place as the opposition sport. This was not purely because football was embraced by a liberal and educated elite, but also because it was the sport of choice for a rising class of Arab clerks, factory workers and dockers growing up in the triangle made by Jaffa, Haifa and Jerusalem.

The year after the formation of Nusseibeh's al-Araby team, Sir Alfred Mond returned to Palestine for his second tour of the country. The visit was treated as a state event by the Maccabi. Parades took place around the country, and new clubs were created in his honour, including a new Maccabi football team in the Galilee. Sir Arthur promoted his long-term plan for a new 'Land of Israel' team to tour Britain, and supported Yosef Yekutieli's attempts to fashion a football association that would win FIFA approval.

Sir Alfred arrived against the backdrop of changes brought in by Stanley Baldwin's new Tory government. The new Foreign Secretary, Austen Chamberlain, installed a military figure as High Commissioner, Field Marshal Herbert Plumer, with instructions to slash the military presence in Palestine. This alarmed the Yishuv, who worried about security without British backing. The economy tanked, and faith in the British declined within the Yishuv. But among all these pessimistic signs, Sir Arthur recognised an upside. Chamberlain had placed Leo Amery in charge of the Colonial Office. Amery was a long-time member of the ZO party who, back in 1917, had written the final version of the Balfour Declaration, presented to the British cabinet. Now, Amery was in charge of Palestine from within the British government. His policy aim was to devolve power to local administrators. It was proposed that Yosef and the Maccabi take over the existing football league run from Storrs's Jerusalem Sports Club. If a new Maccabi-led Palestine FA was already running a football league, this would strengthen its cause with FIFA.

As Chamberlain and Plumer downsized the military, the country lost many of the best teams and most talented players. Ronald Storrs had moved on to Cyprus, but his sports club continued. Yosef took over the league's affairs, and even brought in new sponsors. The Palestine Cup trophy was donated by the Carmel winery, established by Baron de Rothschild and now co-owned by the Jewish Agency. But before the new league could get underway, the Hapoel and Maccabi had to make friends. With Sir Alfred's backing, Yosef approached Hapoel with the idea of a Tel Aviv derby: Maccabi Tel Aviv vs Hapoel Allenby. Hapoel agreed.

The match took place on 25 February 1928. Posters were plastered across Tel Aviv and Jaffa. On the day of the match, Allenby fans gathered on Allenby Street, while Maccabi supporters gathered at a bar on Shabazi Street, the red-light district on the edge of Manshiyya. The likelihood of violence brought the police out in force, and heavy-wooden football rattles were banned in case they were used as weapons. Three thousand fans made their way to the Palm Court. This first Tel Aviv derby ended with a 3–0 victory to the Maccabi team. The Maccabi player-coach Lumek Ratner was agreed to be the best player on the field, but Allenby suffered because they were missing their attacking midfielder Avraham Nudelman and goalkeeper Willy Berger. Berger was a particular loss. He was the Allenby boys' secret weapon, a Hungarian professional who had played for the Vívó és Atlétikai Club in his homeland. Berger arrived in Palestine 1927 to take up an invitation from Maccabi Haifa to tour the United States. He soon discovered the tour was a fantasy, and so took a job in the Galilee coaching the new Maccabi side. The Allenby boys recruited him from the Maccabi, but he was unavailable for this first Tel Aviv derby.

The game at the Palm Court launched an era of friendship and collaboration between the Maccabi and Hapoel that lasted almost two months.

Yosef Yekutieli would write an article, three years later, for the FIFA yearbook that provided a short account of the history of football in Palestine prior to his takeover. He noted the sport began at St George's School, and gave credit to the British for bringing a national league to the country through the Jerusalem Sports Club. He also noted the existence of the local leagues, such as the al-Zahra league of Jerusalem and the Jaffa League, home of the Orthodox Christian club and the Islamic club. However, Yosef invited none of these clubs to play in the first year of his national league. Rather, he brought in five military sides, six Yishuv teams, and one club fielding Palestinian players, Sporting el-Carmel, a sports club from Haifa.

The competition kicked off on 7 April 1928, beginning a series of elimination rounds over six weeks. Sporting el-Carmel was the first to be knocked out. The military teams were RAF Gaza, playing as the Gaza Bedouins; the RAF Amman side known as Flying Amman; PGH Sarafand from the city's military hospital; and two police teams. When one police team failed to turn up for its match, Jerusalem's Mount Scopus station was given a bye to the next round. The Yishuv was represented by Hapoel Haifa, Hapoel Jerusalem and Allenby Tel Aviv from the Hapoel association, while the Maccabi clubs were Maccabi Tel Aviv, Hasmonean Jerusalem and Avshalom Petah Tikvah. The final on 26 May 1928 saw the Allenby boys face Hasmonean Jerusalem in front of a crowd of 6,000 at the Palm Court, with the match refereed by an Englishman named Adams, who may have been the chauffeur to the new High Commissioner. Allenby's Shlomo Poliakov scored twenty minutes into the second half, leaving the Jerusalem team to chase the game. This time, Allenby had Willy Berger, their first-choice goalkeeper, and he kept out three clear shots. In the eighty-first minute, Allenby got a second goal from Poliakov's brother-in-law, Avraham Nudelman, who was playing on the left wing.

The final immediately led to a new argument between the Maccabi and Hapoel. Hasmonean Jerusalem complained that the Allenby boys had fielded an unregistered player, a man named Moshe Mayer. When they took their complaint to the Palestine Football Association – which is to say, to Yosef and his friends in the Maccabi – the judgement was fudged and led to the bizarre decision to share the cup. The Carmel company's trophy spent six months in Jerusalem and six months in Tel Aviv. This soured relationships so badly that when Sir Alfred offered to pay to bring an English coach to Palestine to train a joint Hapoel and Maccabi team for a British tour, the proposal was rejected. The dream of a 'national' Yishuv side seemed to be in tatters.

This was not the only blow Yosef faced around this time. He had seen FIFA as a back door into the Olympics, but this hope ended in 1928 when FIFA resigned from the Olympic movement. As Henri Delaunay of FIFA said, now that the world's best players were all professionals, 'football can no longer be held within the confines of the Olympics'.

The only hopeful news was that FIFA announced its plans for a future outside the Olympic movement. At its International Congress, held in Amsterdam two days after the May Palestine Cup final, FIFA announced plans for a first World Cup. This presented a new opportunity for Yosef. If he could meet a tight deadline, he stood a good chance of leading a Yishuv side at the first FIFA World Cup in 1930. He hosted the inaugural meeting of the Palestine Football Association that summer.

Yosef's application to FIFA lists the founder members in

attendance that day, and it includes a Palestinian referee named Nusseibeh. Everyone who has written on the subject has naturally identified the referee as Ibrahim Nusseibeh; after all, he was the sole qualified official in the country. The only evidence Nusseibeh was in attendance, however, is Yosef's list. The meeting was conducted in Hebrew, a language Nusseibeh could not speak; if he had been there, he would have understood nothing. It is also worth noting that Nusseibeh's name is the only one not given in full. As Palestinians rarely use their first names, it is possible that Yosef did not know Nusseibeh's name. Yosef is frank in his memoirs that he bent the truth in all his dealings with FIFA. All in all, it seems likely Nusseibeh was added to the list without his knowledge, and he never knew about the meeting. When I began to nurse doubts about Yosef's minutes, I contacted Nusseibeh's family. His cousin, Hazem Nusseibeh, was only a child at the time but has no knowledge of the meeting. If Nusseibeh attended, he seems to have told no one, and certainly never went to another: his name never appears on any further minutes from Yosef's organisation. His attendance is especially unlikely given his family's role within the Opposition that took such a strong anti-Yishuv line (though he was never anti-Jewish, as the bye-laws of the al-Araby Sports Club make clear).

Perhaps the strongest reason to assume that Nusseibeh was never at the meeting is that nothing else in the application is true. The document is a fiction from start to finish. Yosef backdated the formation of the Palestine Football Association to 1927, in order that the organisation could take credit for the 1927 Palestine Cup, as well as the 1928 version. The letter assures FIFA that both tournaments were a great success. The application sets out the structure of what Yosef claims are existing, functioning Palestinian leagues. He states that there are ten teams in Division 1, twenty in the Division 2 and thirty-nine in Division 3. This makes a total of sixty-nine teams, which is far more than the country could support, and way more than the number Yosef recalled when he wrote about the state of football in Palestine in the 1931 FIFA yearbook. The application claims that eleven of these teams are run by Palestinian clubs, with five playing in Division Two and six in Division Three (in his imagination, none are good enough to play in the top division!). If this were true, then the league would contain a staggering fifty-eight Jewish teams in 1928. Yet when Yosef organised the Palestine Cup competition, he only managed to scrape together six teams.

The application claimed that the Palestine Football Association oversaw multiple divisions, with promotion and demotion each season, and an established national knockout competition. It was exactly what FIFA required, but none of it was true. Yosef's letter pulls teams and even whole leagues out of thin air. If the package seemed dubious, it came with the backing of the British military, who had teams in the league. It was also backed by Colonel Kisch, sponsor of the Magen Shimson tournament, and by the Paris-based Baron de Rothschild, whose winery sponsored the Palestine Cup. Finally, the application carried the imprimatur of Sir Alfred Mond, whose sponsorship of the Mond Cup made him a key figure in the British Home Nations football associations. FIFA was struggling to keep the four British Home Nations within the international organisation. Signing up a British colony must have looked like a good way to appease the British associations.

In December 1928, FIFA voted to admit Palestine on a trial basis.

Chapter Eleven:

From Hebron to Cairo

Yosef had faked and forged his way into FIFA, yet at the moment the Maccabi won acceptance, the Home Nations pulled out of FIFA. The British ostensibly withdrew in 1928 over the issue of amateurism, although there were no material differences between the British and FIFA positions. In truth, it was an early example of the arrogant self-harm that would become a hallmark of British diplomacy. The new Palestine FA was left without a champion in Paris. The 1930 World Cup would be held in Uruguay, and without British backing Yosef saw little hope of making it to Montevideo. The teams had to pay their own sea passage and commit to two months away from home. There were problems at home, too, as the Maccabi and Hapoel continued to squabble over the 1928 Palestine Cup final.

There was worse to come. In 1929, football was banned following a fresh outbreak of rioting in 1929. Palestine saw no league football for the next three years. It was a disaster for the nascent leagues. It must have seemed to Yosef that all his invention and all his efforts were in vain. His Palestine FA was only a provisional member of FIFA. If Yosef failed to operate a league and tournaments, he risked being thrown out of the world body.

A solution of sorts came from Yosef's old friend, David Tidhar. David had been a big noise as a kid but he found adult life tougher than he expected. His mouth had soon got him into trouble in the police force. He fell out with his superiors, lost his command in Jerusalem, and by 1924 was living back in Tel Aviv. He set up what he later claimed to be the first private eye agency in Palestine. This was the age of Agatha Christie's Hercule Poirot and Dashiell Hammett's Continental Op. The ever self-aggrandising David always enjoyed posing as an omniscient man of action, but in reality the work was providing checks on prospective investors in the real-estate deals shaping the growth of Tel Aviv. Yosef's letters, stored in the Maccabi library in Ramat Gan, invariably contain digressions away from sport matters to advise correspondents on the investment opportunities of Tel Aviv's real-estate market. David scrutinised clients for Yosef, as well as other old friends such as the Danin family. At the same time, he found a new outlet for his observations and opinions in writing. Tel Aviv's burgeoning Hebrew-language newspapers became an outlet for his continued polemics against the British officers in the Palestine Police Force, whom he portrayed as fools. Predictably, this made him unpopular.

By 1927, even Tel Aviv had become too hot for David. He and his wife Rebecca moved to Cairo and took work in the downtown pharmacy run by Rebecca's brother. Cairo was thriving in the 1920s. The Egyptian capital is really a string of cities, each with its own character, from the medieval Islamic capital, through the citadel and, by the 1920s, a fascinating art deco downtown district. Egypt had the first democratically elected government in the Middle East, which existed in an uneasy alliance with the colonial British powers. British and Australian soldiers filled the bars and the brothels. Cairo seemed a city bursting with opportunities, and a magnet for political and international intrigues. In his own account of his Cairo years, David was the eyes and ears of Colonel Kisch, spying on the comings and goings of Syrian and Palestinian delegations to the Egyptian government. Like so many of his tales, this may have been an attempt to retro-engineer a heroic past. David was still looking for the main chance to leave his mark on the world. But he was in contact with Kisch in 1929, when the violence came.

Rebecca Tidhar and her brother Benzion Capiloto were born in Hebron, twenty miles south of Jerusalem, in the Sephardic Jewish community that had made the city their home from the 1840s onwards, after leaving Rhodes with the help of the English industrialist Moses Montefiore. By 1929, the community numbered around 500 in a city of 20,000. In August 1929, David and Rebecca were opening their Cairo pharmacy when they heard rumours of a massacre in Hebron. Somehow, David managed to contact his wife's family in the city, and learned that the British had cut communications across Palestine, hoping to control the news of the murders before it inspired more violence. David claimed that he was the only conduit for information from Hebron, and for once he was perhaps right.

The violence had begun in Jerusalem a week earlier with a march by a new youth party, backed by Menachem Arber. The party was another of these sporting-scouting-paramilitary organisations that were springing up across Europe. It had been founded in newly independent Latvia, where its leaders had taken inspiration from a 1923 speech by Vladimir Jabotinsky. In his speech, Jabotinsky asked for a 'Covenant' with the memory of a fallen comrade, Joseph Trumpeldor, a Jewish-Russian soldier who had died in a firefight in the Galilee in 1920 with a Lebanese Shi-ite militia. Trumpeldor's covenant, or *Brit* in Hebrew, became the sacred oath that defined party membership. The initial letter of Brit, 'B', led the new party to pose as a secondary 'B' force to the existing Haganah, the militia of their loathed socialist rivals. But because the Hebrew letter 'B', or *'Beit'*, is also the Hebrew word for 'house', this allowed party members to pose as both a back-up force and simultaneously as a more patriotic 'Home Guard'. In due course, Arber's party took the name *Beitar*, which means a fortified homestead.

Arber had established the initial Brit Trumpeldor society in Tel Aviv in 1926. Arber held a great deal of affection for Jabotinsky, the man who had recruited him into the British Army. As an industrialist, he also shared Jabotinsky's right-wing, anti-socialist and anti-union politics. There was an additional bond: Arber and Jabotinsky both hailed from Odessa, the port city in Russia's lawless 'wild east', rather than the Pale of Settlement that had produced so many leaders of the close-knit Yishuv. But Arber's main reason for creating the party was nostalgia for the old fighting Maccabi he had joined as a boy.

Arber's youth party opened a training programme for instructors in 1928 in Tel Aviv, focusing on civil disobedience and demonstration tactics, rather than sports and exercise. The course leader was Jeremiah Halpern, who had recently graduated from Lazio's naval academy in Italy. His contacts in Mussolini's regime brought Italian state funding to the new party. On Thursday 15 August, 1929, Halpern led a gang from

Tel Aviv to a demonstration in Jerusalem. The group unfurled banners at the wall – then known as the 'Wailing Wall' – while shouting, 'The Wall is ours.' The wall surrounds the holy sanctuary in Jerusalem, and is said to date to the Roman-era temple built by Herod the Great. The area now holds both the al-Aqsa Mosque and the mosque of the Dome of the Rock. Any attempt to claim ownership of the mosque area is a reliable way to provoke violence. The Beitar demonstration soon brought a confrontation between the police, as well as local Palestinians. The first murder happened away from the march, however, when a young Palestinian grocer's assistant was kidnapped while pushing his wheelbarrow in the Old City's narrow market streets. The boy had been chosen at random and was lynched.

The next week saw a series of random murders. Everyone expected Beitar to attempt another demonstration on the following sabbath. The next Friday, 23 August, 700 men from Hebron tried to get to Jerusalem to confront Beitar. When they were blocked from leaving Hebron by the police, they turned on their own city. The target was a recently established yeshiva – a Jewish religious learning institution – in the downtown souk area of Hebron. This residential seminary was five years old, and had been built to train rabbis in Rabbi Kook's innovative Bible-based sect. Stones were thrown at the building, and when a student was discovered in the street he was set upon and stabbed to death.

The worst of the Hebron massacres began early the next day, the Saturday. The rioters returned to the seminary, which was the only Jewish residence in the downtown area. Twenty-four young Lithuanian men were murdered, seven of whom held US or Canadian citizenship, which made the killings international news. There were sixty-seven fatalities in total across Hebron, with another fifty-eight people receiving injuries. The Hebron massacre became a symbol of the 1929 riots, but took place against a wider backdrop of confrontations and lynchings, notably in Jerusalem and Jaffa. The police struggled to maintain order as both Palestinian and Jewish policemen joined the rioters. In Hebron, the British chief of police claimed that Arab policemen sent from Jerusalem to the city were responsible for some of the worst of the murders.

Simcha Hinkis, a Jewish policeman from Tel Aviv who was also in the Haganah, led an attack on the house of the sheikh of the mosque in al-Manshiyya, Jaffa. Hinkis was also a football player, part of the squad of Hapoel Allenby FC. The attack saw Hinkis personally murder the five adults and injure two children. As the violence spread through al-Manshiyya, the Haganah set up patrols to guard Jewish neighbourhoods. Arber and Halpern responded by setting up the Beitar-based rival, Haganah Beit, and disaffected Russians and right-wingers flocked to this force in preference to the socialist-led Haganah. The riots opened the way for the new Beitar party to challenge the socialists, importing Europe's well-established fascist versus socialist dynamic into Palestine.

David Tidhar reacted to the massacre in Hebron with telegrams to Palestine, asking everyone to support his bid to be placed at the head of a security force to restore order in Palestine. No one responded.

His next idea was even more quixotic: a football tour of Egypt.

*

David had convinced himself that a tour of Egypt could be a money-spinner. As unlikely as it sounds, he seems to have shouldered the cost of the tour alone. The Palestine FA was not wealthy: it had been unable to finance the trip to the Uruguay World Cup. David believed that the earlier tours of Egypt by Hakoah Vienna had turned a profit and was impetuous enough to believe a tour by a Palestine FA side could also make money. To Yosef, the proposed tour came at a good time, when football was impossible in Palestine. However, Yosef misjudged the mood and blundered by turning the tour into a celebration of the close links between the Yishuv and the British authorities. It was the wrong time for such a gesture. Both the socialists and the new Beitar party were blaming the British for the security situation in Palestine. The tour proved to be a disastrous misstep, politically for Yosef and financially for David.

In 1930, as other footballing nations boarded ships for Uruguay, a hastily assembled side boarded a train for Egypt. The team included nine British soldiers and five members of the Maccabi. The specially designed strip featured a new insignia sewn over the left breast, incorporating a large 'P' for Palestine, beside a smaller 'LD' placed in the angle formed by the taller letter. The LD apparently stood for Land of Israel. The team photograph shows the fifteen-strong squad, fourteen wearing this new strip and a goalkeeper who is so wrapped up in a thick two-ply sweater and a flat cap that he looks as if he is ready to play through an English winter. Some reports state that an Arab Palestinian was included in the squad, possibly as a translator, which allowed Yosef to continue the deception that his association represented all parts of Palestinian society.

The touring team played three matches, losing 5–0 against a side described as a Cairo XI, then 2–0 against an Alexandria XI, and finally 5–2 against a British Army XI. There is no information on the teams representing Cairo or Alexandria, and whether they were drawn from professional sides or the universities. The games were not popular spectator events and the tour left David bankrupt. The size of the three defeats also brought a savage reaction from the Yishuv. People were offended by almost every aspect of the tour, not simply the scale of the defeats.

The greatest attacks came from *Doar Hayom*, a popular newspaper modelled on the British *Daily Mail*. This criticism was all the more bitter because *Doar Hayom* was the paper of the landowners and citrus growers, the stalwarts of the Maccabi movement from its earliest days. However, the paper was now edited by one of Halpern's recruits, named Abba Ahimeir (born Geisinovich). Abba was older than many of the early Beitar boys, at thirty-one years old, and already a self-declared fascist. He had written his PhD on the fascist philosopher Oswald Spengler. The Beitar party had bought *Doar Hayom* and appointed Abba as editor in 1929, with the idea of wooing the old Russian establishment, the paper's readership. Abba began his editorship with passionate apologies for the Beitar demonstrators, who he claimed were not agents provocateurs but Jewish patriots acting in defence of a Jewish wall. When he turned his invective on the Maccabi in 1930, he criticised the tiny letters of the cryptic LD insignia, the poor quality of the team, and the decision to run a tour with a team that included so many British soldiers: 'the team had to comprise the inhabitants of the country . . . not military people who travel here and there, and due to their temporary status in the land cannot be representatives of the country', he blasted.

The judgement against Yosef and the Maccabi was even harsher in Hapoel circles. David Tidhar responded by writing his own defence of the tour as an example of Jewish pride in an article in the rival *Davar* paper, but he had left it too late to change opinion.

David's money problems drove him back to Palestine. He teamed up with a journalist named Shlomo Gelfer (whose pen-name was Shlomo Ben-Israel) and began to supply stories for a series of pulp detective novellas. In the books, a private eye named David Tidhar performs exploits that are considerably more exciting than David's real-life time as a financial investigator. His villains tended to be Jewish: shadowy criminal figures with agendas that undercut the happy and stable life of the Yishuv, whether as agitators, underhand speculators or foreign emissaries. The stories represent a graphic picture of the insularity of the Yishuv. The rivalries and enmities of Tel Aviv took place within a bubble, occasionally buffeted by the street politics in Europe, but rarely affected by any interface with the Palestinians.

Chapter Twelve:

The Arse

The football stadium used by both the Jaffa Orthodox club and the Islamic Sports Club from the late 1920s to the 1940s was known as the Basa, which can be translated as 'arse'. It stands on the same low-lying plane as the Palm Court stadium, and perhaps got its name because it was also prone to floods. Yosef Yekutieli had won membership of FIFA in 1928 by conjuring teams out of thin air. He seemed to know nothing of the reality of Palestinian football, and it is unlikely he saw any games at the Basa during its time as Jaffa's stadium. After the 1929 riots, there was nothing to see, thanks to the ban on football imposed by John Chancellor, the third High Commissioner of Palestine. The ban was relaxed briefly in March 1931, to allow a side from Cairo University to play a number of games against Yishuv sides and British military personnel. *Falastin* seized on the tour with a demand that the Egyptian side play Jaffa Orthodox. For a brief afternoon, the arse was reopened. As it were.

Issa al-Issa had written a series of critical editorials against Amin al-Husseini, which earned him death threats. He took the threats seriously enough to move temporarily to Beirut and his nephew Daoud al-Issa took over as editor of *Falastin*. Daoud had founded and played for the Jaffa Orthodox boys' club, and his paper enthusiastically supported his old team. The match report declared the team gave such a good account against the Egyptians that the opposition learned the quality of Palestinian football, which is a bold way to report a defeat. For good measure, Daoud lambasted other Palestinian teams for not also stepping up and giving the Egyptians a game.

The period of the shutdown had a bizarrely positive effect on Palestinian football. March 1931 saw the formation of a first national team, created to represent Palestine on a trip to Lebanon to play the American College. The team was drawn from five teams: Jaffa Orthodox; Jaffa's Islamic Sports Club; Ibrahim Nusseibeh's al-Araby Sports Club; the team of St George's School; and finally from Jerusalem's new YMCA. *Falastin* reported the event with excitement, insisting 'this team would be the strongest team in Palestine'. There are, however, no reports on how this team fared against the Beirut players.

The creation of a Palestinian national team ignited a new era for football. In June 1931, all the Palestinian teams met to launch the Arab Palestine Sports Federation, also known as the Palestine Sports Federation or PSF. The federation comprised ten teams, two from Jaffa, four from Jerusalem and four from Haifa. Palestine now had two rival league organisations, the Palestine FA and the PSF, though still no actual leagues and no tournaments as long as the ban on football persisted.

Yosef had only won provisional membership of FIFA, and since joining there had been no league games or tournaments; nothing, in fact, but the Egyptian tour. The risk of expulsion must have seemed all the greater now that a rival organisation existed. Especially as this new league had a genuinely multifaith membership. It not only included Muslim and Christian teams, but as the decade progressed the league included non-Arab sides from the Syriac and Armenian communities. The PSF made no secret of its ambition to join FIFA, and so Yosef needed the British to lift the ban on football to prove that his FA was a functioning organisation. He still needed British help to run the leagues: almost all the qualified referees were British soldiers. Yosef stated there were only two civilian referees in the country in 1931, and he was probably thinking of Adams, the High Commissioner's chauffeur, and Ibrahim Nusseibeh.

The problem was that relations between the Yishuv and the British had soured considerably since the riots, fuelled by attacks in Abba Ahimeir's editorials in the Beitar newspapers, and by parallel criticisms from the left. Army cutbacks were blamed for the lack of security, while the Jewish Agency was attacked for being too close to the British – which, of course, it was, having been created by the British. Weizmann took the protests personally and resigned as head of the Jewish Agency and the ZO in 1931, to be replaced by his deputy Nahum Sokolow. Ben Gurion's socialists only formally took over the Jewish Agency in 1933, the start of their forty-five-year domination of the Yishuv and, subsequently, Israeli politics. The shake-up at the Jewish Agency meant that Colonel Kisch lost his job as the Agency's spy chief. He retired to Haifa, where he still exerted influence over the British. When John Chancellor was replaced as the High Commissioner by General Sir Arthur Grenfell Wauchope, a career soldier whose previous job had been Commander in

Chief of Northern Ireland, Kisch personally asked for the ban on football to be lifted. Wauchope acquiesced.

The second year of the Palestine Cup ran from November 1931 to May 1932 with eight Jewish sides and a ninth team drawn from the Palestine Police. Nine is an awkward number for staging a knockout tournament, but in his letters to FIFA Yosef continued to insist there were no Palestinian sides of sufficient quality to compete at the top level. Five of the teams were from the Maccabi: Petah Tikva, Jerusalem, Tel Aviv, Nes Tziona and Haifa. Three represented the Hapoel association: Haifa, Allenby and Jerusalem. The matches began with the old tradition of playing both 'God Save the King' and 'Hatikvah'. In another bow to tradition, the tournament was marred by violence between Hapoel and Maccabi, and also between the British and Hapoel supporters. The resentment boiled over in the Cup final when Hapoel Haifa were defeated by the Palestine Police. Angry fans from Hapoel Haifa, the dockworkers' side, stole the trophy. Though the cup has never been recovered, it is not exactly lost, either. There have been numerous sightings over the past eighty years. Like a mystical object, the cup is not missing so much as occluded from the eyes of anyone not Hapoel.

Once the ban on football was lifted, Palestinian teams began matching and defeating British teams. In February 1932, the Jaffa Orthodox boys beat the Royal Air Force, once the best team in Palestine. They did it in style, running out 5–1 winners. Jerusalem's al-Araby also beat the Air Force and a combined army side 5–2 and 4–2 respectively in 1934. The Palestinian teams continued to tour neighbouring countries, playing regularly in Syria and Egypt. A national Palestinian side made up of al-Araby and Jaffa's Islamic Sports Club played the top

Egyptian team Alexandria United in August 1933, losing 4–1. The same team played a side in Amman the next year, winning by five goals to one. The Lebanese club al-Nahda visited Palestine in 1935, and were soundly beaten by al-Araby (5–0). Jaffa's Islamic Sports Club visited Beirut to play al-Nahda and also won (0–1).

Falastin's sports columnist Hussein Husni continued to berate Palestinian footballers for their lack of quality but the results suggest there were decent teams. The game had been embraced by a rising working class, especially those in the transport hubs and port cities. The British were building a deep-water port in Haifa to supply the Royal Navy with oil from Iraq's British-controlled oilfields. The oil was pretty much the entire point of the British takeover of Palestine. The German U-boat blockade of the Atlantic during the war had humbled the Royal Navy, at a time when all the world's oil came from Texas. In 1914, the First Lord of the Admiralty, Winston Churchill, had converted the fleet to oil power without plans for how to fuel the ships. The Royal Navy was effectively confined to port for the entire First World War. The British never wanted to be so impotent again.

The three cities where Palestinian football found an audience – the triangle of Jaffa, Haifa and Jerusalem – were also the cities where the Yishuv was strongest, and each year these cities became even more Jewish. Despite the British controls on immigration, 60,000 new immigrants were arriving each year up to the mid-1930s, and numbers increased thereafter. Immigration was spurred by the rise of Nazism, as well as less overt race politics across Europe. The tightening of immigration controls into Britain and the United States made British Palestine an attractive second choice. Outside of the football triangle, there was still little Jewish presence in Palestine. Large cities such as Nablus, Ashdod and Gaza had no Jewish community at all. The survivors of the massacre in Hebron had rebuilt their lives elsewhere. In the countryside, the Palestinian farmhands saw the British as the enemy, and barely experienced the effects of European Jewish colonialism at all.

Football became a marker of an internal political divide among Palestinians, of town and country, and of the central triangle against the cities of the north and the south. In effect, football was popular wherever Amin al-Husseini and his party, the Council Supporters, were weakest. It was clear that football had the potential to mobilise the urban youth. The first serious attempt to harness this power came in 1932 with the creation of the Youth Congress Party, al-Mutamar al-Shabab.

The Youth Congress Party was formed by Yaqub al-Ghusayn, a 33-year-old Cambridge-educated lawyer from Ramle. The city is relatively new by Palestinian standards: it dates back to the seventh century, when the early Muslim armies created it as a transport hub. Ramle was briefly the capital of the Umayyad caliphate. Its role as a logistics centre continued into the twentieth century as Ramle became the country's chief railway hub connecting the coast and Jerusalem with Egypt. Al-Ghusayn's party was formed in reaction to the insularity of the existing two parties, the al-Husseini and Nashashibi factions, and as its name suggests, it was shaped to attract a new constituency of young workers. Young people were flocking to the country's many new social and sports clubs, the vehicles of Palestinian nationalism. The regular scout parades and jamborees, dances and football matches brought out crowds, and saw communities from across the country mix together, party and celebrate.

The Youth Congress Party launched a new football league in 1933 with the help of King Ghazi, the twenty-year-old son of Prince Feisal, who ascended the Iraqi throne that year. King Ghazi already sponsored the Jerusalem team al-Rawda, and increased his commitment by supporting the new competition and providing a shield, known as 'The Armour of King Ghazi'. The competition was adopted as the league tournament of the PSF, but only after tortuous negotiations between the scout movement, the PSF and the Nashashibi 'Opposition' block. The result, however, showed the shape of a new political coalition. The first season began in November 1933 with seven teams on board. Jerusalem was represented by al-Araby and al-Rawda, and Jaffa by the Islamic and the Christian Orthodox clubs. Haifa had three teams: White Star, Haifa Islamic Club and a team of old boys from the Christian Salesian school. The following summer, the Salesian boys ditched the name of the school in a symbolic protest against European meddling in Palestine. They became al-Shabab al-Arab, meaning Arab Boys or Arab Youth, signalling that they shared the same nationalist politics as Ghusayn's party, al-Mutamar al-Shabab.

In May 1935, the Youth Congress Party mounted a national festival of sport in Jaffa at the Basa stadium. The motivation for the event came from the Maccabiah Games. The PSF faced opposition from the British, who were worried about spectators from across Palestine descending on Jaffa. Overt pressure was backed by appeals to the owners of the stadium to pull the event. The Palestinian newspapers took up the cause, arguing that the Basa was the only stadium capable of holding a national festival, as there were so few stadiums available to Palestinians. The newspaper *Difa'*, the paper of the Opposition, ran a campaign to highlight the lack of Palestinian sports facilities. The accusation hit home because land acquired by the British Army to the north of Tel Aviv had been donated to the Maccabi for the 1932 Maccabiah Games by High Commissioner Wauchope. After the games were over, the stadium became the home of Maccabi Tel Aviv FC. The development included new apartment blocks created by the Sports Stadium Corporation, a company operated by Yosef Yekutieli and the Maccabi. The Palm Court was donated to Hapoel Allenby FC. It became the Hapoel home stadium.

On the creation of Israel in 1948, the new state confiscated the Basa stadium and donated it to Hapoel. It remains the Hapoel Tel Aviv home ground to this day.

Chapter Thirteen:

The World Cup

The threat from the new Palestine Sports Federation seemed so great that the Maccabi waged a covert war against it throughout the 1930s. The rules of FIFA forbid the associations' members from playing non-FIFA sides without special permission. When Syria was being considered for membership in 1933, the Maccabi demanded that any match between a Syrian club and a team from Palestine be submitted to Tel Aviv for approval, which would be withheld if the side was a member of the rival PSF. Another letter from Tel Aviv to Paris dated September 1933 goes even further, demanding any fixture between a Syrian team and a club from any third country be regarded as an extraordinary match and require special permission to go ahead. When Lebanon's Football Association also applied to join FIFA, Yosef wrote to Paris offering to vet all of the Lebanese and Syrian teams to see if the countries' football were truly worthy of international recognition.

The year 1934 saw the Yishuv teams gearing up for the second World Cup. Lumek Ratner, now thirty-five, was brought in as coach for the qualifying match against the Egyptian national side in Cairo. Hapoel Allenby were in the middle of a barnstorming season, and would win the Palestine Cup that year. Lumek was a Maccabi man through and through. After his stint as the player-coach of Maccabi Tel Aviv, he had gone on to coach Maccabi Avshalom Petah Tikvah. But he showed he was evenhanded by building his World Cup squad around the Allenby rebels.

Yohanan Sukenik, the forward, was the best player, followed by Avraham Nudelman, who played on the left. Nudelman was so small he was nicknamed 'Feather', and had been immortalised under that name by the flamboyant Tel Aviv poet Alexander Penn in a verse celebrating the Cup final win published in the *Davar* newspaper.

Lumek complemented Nudelman by picking a giant to play on Sukenik's right, Amnon Harlap. The 25-year-old from Rehovot was so tall that he is only ever pictured sitting in team photographs. Amnon was known for his boast that he was descended from King David and carried a family tree in his pocket to prove the connection whenever he was challenged. Amon was more of an athlete than a footballer, though he had been good enough to make the reserves of the Belgian team KAA when he was an engineering student in Ghent. He later said he could not pass the ball: 'I could receive a pass and I could use my head and especially my legs, that was all.' He claimed that only Sukenik and the goalkeeper Willy Berger had the skills to implement Lumek's game plans. Everyone else was in the business of kicking and running. But it was a happy team. Berger was Ratner's oldest pick at twenty-eight, with all the others either Amon's age or younger. Maccabi Tel Aviv was represented by the popular Avraham Reznik, who was twenty-five. Hapoel Haifa supplied 23-year-old Gedalyahu Fuchs, a Romanian who had only arrived in Palestine in 1931, but was already the mainstay of the port dockers' team.

The 23-year-old defender Pinhas Fiedler from Jerusalem had played for Maccabi Hasmonean Jerusalem, but just a month earlier had switched to Menachem Arber's team, Beitar Tel Aviv. The 1930s saw the Maccabi effectively driven out of Jerusalem. The problem was that the Maccabi ground on Mea She'arim Street ran by the Geula neighbourhood, which was home to the devout Bukharan Jewish sect. The quarter had grown since the 1880s, and besides the Bukharan Jews had begun to attract Hasidic Jews from Poland and Ukraine. Football is a game traditionally played at the weekend, and the regular Saturday football games became the focus of ultra-Orthodox protests to defend the sabbath. Pictures capture the Palestinian police on horseback, wearing uniforms more reminiscent of Ottoman times than anything associated with the British Empire. The players are lost in the large crowds of the Hasidim, identifiable by their tall black hats, and the Bukharans by their broad, fur-trimmed cartwheels. The unrelenting hostility of the religious Jews had a profound effect on football in Jerusalem. The city is the site of the mythical hill of Zion, a term that had come to function as a synecdoche for the entire city, and been adopted as the name of the Jewish nationalist movement. Yet from the 1930s onwards, the Maccabi and Hapoel struggled to build a significant football team in the city. The protests ultimately saw the Maccabi disappear from Jerusalem. The irony was that the completion of the new YMCA in 1933 meant there was a fine football stadium, right in the centre of the city. If only the

Maccabi had consented to play non-Jewish sides, they might have built a thriving football club in the city.

On Amnon Harlap's account, the only conflicts of the 1934 World Cup campaign were with the PFA officials. Interviewed in 2001 when he was ninety-one years old, Harlap was still bitter about the Maccabi-appointed men, claiming they were interested only in collecting subscriptions. The party of players and PFA officials was led by Yehoshuah Aluf (previously known as Wolfiansky), one of Yosef's childhood friends from Zvi Nishri's gym club. Aluf had worked with Nishri at the Gymnasia Herzliya, before moving to a high school in Jerusalem. Hapoel were represented by a Histadrut man, Morris Weintraub. There was also an Arab Christian translator named Elias Charbelos. The name Charbelos is Aramaic, suggesting that his family were Lebanese Maronites, or perhaps Syriac refugees who suffered during the same massacres as the Armenians. His inclusion maintained the illusion that the team represented all of Palestine.

The thirteen-hour journey to the match in Cairo required a change at Ashdod, a city that is only twenty-six miles south of Tel Aviv yet seemed like a foreign city to Harlap because he had never visited a wholly Palestinian city before. The party changed trains again at Rafah, the border town between Gaza and the Sinai, and changed for a third time at the Suez Canal. They passed the time by flirting with three actresses who were also making the journey to Cairo. The players often struggled to understand each other, because the team included native Hebrew speakers such as Harlap and others who barely spoke the language at all and had to resort to German and Yiddish.

The match, played at the Prince Farouk stadium, was a disaster: the Yishuv team lost 7–1. Nudelman scored the visitors'

George's School team, 1908–9 season.

Izzat Tannous and friend,
St George's School, 1913.

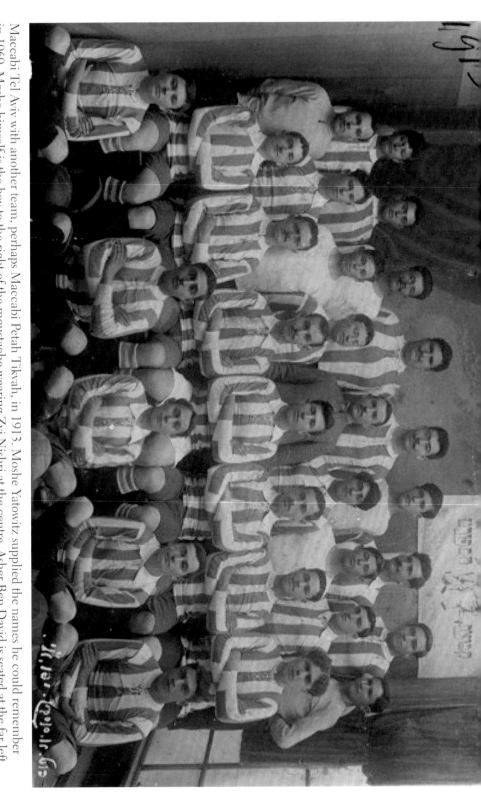

Maccabi Tel Aviv with another team, perhaps Maccabi Petah Tikvah, in 1913. Moshe Yatowitz supplied the names he could remember in 1969. Moshe himself is the boy to the right of the moustache-wearing Zvi Nishri at the centre. Asher Ben David is seated at the far left. Menachem Arber and David Tidhar are seated on the ground at the extreme right.

Yosef Yekutieli, David Tidhar and
Yehuda Hezroni, 1914.

אבנריאל "צבי יולום, בביתו תל-אביב
1919. תל.

i Nishri, 1919.

Palestino FC, Santiago, 1920: Elias Zaror, Miguel Saffie, Nicolás Hirmas; Rafael Hirmas, Elías Hirmas, Antonio Sarah; José Yunis, Victor Panayotti, Emilio Deik, Jorge Lama and Elias Deik.

Yosef Yekutieli, founder of the Palestine Football Association, in the dress whites of the Maccabi Association, pictured with two of his children in 1929.

he 'Palestine' team on its 1931 Egyptian tour.

man stands in front of various posters on Allenby Street, at Bet-B November Square. The
osters include an advert for the football game in honour of Simcha Hinkis, 1935 (bottom right).
rde Collection, Israel Museum, Tel Aviv)

Ultra-Orthodox protestors at Geula, Jerusalem, around 1935.

Koko Kalalian in 1969 playing for Hapoel Antonio, a Catholic team from Jaffa.

Rami Mansour, Koko Kalalian and David Mansour in Jaffa, 2018.

The author with General Jibril Rajoub.

sole goal late in the match. His dribble though the defence so infuriated the Egyptian team, they scored the seventh and final goal immediately in response. The Egyptians were coached by James McCrae, a Scotsman who had served as a Grenadier Guard and played professionally for Clyde as well as a number of English teams. McCrae had modestly predicted a five-goal victory before the game. Harlap best remembered the Port Said forward, Mohammed Hassan, and especially Al Ahly's Mahmoud Mokhtar, a legendary player known as 'El-Tetsh' who served as the Egyptian captain for ten years. Harlap remembered that Mokhtar easily evaded his marker, saying: 'Every kick to the goal was a goal.' Harlap's memory deceived him, though: all seven goals were scored by the Port Said forward, Abdelrahman Fawzi.

The team did not return to Palestine immediately. They played a friendly in Alexandria where they were billed as 'Tel Aviv' and reached a respectable nil–nil draw. The return World Cup qualifier was played at the Palm Court in Jaffa, now the grounds of Hapoel Allenby Tel Aviv. It was the only pitch available as the Maccabi were already rebuilding the 1932 stadium in preparation for the 1935 Maccabiah Games. The Palm Court was already regarded as a faded place. It lay close to the railway tracks, so the trains shook the single stand, running along the western edge. The stand had room for a thousand people on a bleacher of three levels. Ten thousand people turned up for the game, including many Palestinians who wanted to see the big names of Egyptian soccer. The overcrowding led to a roof collapsing behind the stand, as spectators clambered for a view. The game was violent. Abdelrahman Fawzi scored four goals before being taken out with a bone-crunching tackle, and the Egyptians played the second half with ten men as they had no substitute. In the second half, Sukenik delivered a consolation goal, ending the game at 1–4. The stories of the match include an account of a concussion to Harlap that led to him vomiting and being admitted to the new Hadassah hospital. There are stories that even the meal between the players in the evening ended in a fight. The situation may not have been quite as bad as it is portrayed because there was a junior match the next day, a friendly billed as Tel Aviv vs Cairo, which ended 2–2.

Chapter Fourteen:

The Return of Hinkis

The 1930s wave of Jewish immigration into Palestine was the largest yet and the majority were German speakers. Many were medical or teaching professionals. This period saw the creation of a Jewish orchestra, the Palestine Philharmonic, and the adoption of the distinctive modernist architecture seen in Tel Aviv. The 1930s also saw the founding of dozens of new football teams. The Maccabi and Hapoel competed to bring the teams to their associations. Many German immigrants stuck with the familiar Hakoah association, which provided a reminder of the metropolitan life they had left in Berlin and Vienna. The PFA accommodated the new teams with a second Tel Aviv League for the city's youth teams, and a further two regional leagues, termed the Samaria League and the Southern or Sharon League. These 'regions' actually flanked Tel Aviv, with the Samaria League centred on Netanya, the coastal town closest to Tel Aviv. The Southern League was based on Rehovot, the farming district to its south. A map of the clubs of the Jewish Yishuv would show a concentration around the coastal bubble, with Jerusalem no longer fielding teams thanks to the city's religious Jewish protesters.

As the 1930s progressed, the World Maccabi Union consumed more and more of Yosef Yekutieli's time. The Maccabiah Games were his baby, since he and Sir Alfred Mond had persuaded the Maccabi World Union to move the games permanently to Palestine after the first 1928 games in Prague. Preparations for the 1932 games began with a publicity tour: a marathon motorcycle tour through Europe by Maccabi members. Sir Alfred died in 1930 while the convoy was riding to London. Alfred's son Henry was promptly elected as the new president of the Maccabi Union, though only after he went through a speedy Jewish conversion. His German mother had brought him up as a Christian. Yosef invited the Hapoel and the YMCA in Jerusalem to submit athletes to compete for places on the Palestine team. Both declined.

The 1932 Maccabiah Games were celebrated less for their sporting quality than their success in smuggling Jews into Palestine, evading the immigration controls. Spectators and athletes applied for visas to see the games, and then disappeared into the Yishuv. The games proved so contentious that the British placed the 1935 games under a notional ban, without doing anything to prevent them going ahead. The preparations were not subtle, as the stadium was completely rebuilt behind hoardings advertising the games.

The pressure of organising the Games led the Maccabi to cancel the 1934–5 football league halfway through the season. The league leaders at the time, Hapoel Allenby, were announced the winners. Not that this made Hapoel happy: they were outraged, and announced they would boycott the Palestine Cup, which was now a knockout tournament. As a result, Hakoah Tel Aviv received a bye to the finals. This was a new team made up of members of Hakoah Berlin. The 1935 Palestine Cup final was the inaugural event in the new Maccabi stadium. Maccabi Petah Tikvah beat Hakoah by a single goal in the eighty-fifth minute.

The Hapoel teams were happy to boycott the 1935 Maccabiah. They thought they had found a more glamorous date in the 1935 Socialist International Games in Barcelona. Unfortunately, the games were cancelled because of the Spanish Civil War, so Hapoel hurriedly put together their own socialist games at the Palm Court to coincide with the Maccabiah – intending it to be a spoiler. This meant that spring 1935 saw a total of three sporting festivals, all claiming in some way to represent the people of Palestine, while refusing to recognise each other: the socialist games at the Palm Court, the Maccabiah Games at the Maccabi stadium, and the Palestine Sports Federation games at the Basa.

When the summer came, Hapoel Allenby left the country on a tour of Czechoslovakia and Poland. Just as the Maccabiah Games were designed, in part, to bring immigrants to Palestine and circumvent the loose controls in place by the British, the Hapoel tour was partly conceived as a trafficking exercise. Amon Harlap recounted the tricks in his 2001 interview. When the team returned, all but one had acquired new wives, including Harlap, who was actually happily married with a wife in Tel Aviv. He reported that the young Polish girl he brought back was so terrified the entire journey that she was unable to speak to him. Two weeks after they reached Tel Aviv, Harlap sent a letter to the rabbi in Warsaw to ask for help in getting the fake marriage annulled. 'He wrote back testifying that there had been no wedding canopy in the ceremony,' Harlap said in the interview. He was still living with his real wife in the Tel Aviv apartment in which they had begun their married life. Harlap was then his wife's carer, as she was suffering from Alzheimer's.

Though Hapoel and the Maccabi were barely speaking, they briefly buried their differences before the Hapoel European tour. On 8 June 1935, Allenby Tel Aviv and Maccabi Tel Aviv played a special benefit match that ended a week-long celebration to welcome Simcha Hinkis, the murderer of the family in al-Manshiyya in 1929. After his arrest, Hinkis had claimed innocence. It was only when the scale of the violence across Palestine became known that he changed his plea and stated he was acting in reprisal for the Hebron murders. He was sentenced to be hanged, but this was commuted to life imprisonment. He was pardoned by the High Commissioner, Arthur Wauchope. The capacity crowd at the Palm Court greeted him as a hero. He entered the stadium through an honour guard formed by both the Maccabi and Allenby teams, then took the opening kick of the game. Hinkis remained active in sport for the rest of his life, becoming the chairman of the Israel sports association in 1950.

Chapter Fifteen:

Beitar

The 1936 season organised by the Palestine Sports Federation comprised a league sponsored by al-Ghusayn's Youth Congress Party, and a knockout tournament played for the shield of Iraq's King Ghazi. The same year the Nashashibis and al-Husseinis forged a truce and the rival Palestinian political parties formed a united body, the Higher Committee, intended as a kind of parliament or government-in-waiting for Palestine. In the summer of 1936, the committee called a General Strike in protest at Jewish immigration and the requisition of land for the benefit of the Yishuv, and to demand real representative national government.

The strike brought public transport to a halt. Travel between cities became increasingly difficult, especially once the British covered the country in roadblocks. The league was suspended, and the British targeted the Palestinian social and sporting clubs. The *Al-Difa'* newspaper reported that British troops descended on Jaffa, sealing the area around the Islamic Sports Club with armed soldiers at the corners and military vehicles blockading the streets. Soldiers entered the club and arrested the officials, carting out the records and files, which were taken away by military intelligence. The club's doors were sealed and impressed with wax. The Christian Orthodox club fared even worse. The building was requisitioned by the army and became the headquarters of the British forces in Jaffa. When the Islamic Sports Club was allowed to reopen, the two clubs shared the single premises until the end of the strike.

The rival PFA continued to run their league through the first year of the General Strike, but as travelling became difficult the scope of the leagues narrowed once again. Just six Yishuv teams played in the 1935–6 season, and only completed a total of ten matches. Nevertheless, the season lasted well over a year. The first league games took place in the autumn of 1935, and the last match in December 1936. The champions, Maccabi Tel Aviv, took sixteen points from the ten games (two points for a win). Hakoah Tel Aviv were the runners-up, ahead of Hapoel Allenby. There was no knockout Palestine Cup at all.

In Jerusalem, football once again became the preserve of the British military. The city was growing rapidly since it had become the administrative capital of the British. New suburbs spread to the west of the Old City, and attracted both Jewish and Palestinian professionals and their families. The religious Jews were still hostile towards football if it was played close to their neighbourhoods, but they turned a blind eye to the games at the YMCA. The superb new building hosted its own team, as well as a league that included army sides and clubs from the Palestinian Arab, Armenian and Syriac communities.

In 1936, Beitar established a branch in the city. They had come to tackle the strike head-on, with armed violence. Yet, at the same time, the Beitar football team joined the YMCA youth league. It seems odd that a party promoting race politics and segregation was playing football in the only multifaith, multi-ethnic league in the country. The irony never seems to have struck Beitar, however. Football was the least of their activities; from the start, Beitar Jerusalem was a terrorist organisation that played football on the side.

The notional figurehead of Beitar in 1936 was Vladimir Jabotinsky, who took the nom-de-guerre Ze'ev, the Hebrew word for 'wolf'. The name came from an essay entitled 'Man is a Wolf to Man' that he published while writing for the Italian newspaper *Avanti!*, which was edited by Mussolini. However, Jabotinsky was only ever the leader of Beitar in absentia. He never lived in Palestine after 1921. From a home in Paris, he self-published a series of romantic novels under the name Altalena, his old pen-name from the days of *Avanti!*. In the 1930s, much of his energy was spent on the Hollywood adaptation of his novel, *Samson*, the basis for the 1949 film *Samson and Delilah*. Living in Paris, Jabotinsky was not only distant from Palestine, but also from Beitar's true centre of gravity, the newly independent states on the fringes of Russia. In Poland, Beitar had 50,000 members by the mid-1930s, with members performing marching drills in their brownshirt uniforms. The leader of Beitar in Poland was the future Israeli Prime Minister, Menachem Begin.

Beitar in Palestine may have been founded by Menachem Arber, but after 1929 its effective leader was Jeremiah Halpern. In 1934, however, Halpern moved to Italy to set up a Beitar training academy funded by the fascist government. From 1934, the political head of Beitar was the journalist-activist Abba

Ahimeir, aided by his 24-year-old lieutenant Benzion Mileikowsky. Beitar's military wing was led by a renegade from the official Haganah named Avraham Tehomi, who, like Arber and Jabotinsky, also hailed from Odessa. Tehomi gave Beitar's gunmen the sonorous name of 'The National Military Organisation in the Land of Israel', a tongue-twister that was abbreviated to Irgun, Hebrew for 'military', and also to Edzel, the phonetic pronunciation of the abbreviation 'IZL' (that is, *Irgun Tzva'i Leumi*, 'Military Organisation National'). Arber brought in an old footballing friend named Uri Nadav to help smuggle guns in from Finland. Later, Arber began to manufacture weapons in his factories.

Tehomi was based in Tel Aviv. He needed to recruit an Irgun organiser in Jerusalem and found his man in Avraham Stern, who was then at university in Florence. Like Abba Ahimeir, Stern was a self-declared fascist. He was living in Italy as part of a large contingent of young Yishuv men who admired Mussolini's Italy. Jeremiah Halpern's new Beitar training academy was not only sponsored by the Italians, it was based inside the military naval port in Lazio.

Football was regarded as a key pillar of Italian fascism. The naval team, Lazio, was the exemplary 'national' side. It was run by a fascist politician, Giorgio Vaccaro, who also served as the President of the Italian Football Association and sat on the International Olympics Committee. Vaccaro's dominance of Italy's football structure allowed him to take credit for the global success of Italian teams in the 1930s. Mussolini's government had essentially nationalised the game, and Italy had become the dominant force in world football, winning the 1934 and 1938 World Cup with professional teams, and the 1936 Olympics with an amateur side. The Italian teams were multinational affairs, as the sports minister looked for the best footballers around the world, especially Latin American players of Italian heritage. The Italian sports ministry retro-engineered a new history for football, claiming that its roots lay in medieval Italy. The claim was supposed to usurp Britain's claim on the game. England was again cast as perfidious Albion, and as England was no longer a member of FIFA, there was no chance of the true ownership of football being settled, duel-like, on the pitch.

Beitar followed the Italian lead by launching a number of football clubs through the 1930s: Beitar Tel Aviv in 1934; Beitar Jerusalem in 1936; and Beitar Haifa, Beitar Netanya and Beitar Rishon LeZion, all in 1939. From the start, however, Beitar Jerusalem was different to the other Beitar sides. In part, this is because of Jerusalem's difference from the coastal towns. Jerusalem of the 1930s was the only city where Jews and Palestinians lived in the same neighbourhoods. Their lives were intertwined, and while there were many individual friendships, there were tension and enmity, also. The communities became increasingly polarised as the General Strike dragged on, year on year. Beitar Jerusalem were aggressively sectarian, in a city where sectarianism actually meant something: it had consequences because the communities shared so much space together.

Another reason for Beitar Jerusalem's difference is that Jerusalem had become yet more isolated thanks to the travel restrictions during the strike. This allowed the club to develop its own culture and character under its younger leadership. Beitar Jerusalem aimed to stand out. It was the noisiest, the most extreme, the most nationalistic, the most confrontational, the most competitive of teams. Being based in multicultural Jerusalem offered Beitar an opportunity to get in the face of every other community and scream its superiority.

It is customary to talk of Tel Aviv as a bubble, and it certainly does have its own mores and culture. But it is an open port city, connected to the world and the string of old and new cities that stretch around the Mediterranean coast. Jerusalem is arguably far more insular. For one thing, it has always been difficult to get to. Jerusalem is not a natural capital in an age of communication and transport. It lies at the centre of a long mountain range, accessible only by steep slow roads or else by a meandering train from Jaffa/Tel Aviv that chugs through hidden valleys following a route laid down in Ottoman times. A direct high-speed rail line connecting Tel Aviv and Jerusalem is on the verge of completion, but it has faced so many difficult engineering problems that when I visited in 2018 delays were pushing the full opening into the 2020s. The line needs ten bridges and four tunnels. The Jerusalem tunnel alone is almost two miles long.

In the 1930s, Jerusalem's isolation was compounded by the military checkpoints. Beitar Jerusalem was a very young team, founded by a sixteen-year-old named David Horn, and its teenage members were in thrall to Beitar's local leaders, who proved to be the most radical of the Irgun. In 1936, the gunmen were led by a 26-year-old religious student named David Raziel, recruited from a yeshiva attached to Rabbi Kook's sect, and by Avraham Stern, who was then twenty-eight. These leaders regarded themselves as intellectuals. They talked history and philosophy, and many, such as Ahimeir, Mileikowsky and Stern, had PhDs or were working on them. They saw Europe being dragged into a race war, and responded by creating their own politics of racial identity.

Jabotinsky's role in this was as a Wizard of Oz-type figure. He was permanently absent, which allowed the young leaders to project their own ideas onto an empty space. Yet his romantic rhetoric was often inspiring. The 'Beitar Anthem', written in 1932, states: 'Whether you rise or fall, hold the torch of revolution high to proclaim: No Regrets! Silence is for the scum. Give up your blood and soul . . . to die, or to conquer the Mount.' The great recurring theme in Jabotinsky's rhetoric is the suicidal risk that aims to capture the mythical heights of Zion. The path to victory is prepared by suicidal martyrs. This is the story of Samson in Jabotinsky's novel, as well as the meaning of the Covenant to the memory of Trumpeldor, and of the 'death or conquest' message of the Beitar song. The death rhetoric proved intoxicating to some very disturbed young men who were searching for personal validation in a violent age. No one was more disturbed than Avraham Stern. As a thirteen-year-old child in a disputed area of Poland, he was separated from his mother during the Polish–Soviet war of 1919–21. He was forced to live on his wits, wandering vast tracts of Russia alone to find remnants of his family. In 1925, he set out for Palestine, also alone, aged just eighteen. He took charge of his own education, which is how he ended up in Florence when Tehomi came calling, looking for a man to organise in Jerusalem.

As the General Strike turned violent, these men moulded Beitar Jerusalem's young recruits into terrorists.

Chapter Sixteen:

The General Strike

A year into the General Strike, the British attempted to destroy the Palestinians' unity by outlawing the Higher Committee. The politicians were arrested, some imprisoned, others deported to remote British colonies. Amin al-Husseini was visiting Beirut in 1937 when the arrests came, and he chose to remain in exile for more than a decade. The young politician behind the Youth Congress Party and the new football league, Yaqub al-Ghusayn, was one of a number of Palestinian leaders who ended up in the Seychelles, used by the British as a place to detain hostile leaders in the countries they colonised.

The only politicians to survive the cull were members of the Nashashibi family who had chosen to cooperate with the British. The Palestine Sports Federation league continued after a fashion. Jaffa Orthodox is missing from the list of league members for 1937, but Jaffa's Islamic Sports Club appears under a new name, al-Qawmi, which means the People's Club. The records of the players are now lost, but as the Christian and Islamic clubs were sharing premises, the change suggests they

were sending out a united team. The name al-Qawmi points to
the spread of socialist-style politics, which became a feature of
Palestinian nationalism through the twentieth century. As early
as 1928, Palestinians were represented at the Comintern, the
Soviet-sponsored Communist International organisation, by a
Gazan socialist leader named Hamdi Husseini (no relation to
Amin al-Husseini and his Jerusalem family). The year 1937 also
saw the creation of Haifa's socialist club, the Arab Workers'
Society of Haifa. The football team was imaginatively named
the Workers' Team (Nadi al-Ummal). Palestine's socialists,
however, were often ignored by the wider international movement. The 1937 International Workers' Olympiad in Belgium
(rescheduled from 1935 in Barcelona) saw a football team drawn
from Hapoel teams compete under the name 'Palestine', and no
one seems to have pointed out the obvious parallels with
colonialism, as a team of recent emigrants represented the
whole country. The Hapoel team was soundly beaten 7–1 by
Norway, who went on to play Russia in the finals (losing 2–0).
The players once again returned to Palestine with new wives.
Harlap contracted another fake marriage, but always remained
with his real first wife.

In the Yishuv, the 1937 league started in January, just one
month after the end of the 1935–6 season. The only team from
outside the greater Tel Aviv area was Hapoel Haifa, and the
league was won by Maccabi Tel Aviv, who took fourteen points
from eight games, suggesting a commanding performance.
Hapoel Allenby were runners-up with eleven points (five wins
and a draw). The Palestine Cup 1937 included Hapoel and
Maccabi teams from Jerusalem, as both associations tried once
more to establish a presence in the city. Both were eliminated in

the first round, Maccabi Jerusalem by 10–0, as the weekly demonstrations against them continued to take their toll. The demonstrations were frequently violent, and the religious Jews would happily turn on the police.

The score line in Maccabi Jerusalem's 10–0 defeat by Maccabi Tel Aviv does not even do justice to the game: Maccabi Tel Aviv were banned from fielding the senior team, so a youth team had entered the Cup. The PFA were punishing Maccabi Tel Aviv senior players for going on strike over the non-payment of wages. The strike had led to the cancellation of an international fixture against a visiting Greek team, Aris Thessaloniki. The officials were so worried that FIFA would fine them for failing to honour an international commitment that they imposed a penalty on the Maccabi team, as well as banning them from the Cup. The Palestine Cup winners were Hapoel Allenby, a feat they would repeat for the next three years.

The Palestine Sports Federation managed to run a nationwide league and knockout cup in 1938. The league comprised just four teams: Jerusalem's al-Araby Sports Club, Jaffa's al-Qawmi, Haifa's Islamic Sports Club, and Haifa's Scouts. Al-Araby beat al-Qawmi in the final to take the title. In the finals of the knockout tournament for the Ghazi Shield, the al-Qawmi Club lost again, 3–1, to Jerusalem's al-Rawda club. This would be the last year of Palestinian football until the 1940s, as the British Army shut down the PSF in 1938.

The lack of football led Palestinian sportsmen to look abroad. Teams played in Lebanon and Syria while it was impossible in Palestine. Haifa's Islamic Sports Club (winners of the 1937 Ghazi

Shield) led the way. The club's owner, a businessman named Shafiq Addik, tried to re-establish a national side to play neighbouring countries. This idea immediately ran into problems with FIFA. The Palestine Sports Federation responded by exploring the possibility of playing internationals with FIFA's permission.

The PSF's new secretary, Khader Kamal of Jerusalem's al-Araby Sports Club, wrote to Paris asking for local and national teams of the neighbouring countries to be allowed to play FIFA-affiliated countries. Kamal was unaware of the history of communication between Paris and Tel Aviv. Indeed, Kamal's letters to FIFA were immediately shared with Yosef Yekutieli and his board. The idea of Palestinian teams touring the region so alarmed Tel Aviv, the PFA secretary demanded FIFA ban any game between Lebanese teams and teams from the Palestine Sports Federation. The letter again asked for the right to veto matches between Syrian and Lebanese teams, and between any other FIFA member in the region. The only other FIFA members in the region were Egypt and Turkey, so Tel Aviv was effectively demanding that they approve internationals between these teams. The Lebanon Football Association had an application to join FIFA pending, and in 1937 FIFA sent Beirut a formal letter instructing the Lebanese Football Association to run any games with Palestinian sides by the Tel Aviv association. The letter acknowledged that the 'situation' was making life difficult in Palestine but assured the Lebanese that the PFA officials in Tel Aviv were talking in a 'broadminded way' to bring all the remaining Palestinian teams into its sphere. No such talks ever took place, and there is no sign that FIFA ever enquired if they were. The letters between Tel Aviv, FIFA, Beirut and Damascus were uncovered in FIFA's library by the sports historian Issam Khalidi. They make dramatic reading. Tel Aviv insisted throughout the 1930s there were only three Arab teams in Palestine, and of such poor quality that they could not win a place in the PFA leagues. The letters also claim, however, that there were no Palestinian teams in the leagues because their political masters had forbidden them to join a Jewish organisation. The claims that Palestinian teams were both too feeble to be included and too political to play nicely were accepted by FIFA, without investigation, though clearly both could not be true.

The Palestine Sports Federation was one of the last Palestinian organisations to be closed in the strike. The British policy was to dismantle every Palestinian institution, regardless of its aims or politics. This left the Palestinians unable to create a state-in-waiting to compete with the Yishuv, now led by the dynamic David Ben Gurion. In 1935, Ben Gurion became head of the Jewish Agency. After the British deported the members of the Palestinian Higher Committee, thereby proving they had no intention of finding concessions or looking for negotiations, Ben Gurion pursued a policy of collaboration and friendship. The policy was couched as 'restraint', by which he meant that Palestinian attacks on the Yishuv would not elicit a response from the Haganah. This undersold the actual deal: the expansion and arming of a Jewish-led police force meant the better part of the Haganah was, in practice, now part of the British Army. A central policy goal of Weizmann and Kisch had been to create a 'Jewish Legion', a colonial gendarmerie backed by the British, similar to the British-run 'Arab Legion' in Jordan. Ben Gurion had delivered where this previous generation of leaders had failed. The Yishuv gendarmerie numbered 19,000, making it around four times the size of Jordan's Arab Legion.

Security deteriorated drastically after the Palestinian leadership was exiled, as the lack of central command and clear political goals created a chaotic situation. Palestinian groups launched attacks on police, army and civilians. The British used the Yishuv force for crowd control and roadblocks, putting armed Jewish men in face-to-face contact with Arab civilians. The British also employed Arabic-speaking Jews in their military intelligence network both as spies and interrogators. Ezra Danin, brother of Moshe Danin, swiftly rose through British intelligence.

The emergency situation allowed Ben Gurion to militarise his own political structure, and adopt a more centralised command of the Yishuv. The militarisation of Yishuv life did not stop at the level of uniformed enlisted men, but extended deep into everyday life. The football association merged with the British army in the coastal cities. A Maccabi official, Nachum Chet, outlined the policy in a 1936 letter to Colonel Kisch, stating that the British were only interested in women and sport, 'and the first way not being open to us, then the field of sport represents the only common ground between our youth and the British army and navy'.

Outside the coastal cities, all football matches took place under the supervision of the British military. In Jerusalem, the only sports ground was the Jerusalem YMCA, opposite the King David Hotel. The hotel was then home to Emperor Haile Selassie of Ethiopia, who was in exile following the 1936 Italian invasion of his kingdom. The British Army took over an entire floor of the hotel during the strike, and this became military intelligence headquarters.

*

Ben Gurion had persuaded Avraham Tehomi to merge the Irgun with the Haganah in 1937, and Tehomi took up a senior role under Ben Gurion's command. Most Irgun recruits followed Tehomi, but the deal was treated with dismay and incredulity in Jerusalem by Stern and Raziel.

Beitar in Jerusalem rejected the idea of collaborating with Ben Gurion's socialists. They were backed by Menachem Arber, who continued to support them, bringing money and technical know-how to the operation. In 1937, Stern persuaded Jabotinsky to meet him in Egypt's port of Alexandria, where Stern decried Tehomi's surrender to Ben Gurion's socialists, and proposed to create murder and mayhem to discredit the collaborationist policy of 'restraint'. Jabotinsky gave Stern the green light to run the Irgun in Jerusalem as he saw fit. As always, Jabotinsky remained an empty suit, offering no strategy nor asking for details. Stern and Raziel were the youngest and most inexperienced leaders in the Irgun, and Jabotinsky had given them a free hand to do as they wished.

Stern declared the end of Ben Gurion's policy. Instead of restraint, the Irgun would adopt a new strategy of 'sacrifice and endangerment', which was deliberately couched in the language of theatrical martyrdom so loved by Beitar members. These were high words for naked terrorism, and Raziel and Stern's bombing campaign soon brought an exponential escalation of violence. When we write about violence between Palestinian and Jewish groups, events so often blur into cycles that it is difficult to point to their origins; to determine which side might be guilty of incitement, or decide what event could mark a new stage of escalation. The 1937 Beitar campaign of 'abandonment'

introduced several elements now associated with modern terrorism that were absent before that date. Firstly, there was the
centralised political direction of the terrorist campaign, author-
ised by Jabotinsky but organised by Raziel and Stern, the cell
commanders. Secondly, the targets were chosen for the max-
imum loss of life, with no other criteria. Thirdly, Raziel and
Stern commissioned explosives that detonated only after the
bombers had left the scene: this was entirely new.

The events later known as Black Sunday, on 14 November
1937, saw countrywide, near-simultaneous attacks on buses and
coffee shops. Raziel's aim was to kill as many Palestinians as
possible, and while the Black Sunday attacks were carried out
with machine guns and grenades, subsequent attacks achieved
the same results with timed explosives. The three-week campaign by the Jerusalem cell saw 140 Palestinian deaths. This
exceeded the number of Jewish fatalities of the previous
eighteen months. Indeed, as Israeli historian Benny Morris has
noted, Raziel and Stern killed more Palestinians in three weeks
than Palestinians had killed in all the riots of 1920 and 1929 put
together. Two bombs in Haifa market alone saw 74 Palestinians
killed and a further 129 wounded, an unimaginably high number
for terrorism in the mid-1930s, far in excess of anything the world
had seen before.

Beitar supporters claimed their violence was intended as a
deterrent, to ward off future violence. The tactics only fuelled
more violence, of course, as Palestinians began targeting
government buildings, and also using high explosives and car
bombs for the first time. The three-week campaign persuaded
many that the country was gripped by an uncontrollable spiral
of violence.

Yet throughout the terror campaign, Beitar Jerusalem continued to play football in the YMCA league against Palestinian
teams. British police decided to allow Beitar to play league
fixtures in the hope of gathering intelligence at the games.
Undercover officers joined the fans at the YMCA ground to spot
Irgun/Beitar operatives in the crowd. Beitar Jerusalem was only
outlawed in 1938, a decision that was not extended to any of the
other Beitar teams in the country: Beitar Jerusalem alone was
regarded as a terror organisation. For a year, Beitar Jerusalem
only played non-Jewish sides, a point that has occasionally been
raised to suggest that the team was less racist in practice than its
peers in the insular Yishuv-only leagues. But the Beitar boys
should be seen in the context of the 1930s. The old ideals of
friendship-through-sport, voiced by Muscular Christians and
Olympians alike, were being turned on their head by race
politics. This was an age when Italian football teams were
dominating the sport, and despite the best efforts of the African-
American athlete Jesse Owens, Nazi Germany was miles ahead
of every other nation in the 1936 medals table at the Berlin
Olympics. In 1920s America, at a time when baseball was
racially segregated, the Ku Klux Klan alone went out of their
way to play black teams and Jewish teams. Beitar Jerusalem
chose to play football as Jerusalem's lone Jewish side because
they thrived on the sense of competition, risk and sectarian
face-offs.

Beitar Jerusalem was a youth team and its members were the
foot soldiers of the terror campaign. They included fifteen-year-
old Shmuel Tamir (born 1923), the nephew of Joseph Katzenelson,
a long-time associate of Jabotinsky; and Dov Milman, born 1919,
who was eighteen when he arrived in Jerusalem and joined Beitar.

A nationwide terror campaign was facilitated by teenagers who played football at the weekends against their targets.

I wanted to find out more about the experiences of these teenage Irgun/Beitar recruits, and so on a bright spring morning in 2018, I visited the Irgun museum in Tel Aviv. The heavy concrete building resembles a bunker, with the ground floor and basement devoted to the Irgun, and the top floor a museum to Jabotinsky. The man at the desk was thickset with a pugnacious face in the way of an Eastern European tough guy. He seemed wary, and I wondered if my discomfort with the building had put him on alert. He asked me to wait: a sign on the wall stated all bags will be inspected. A slim Ethiopian guy appeared and pushed a probe inside the pouches of my grey rucksack.

The Jabotinsky exhibits on the museum's top floor seemed miscellaneous, even random. How can you repackage the biography of a dreamer and romantic novelist as though he was a major military figure? Jabotinsky is treated with reverence in Israel, yet I always find something inescapably buffoonish about the man, and his writing. So many figures in Israel's history have a genius for politics and for organisation. Jabotinsky is different. Men such as Ben Gurion or even Yosef Yekutieli fill the space they create, but all you get with Jabotinsky is a vacancy. It is unclear who he really is, or what he stands for. This in turn serves to disguise what his followers believed in.

I returned to the ground floor. The museum was unusually gloomy. The lighting was so low that I struggled to see the details on smaller exhibits such as athletics trophies and membership cards. As I peered into a glass case, the tough-looking guy came to warn me that a party of kids were booked for a tour. If I wanted to see the museum film it would be better to do it before they arrived. The film was screened in the basement and told the history of Beitar/Irgun. I took my seat, alone, and the guy popped into a cupboard to start the projection. The film flickered into life, and a Hebrew speaker began the voiceover. Immediately, the guy popped back into the cupboard and restarted the film, selecting the English-language version.

The film tells its story through newsreel footage and slide-shows, but ends with a short dramatised piece in which an actor plays an undercover Irgun operative running a printing press. There are any number of incidents in the history of Beitar that might make exciting dramas. I could imagine a scene of men planting explosives, or robbing banks with their tommy guns, or a scene of young activists being arrested, interrogated and sentenced to be hanged. There are ways to frame real-life episodes to make Beitar's myths seem like heroic dedication to the ultimate prize: a Jewish state. So as I watched the scene, I wondered why the writers had concocted such a low-key moment. To be frank, something a bit on the boring side.

In the film, the printer is passed a piece of paper by a man on the street, who must crouch to pass the message through a grille on the window. We are in what looks like a stone basement, suggesting the setting is Jerusalem rather than Tel Aviv. My first thought was that the printer was running an underground press, printing secret samizdat for the Beitar cause. But I was mistaken: this is a commercial press. The secret message is not a rush order for propaganda leaflets. It concerns the printer's young apprentice. He is a Beitar boy who has recently arrived from Europe and asked to join the Irgun.

The message asks, *Is the boy made of the right stuff? Can he be trusted to keep a secret?*

That is the entire drama.

The printer stands in the gloom, his expression fixed between a glower and a smile as he contemplates the boy with grim pleasure. The reverse shot shows the boy looking back with fear, wilting under the gaze of his master who would judge and groom him. It struck me how easy it would be to overdub the scene with a warning about the dangers of predatory sexual abusers. It was a facetious thought, but having once seen the film this way, it was lodged in my imagination. Anyone would find the film cold and suspenseful, though there is no action. Why dramatise the recruitment, alone? Why emphasise the secrecy of Beitar above any of its other qualities? The secrecy and the implicit threat of retribution if the codes of secrecy are broken?

Beitar Jerusalem ended up splitting over the issue of secrecy. The film is possibly designed to reflect the final argument between its two leaders, Stern and Raziel. They were very different characters, one a fascist and the other a Bible scholar. The two were not arrested until 1939. Despite the horror of their terror campaign, they were released in a wartime deal in June 1940. Jabotinsky had left Paris to open a Beitar office in New York, with British assistance, to lobby the Americans to join the war. Two months later, he died suddenly of a heart attack. This left the Jerusalem attackers without even a titular commander. Raziel argued the Jerusalem cell must recognise the authority of the international Beitar movement, whose leaders were abroad. Benzion Mileikowsky, now known as Benzion Netanyahu, succeeded Jabotinsky as head of the US office. Menachem Begin led Beitar's largest branch in Europe. Raziel believed the party hierarchy was a source of legitimacy, as well as funding and new recruits.

Stern disagreed.

He refused point-blank to recognise any new leader. He argued that deferring to anyone outside the country would break the essential secrecy of the underground. The focus on secrecy in the museum film reflects Stern's view of the organisation: Beitar is persecuted, paranoid and uncompromising. The little drama shows the operatives on the ground making the big decisions by weeding out the bad Jews: the rotten apples and the weaklings. The Beitar worldview foregrounds resentment and betrayal. It is a story that can be constantly renewed in an immigrant nation with little institutional memory. There is always a new betrayal to be feared. There is always a new elite to be attacked. The enemy is always internal: the threat comes from Jews who don't have the backbone that Beitar demands. In the film, the prospect might seem trustworthy: he is a Jewish child, a Beitar boy. He wants to help, he looks earnest, but can he be trusted? In Beitar's world, it is always other Jews who will betray the movement.

One of the reasons that football has been important to so many revolutions and terror groups is that it brings committed youngsters together. Across Europe in the 1930s, socialist, nationalist and fascist organisations were creating uniformed youth movements that learned marching drills, and played football on the side (in America, the Ku Klux Klan wore the distinctive Inquisition-style robes and played baseball, and to a lesser extent soccer). The Palestinian Youth Congress Party and Beitar alike used football to attract young men and break the hold of older political parties. Children have no knowledge of the way things have been done in the past, and they are willing to take the greatest risks on the flimsiest hopes. As Egypt proved in 1919, and Italy in 1922, once a youth party gets out on the street, the older parties are forced to take notice. But placing the entire emphasis on kids in this way has its sinister side, which is what comes out of the museum film. The abusive aspect, the sense that a child is being groomed, is deeply unsettling.

As I left the museum, the party of kids arrived. It hadn't occurred to me that they would be soldiers on military service. Their coach was parked in the sunlight of King George Street, and the kids streamed out towards the museum, all in uniform, boys and girls, kitbags and guns on their shoulders, ready to learn about the underground movement whose spirit, they would be told, they now embodied.

Chapter Seventeen:

Australia!

The General Strike led to one of the more curious events in the history of the Palestine Football Association: a 1939 tour of Australia by Maccabi Tel Aviv as last-minute stand-ins for the Austrian national side. Austria had ceased to exist following unification with Hitler's Germany, leaving the Australian FA with a big blank in the diary. An Australian Jewish association came up with the idea of a series of Palestine–Australia internationals. The tour came at a good time for the Maccabi. There was so little football in Palestine, thanks to the strike, that the Maccabi was struggling to keep its flagship team happy. Maccabi Tel Aviv had already gone on strike over the non-payment of wages, and the players remained fractious. The players agreed to go, and they were booked onto an all-expenses-paid three-month tour of Australia, billed as the Palestinian national side.

The tour ran from 24 June to 28 August 1939. It took the Maccabi boys from Perth to New South Wales and Queensland to South Australia. The first game in Sydney received the most attention, and Pathé News footage of the game survives on the internet. At half time, Australia were leading 6–1 and the sizeable crowd grew bored. The Australians gave up defending after half time, and spent the second half high up the pitch. This left the Australian goalkeeper Jimmy McNabb with more work than he might have expected, or even wanted as he was suffering from the flu. The final score was 8–5, and the report in the next day's *Sydney Herald* was scathing. The newspaper received a telegram from Amin al-Husseini, still in exile outside of Palestine, sourly congratulating them on welcoming a team of terrorists into their country.

Australia was as obsessive about its sports in the 1930s as it is today, though soccer came a long way behind Australian rules football, rugby and cricket in popularity. The national soccer team often played what were termed 'exhibitions' against South Africa and New Zealand. In 1938, Australia played five matches against a visiting Indian team (5–3; 4–4; 1–4; 5–4; 3–1). These were India's first ever international soccer fixtures and the size of the crowds made the tour a financial hit. The newspapers reported that 25,000 spectators watched the first Australia–India exhibition in Sydney, and though the official figures put the crowd closer to 13,000, attendances everywhere were good, with crowds ranging from 9,000 to 18,000. It was these figures that persuaded the Australian promoters that a tour by Palestine could work. However, to keep the costs down, the Maccabi boys were presented with a daunting schedule that also involved fourteen games against local sides, where they would play as Maccabi Tel Aviv. The travel was all by second-class train, and though the internationals took place in the more populated south-eastern cities, the remaining dates took the team across the country, criss-crossing the vast interior and often playing after a sleepless night on hard train seats. The second international was in Brisbane and the team lost again by a more reasonable score of 2–1. The third, back in Sydney, produced a victory (1–2). The newspaper report of the fourth game, in Newcastle, declared: 'The Australian Soccer eleven clinched the rubber against Palestine by a 4–1 victory at Newcastle on Saturday in the fourth test match which like the earlier games of the series was unworthy of test status. The largest northern crowd attracted by any code of football this season spent a bored afternoon watching.' Yet the fact that the crowd exceeded that for Australian rules or rugby suggests the tour was far from a failure. The final game in Melbourne saw the Maccabi hold on for a 4–4 draw.

The Pathé footage has had a second life in the age of YouTube. The film gives no clue that the team is actually Maccabi Tel Aviv, and I've seen it shared by Palestinians who take it at face value and believe a Palestine national team toured the world before the creation of Israel. The Maccabi seem to have enjoyed their taste of Australia. A few took lifeguard badges on Sydney's beaches and returned to work as lifeguards in Tel Aviv. The defender Avraham Beit-Halevi liked the country so much that he stayed at the end of the tour. Avraham was the brother of the more famous Jerry, who later managed both Maccabi Tel Aviv and the Israeli national side, pioneering a style so defensive that it was known as 'Jerry Bunker'. The two brothers never saw each other again, as Avraham joined the Australian Army and was killed fighting in south-east Asia.

The Maccabi's chance to tour had only come because of the Anschluss. As the tour finished, it was becoming clear that war was inevitable. Britain's declaration of war came on 1 September 1939 while the team was at sea. The ship was diverted from its course to Singapore and put in at Bombay, where the team played two matches against a local pick-up team, winning by large margins. They continued to Palestine via the Yemen and Egypt's Port Said, returning to a country at war.

The war led to an amnesty of imprisoned and exiled leaders in return for an end to terrorism, the support of the Allied war effort and the end of the General Strike. In August 1940, the unexpected death of Vladimir Jabotinsky (he was fifty-nine) in New York, while he was petitioning for the US to join the war, pushed Benzion Netanyahu into the Beitar leadership where he headed an office comprising Jabotinsky's son, Ari Jabotinsky, Hillel Kook, the son of Rabbi Avraham Kook, and the British soldier Lieutenant-Colonel John Patterson. Patterson was a colonial officer and big-game hunter (he is played by Val Kilmer in the 1996 film *The Ghost and the Darkness*). He was also an evangelical Christian and the commanding officer of the 38th 'Jewish' Battalion in the First World War. The coalition put together for Beitar's American mission proved to be a powerful political nexus. In its own view, it was part of a Judaeo-Christian partnership that made a claim to a deep and historical 'civilisation', though its actual roots are no older than the nineteenth century. The Netanyahu family story is the tale of this blossoming coalition. Benzion Netanyahu asked Patterson to stand as godfather to his eldest son Jonathan, who was named in John Patterson's honour. His younger son, of course, is Benjamin Netanyahu, Prime Minister of Israel.

Izzat Tannous was allowed to return from exile in England, where he joined other returnees from the Seychelles, including the politicians Ahmed Hilmi and Yaqub al-Ghusayn. As I was recounting the story of al-Ghusayn's exile to a friend in London, she declared that her great-grandfather had been imprisoned in the Seychelles at the same time. I was amazed to discover that the entire aristocracy of Ghana, including Ingrid Karikari's great-grandfather, was exiled to the Indian Ocean archipelago in 1900. Many were still there thirty-six years later. The image of Palestinian politicians and African royalty wandering the white beaches, playing cards in the evening on the verandas of tin-roofed colonial bungalows, is somehow comic. Yet the wholesale and systematic destruction of existing political orders was evidently something the British Colonial Office had turned into an art.

The General Strike ended in defeat for the Palestinians. The climbdown was humiliating, but the war brought an industrial boom that was welcomed after the years of extreme hardship. Airstrips, oil ports and roads all received upgrades, and new troops flooded into the country, needing to be fed and housed. The war also created a fresh appetite for entertainment. The radio station, the Voice of Palestine, was based in Ramallah and pumped out not only news but popular entertainment shows. There were tours by concert parties and theatrical shows, and once again football tournaments filled the stadiums to entertain British servicemen who loved football both as a pastime and a spectator sport. The British had outlawed the Palestine Sports Federation leagues during the strike, but now Palestinian teams were encouraged to play against an array of new military and government sides. The Armenian Homenetmen club of Jerusalem and Shabab al-Arabiya in Haifa both joined military leagues.

The resurgence of interest in football after years of strikes represented both a risk and an opportunity for the Palestine Football Association. The war began with a familiar and self-inflicted crisis within the Yishuv; the Maccabi and Hapoel refused to play each other. The reason for this particular dispute is obscure, though the tour of Australia must have been a factor. The 1940 season saw two Maccabi-only competitions, sponsored by Henry Mond, the son of Alfred and by now the second Baron Melchett. The league was played for the National Shield, reviving memories of the 1920s 'Shield of Samson' tournament sponsored by Colonel Kisch. The Palestine Cup was replaced by the Melchett Cup. The émigrés of the Hakoah sports club tried to mediate between Maccabi and Hapoel and invited both to join their own competition, the Autumn Cup. The Maccabi boycotted the tournament. The final took place over two legs. Hapoel Allenby (now more commonly known as Hapoel Tel Aviv, as the original Allenby boys had retired) faced a British military side, the Captain Watson XI. The teams won a game each, but Hapoel Tel Aviv took the trophy on goal difference.

The Maccabi-run Palestine Football Association gained its prestige and authority both from being recognised by the British as the official football association in Palestine, and from its membership of FIFA. FIFA, however, no longer carried much weight when Paris was occupied by Germans, and the British were not part of FIFA anyway. With Palestinian sides competing against military sides, and Hapoel and Hakoah happy to go it alone, the Maccabi were in danger of squandering the work of the past twenty years and losing their grip on football. In 1942, they saw sense and started operating a national league that would be open to everyone, regardless of faith or ethnicity. For the first time in Palestine's history, there was a countrywide league featuring Yishuv and Palestinian sides. This might have been a glorious turnaround, except that the Maccabi proved extraordinarily inept.

Chapter Eighteen:

The Wartime Leagues

In 1942, the Tel-Aviv based FA embraced the spirit of wartime togetherness by inviting the military and all the civilian sides into its leagues, and also donating gate receipts to the war effort. The leagues only lasted two seasons and proved a fiasco, squandering the chance to foster a space that brought the Yishuv and the Palestinians together.

The season began badly, with a vastly over-complicated system. The country was divided into three territories, each with its own league: Tel Aviv, Haifa and Jerusalem. The national champion would be decided by a series of home and away play-offs between the league winners. Al-Qawmi from Jaffa joined the Tel Aviv league and ended the season mid-table with Maccabi Rishon LeZion taking top spot. The Jerusalem league included teams from both the Maccabi and Hapoel associations, as wartime security clamped down on the religious protesters in the city. There were three rival Armenian teams, a schoolboy side from the De La Salle College, and a team of Greek Jews who had fled the Nazi takeover of Greece. The Armenian Homenetmen ended the season as Jerusalem champions. The Haifa league was abandoned part way through the season, which led the PFA to hand what should have been the Haifa spot in the play-offs to Maccabi Tel Aviv, the runners up of the Tel Aviv league. Inevitably, Maccabi Tel Aviv won the championship, despite effectively gate-crashing the finals.

If the league was poorly run, the 1942 Palestine Cup might count as the worst-organised tournament in football history. Twenty-two teams played in the first round on 14 February. The sides included two British military teams, and a team of the Greek Royal Air Force, which had been stationed in Palestine after helping King George II of Greece escape the Nazi invasion (King George was living in exile in Jerusalem). Haifa was represented by six teams, including two Palestinian sides, Haifa's Islamic Sports Club and Tirsana (which means 'Arsenal'). The city was also represented by Imperial Haifa, on behalf of the oil depot, and two separate Hapoel sides. Tel Aviv fielded four teams, Netanya three, Jerusalem and Petah Tikvah each fielded two teams, and there was also a team each from Rishon LeZion, Nes Tziona and Rehovot.

The problems began with the replay of a game between Maccabi Haifa and Hapoel Petah Tikvah. The first meeting had ended in a nil–nil draw, even after extra time. The replay also went to extra time, despite Maccabi Haifa losing a player to a red card. When the game restarted in extra time, the dismissed Maccabi player returned with no objection from the referee. Maccabi Haifa won the match 3–2 but Hapoel Petah Tikvah lodged a complaint. The resulting argument dragged on for two months, and was finally resolved by a process of mediation that saw both sides agree to play yet another match on 25 April.

As the teams began the mediation process, the PFA decided to expand the tournament to bring in three new Palestinian sides: De La Salle College from Jerusalem; al-Qawmi Sports Club of Jaffa; and Shabab al-Arabiya of Haifa. Maccabi Haifa played the De La Salle boys on 14 March, despite the unresolved argument with Hapoel Petah Tikvah. After they had beaten the schoolboys of De La Salle 1–0, Maccabi Haifa learned they were to play Hapoel Petah Tikvah for a third time.

When the second replay finally came around, Maccabi Haifa failed to show up. They were penalised by being kicked out of the tournament, and the De La Salle boys were invited to re-enter the tournament and play Hapoel Petah Tikvah. This time, the schoolboys lost 2–1.

Maccabi Haifa were furious at being expelled for the no-show. They continued to fight, taking the decision to arbitration. The panel upheld their appeal by ruling that the first victory over Hapoel Petah Tikvah should stand: this was the game Maccabi Haifa had only won in extra time with the help of a player who should not have been on the pitch, following his red card. Now, Hapoel Petah Tikvah were out of the tournament, which meant that Maccabi Haifa's original 1–0 victory over the De La Salle boys once again stood.

Shabab al-Arabiya beat a British Army team and progressed to the quarter-finals to face Maccabi Tel Aviv. This game also went to extra time, eventually ending with a Maccabi Tel Aviv victory, 7–4. Soon after the game, however, Shabab al-Arabiya discovered that four members of Maccabi Tel Aviv's squad were ineligible to play. They complained and the Palestine Football Association upheld their complaint. Maccabi Tel Aviv were expelled. Despite ruling that the game was illegal, however, the board simultaneously ruled that the result should stand. Shabab al-Arabiya were bewildered to discover they were also out of the tournament.

These arbitrary rulings made the tournament complicated enough, but things got a lot worse. After beating De La Salle College in March, Maccabi Haifa ought to have played their quarter-final match against the Greek Royal Air Force. When Maccabi Haifa were expelled for failing to turn up for their April rematch against Hapoel Petah Tikvah, the Greek Air Force was given a bye to the semis. This decision had to be reversed once Maccabi Haifa won their appeal, but it was no longer possible for Maccabi Haifa and the Greek airmen to play their match: the Greek Royal Air Force had flown out of Palestine, taking King George to his new home in England. The only solution was to give Maccabi Haifa the bye to the semi-finals. They ought to have faced Maccabi Tel Aviv in the semis, but since Maccabi Tel Aviv had been expelled for fielding unregistered players, Maccabi Haifa got yet another bye. Maccabi Haifa ended up making it all the way to the finals, despite having played only three games, two of them against Hapoel Petah Tikvah, and the other against the schoolboys of De La Salle. The lack of games did not work in their favour. In the final they were hammered 12–1 by Beitar Tel Aviv.

Beitar Tel Aviv had a meteoric rise from winning the Tel Aviv Division 2 in 1939 (Beitar Netanya won the Samaria league in the same year). By 1942, they were probably the best team in the country. The team's strength was a result of two factors. The first was the 1938 closure of Beitar Jerusalem by the security forces, so the most talented of its players gravitated towards the Beitar sister club in Tel Aviv. A second reason was the influx of new Beitar members from Poland who had deserted a Polish-led army in the Middle East. This is a complex and contested story. In outline, the Nazi invasion of Poland meant the country's Jewish communities were faced with the choice of fighting alongside the Poles, knowing they faced extermination in defeat, or fleeing into Russian territory. Most of those who chose to fight were socialists, while many of those who entered Russia were Beitar members. A generation earlier, much of Poland had been Russian territory, but once inside what was now the Soviet Union, the Jewish refugees were interned in camps. The 1941 Nazi invasion of Russia brought the Soviet Union into the war, which led to the creation of a Russian-backed Polish army under General Władysław Anders. This army was sent via Iran and Iraq to Palestine. The force included 4,000 Jewish soldiers, and in addition the Russians had chosen to ship out their wives, children and dependants, too. With their families already in Tel Aviv, about three-quarters of the Jewish soldiers in Anders's army, including the Beitar leader Menachem Begin, went AWOL. They made new lives in Tel Aviv.

Beitar occupied an ambivalent position in British-controlled Palestine. Jeremiah Halpern had switched his support from Mussolini to the Allies, training French frogmen and British seamen. The one-time leader of Beitar Jerusalem, David Raziel, joined a British commando unit and was killed on a mission in Iraq in 1941. On the other hand, many of Beitar's leaders remained true to fascism. Avraham Stern formed a new organisation in 1940, after Jabotinsky's death, named Lehi, an acronym for 'Fighters for the Freedom of Israel' (*Lohamei Herut Israel*), but always better known as the Stern Gang. He aimed to coordinate attacks with Italian and German forces, but his

MORE NOBLE THAN WAR

attempts to contact the fascist states were uncovered by the British in a sting operation and widely publicised. Stern swiftly became the most hated man in Palestine, widely regarded as a 'fifth columnist' who was working for a Nazi victory. In 1942, Stern was arrested and shot in circumstances that strongly suggest his British captors murdered him in cold blood. The Stern Gang was taken over by Yitzhak Shamir and Israel Eldad, who relaunched attacks on the British. Shamir became the Prime Minister of Israel in the 1980s. Eldad, another self-declared fascist, is a revered figure in right-wing settler circles. The Jewish settlement of Kfar Eldad in Bethlehem is named in his honour, built on land seized from Palestinian families.

In 1943, Beitar Tel Aviv was suspended by the Palestine Football Association as a punishment for playing Al Ahly, the great Cairo team. Al Ahly was on a tour of Palestine and played both Shabab al-Arabiya and the Jerusalem YMCA side, as well as three matches against Beitar Tel Aviv. It lost two of those matches to the Beitar boys. The tour was organised with the blessing of the British, over the objections of the Egyptian FA. The Egyptians contacted the Palestine FA and asked if they would forbid their member teams from taking part. I am not clear why the PFA obliged, when FIFA was moribund during the war years; perhaps they simply embraced an opportunity to kick two Arab sides out of the FA and Beitar were caught up in the dispute. In any event, Beitar relished playing Al Ahly, as Beitar Jerusalem had once relished playing Arab and Armenian sides at the YMCA. They took the punishment, even though they were on course to win the 1943 Palestine Cup. The expulsion came on the eve of a semi-final match against Hapoel Jerusalem, who consequently received a bye into the finals only to be defeated 7–1 by the team of the British Royal Artillery.

After the debacle of the 1942 and 1943 seasons, the non-Jewish sides began talking of a breakaway league again. Two teams, the Armenian Homenetmen team of Jerusalem and Shabab Al-Arabiya, were often left angry by refereeing decisions. The Homenetmen were kicked out of the 1943 Palestine Cup when a red-carded player refused to leave the pitch, meaning the game was abandoned and the victory handed to the Hapoel opponents. A derby between Hapoel Haifa and Shabab Al-Arabiya ended in a mass pitch invasion. The Palestinian teams complained of biased referees and favouritism. The most violent scenes of the 1943 season, however, took place between Yishuv teams. Three separate games were abandoned after the referees were attacked by Jewish players.

At the time, Jabra al-Zarqa of Shabab al-Arabiya was widely regarded as the best player in the country. With decent teams and star players, the Palestinians had every reason to be frustrated by the chaos of the Football Association. The teams in Jaffa and Haifa pulled out of their divisions, forming their own local leagues. In Jerusalem, the Palestinian teams returned to playing at the YMCA. But by 1944 plans were already advanced to revive the Palestine Sports Federation, with veterans such as Izzat Tannous and Ibrahim Nusseibeh on board.

Chapter Nineteen:

The Return of the Palestine Sports Federation

In 1944 a meeting at the Islamic Sports Club in Jaffa led to a countrywide league under the resurrected name of the Palestine Sports Federation. The leagues were placed under the stewardship of Abdel Rahman al-Habbab, a teacher and popular footballer who had played for Jaffa's Islamic Sports Club. The board included Izzat Tannous and Ibrahim Nusseibeh, bringing together many of the old names of Palestinian football. A significant new sponsor was found in Ahmed Hilmi, the leader of the Independence Party (Istiqlal). Hilmi had been one of the exiles in 1936, but returned from the Seychelles in 1939 and resumed the directorship of the Arab National Bank, a development bank he had founded to underwrite Palestinian investments and industry. He attempted to centralise power through his new party by building national institutions, in much the same way that Ben Gurion had done in the Yishuv. He also bought the *Falastin* newspaper, retaining Daoud al-Issa as editor. There was a vacuum in Palestinian politics, which Hilmi hoped to fill. The al-Husseinis had declined in power since the war. Amin al-Husseini had never returned from exile, but began a peripatetic life, first seeking help from Mussolini as the potential leader of anti-British forces in Palestine. He moved on to Germany, where he was adopted by the Nazi regime and employed as a highly paid broadcaster on the propaganda station as the Muslim world's equivalent of Lord Haw-Haw.

The 1944–5 season of the Palestine Sports Federation league comprised twenty-five teams. The final was held at the Basa stadium on 3 June, where the Islamic Sports Club played the Jerusalem Orthodox Club for a trophy, 'The Armour of the Arab National Bank', donated by Hilmi. Ten thousand spectators filled the stadium, including all of the Palestinian mayors of the country. The Jaffa side won the title 2–0. Like the Yishuv's league, the Palestinian Sports Federation donated the gate receipts to war causes, but chose charities focused on helping civilians in Syria and Lebanon where there had been fierce fighting between the British and the Vichy French. It proved politically astute to build friendly relations with neighbouring countries. As the war ended the Lebanese Football Association and the Egyptian Football Association championed a new application from the Palestine Sports Federation to join FIFA.

The Palestine Sports Federation divided the country into six regions, Jerusalem, Jaffa, Nablus, Gaza, the Galilee and Haifa. In 1946, membership rose to forty-five clubs, and in 1947 there were sixty-five member clubs. The board might have included names from the old elite families, but football itself was no longer an elite sport: it was the national sport of Palestine, played from Beersheba and Rafah in the south, to Haifa and the

Galilee in the north. Though the bye-laws specifically excluded Jewish teams, all of Palestine's non-Jewish teams – Armenian and Syriac – opted to play in the PSF league rather than the official PFA leagues. Match reports appeared in *Filastin* and the *Palestine Post* (the paper that became the *Jerusalem Post* after the creation of Israel).

The PFA was a far smaller organisation than the PSF, with fewer members and an inferior reach around the country – depleted further because all Beitar teams were now outlawed. By 1944, the leadership of the Stern Gang, Lehi, had become the commanding officers of all Beitar forces and had chosen to revive the terror campaign. The British reacted by rounding up Beitar members and interning them in the prison at Latrun. The team sports continued in prison: the Irgun museum has a cabinet containing a hand-carved wooden cup used as a trophy at Latrun. As the terror campaign continued, the prisoners were moved into exile in Kenya, where the camp in Gilgil became a centre of Beitar sports during the war. Eliezer Spiegel, the lead goal scorer of Beitar Tel Aviv, remained imprisoned in Kenya until 1949 and played football throughout.

It seems inconceivable, today, that a Jewish party would embark on a terror campaign against the British in 1944, when Britain's war against Nazism was far from over. The museum does not gloss over the facts, but argues that Germany was practically defeated, and so the time was right to turn Beitar's guns on the British. The idea that Germany had ceased to be a threat is not a conclusion anyone could have reached with confidence in 1944, even if they had all of the military intelligence at their disposal. It is certainly not a conclusion open to a group of isolated young Jewish men living in wartime

Palestine. The value of the Irgun museum, perhaps, is its ability to convey the inner spirit of Beitar: the refusal to admit mistakes; the belief that its choices were always later proved right; and the angry conviction that it is always persecuted and misunderstood.

In 1946, Beitar in Jerusalem carried out an attack on the King David Hotel, the British military headquarters in Palestine. The attack is described in detail in the museum literature, with a tone of pained injury. The war had seen enormous death and destruction but, even so, the attack was of a scale of magnitude unlike any terrorist bombing seen before. The museum firmly lays the blame on the British for not heeding the group's warnings, an argument no Israeli would accept if they were attacked by terrorists. The moral line is that the fault lies with the aggressors, not with the victims, and I reeled at the museum's shamelessness.

The warnings from Beitar to the British were chaotic. Responsibility was left to the initiative of a child, sixteen-year-old Adina Hay, who phoned in the warnings. Adina's first warning was made to the hotel desk. The museum states she called half an hour before the explosion, a claim first made in the memoirs of Menachem Begin (the political head of Beitar in Israel by 1946; the head of military operations was Yitzhak Shamir). The half-hour warning has gained currency on Begin's authority, but it is false: Adina phoned the first warning fifteen minutes before the explosion. There was a quarter of an hour to begin the evacuation, and the clock ticked down from then on. Her second call was to the French consulate, whose office stood next door to the hotel. Her final call was to the *Palestine Post* newspaper. This left just six minutes to evacuate the largest hotel in the Middle East.

The warning to the newspaper went to the paper's switchboard. The woman working the switchboard called the Jerusalem police. She then made her own decision to call the hotel: an extra warning to the hotel desk. After receiving two warnings, one from Adina Hay and one from the switchboard of the newspaper, the hotel staff began to pay attention. The problem was that the hotel desk had no direct connection to the floors commandeered by the British military; the military HQ had its own switchboard. The clock keeps ticking. The bombs were milk churns, stuffed with high explosives and shrapnel, killing ninety-one people, Jews, Arabs and British personnel alike. This was the highest death toll by a terrorist group by a huge margin. It was not surpassed until the 1983 truck bombing of the American barracks in Beirut, forty years later. Though there is no mention in the display that Adina Hay was sixteen, the museum does not hide Beitar's reliance on children. As its members were arrested, the age of activists was pushed lower still.

Palestinian soccer teams were developing good relations with Allied forces. They played military sides and visiting teams. There were also dozens of games against Jordanian sides. As director of the Palestinian Sports Federation, al-Habbab created a Palestinian national team, which played a charity match against the Free French military in March 1945. Any Egyptian or Lebanese squads that met a Palestinian team were in breach of FIFA's rules, but games were played nevertheless. The year 1945 saw a number of matches. Al-Habbab's national side seems to have played Barada FC in Damascus. A visiting team from Aleppo played in both Jerusalem and Haifa, where a game against the Islamic Club drew 5,000 spectators. The Haifa Homenetmen team played against their sister club in Beirut. In October 1947, al-Arabiya of Aleppo visited Haifa to play both the Islamic Club and Shabab al-Arabiya. In November 1947, Jaffa's Islamic Sports Club went to Damascus to play Barada FC, and the match was refereed by Ibrahim Nusseibeh.

The Palestine FA became aware that the Palestine Sports Federation was planning a new application to FIFA. Tel Aviv responded by writing to FIFA, which was now based in Luxembourg. Abdel Rahman al-Habbab was supposed to appear at the new headquarters to further his application, but his invitation was abruptly withdrawn when he was at the doors to the building. He was told FIFA wished to consider his application in private at a specially convened meeting. The next thing he knew, the application had been rejected, without calling witnesses. Al-Habbab took the first plane to Cairo, where he demanded that the Egyptian Football Association act. Cairo sent a telegram to FIFA to restate the Palestinian case. Al-Habbab followed this up with documents showing the health of the league, and a lengthy letter.

The pressure on FIFA from the neighbouring Arab countries was beginning to tell. In 1947, FIFA agreed to debate the issue of Palestine again. A new British Labour government, however, had signalled that it was ready to quit Palestine, and set a date for withdrawal. The country was plunged into violence again and football was an early victim of the hostilities.

The British Labour government unilaterally set a deadline for withdrawal. The Palestinians were unable to either counter or stymie the British schedule with their own proposals. The Labour Party enjoyed fraternal relations with Ben Gurion's Mapai socialist party. Harold Wilson, the youngest cabinet minister in the 1947 government, gave a taste of the decision-making process in his 1981 book, *The Chariot of Israel*. He admitted his admiration for Jewish nationalism came from the Bible classes of his childhood Sunday school, rather than any knowledge of Yishuv or Palestinian politics. He was not alone, he noted; the British Labour Party owed more to evangelical Methodism than to Marxism.

The British believed Palestine would have to be divided after they left, following the pattern of partition they had tried between communities in India, Ireland and elsewhere. The Palestinian leadership was easily sidelined by the British. The borders of the West Bank were drawn up in secret negotiations between the Yishuv leadership and British military officers attached to the staff of King Abdullah of Jordan. The go-between in these British–Yishuv talks was Ezra Danin. The post-war period brought Yosef Yekutieli his biggest job, as he led an office identifying and nationalising 'abandoned' Palestinian property.

Part 2

Chapter Twenty:

Four-tenths Abandoned

In March 2018, I invited myself to a training session of the Sons of Jaffa Orthodox FC, the current incarnation of the original Jaffa Orthodox Church team. The club was founded in 1924, disappeared in 1948, and was revived by David Mansour, the church scout master, in 1970. David's family are a football dynasty. His grandfather was the parish priest in Jaffa in the 1930s, and his uncle played for the original team in the 1930s and 1940s. The current chairman, Rami Mansour, is David's son. I got Rami's number from the Israel Football Association. After a brief chat, Rami and I arranged to meet before the Thursday evening session. It was only after the call ended that I realised I hadn't bothered to ask for the address of the stadium. I hoped that between Google and common sense, I would find the club.

I was wrong.

I set off in the mid-afternoon heat, keeping to the shade of the awnings above the stalls on Carmel Market. There was no cover on the flat expanse between the bus station and the beach, where the skyline was broken by a few high-rise hotels. Only the Hasan Bey Mosque is a reminder that this was once the densely packed al-Manshiyya district. The area was shelled by combined Haganah and Irgun forces in 1948, and subsequently flattened by bulldozers to prevent the refugees from reclaiming their homes. The Palestinian population of Jaffa was 80,000 in April 1948, and by June fewer than 4,000 remained. The survivors lived on the opposite side of Jaffa old town, beyond a defensive line that was belatedly established by the British Army. Al-Manshiyya was wiped out, renamed, the land nationalised, and the borders of Tel Avivs redrawn, leaving no reminder that a major city district had been expunged from history.

I took a detour to look at the old Basa stadium. Following the creation of Israel, on 14 May 1948, the Basa was nationalised. In 1950, it became the home of Hapoel Tel Aviv. In 1962, the Basa lost its semi-obscene name and was renamed the Bloomfield Stadium to commemorate a gift from a Canadian benefactor, Louis Bloomfield, director of a Canadian Jewish labour fund. In 2000, Maccabi Tel Aviv also moved into the stadium. When I visited, in March 2018, the stadium was two years into a rebuild that is intended to double its capacity to 29,000. I took a walk around the site and found a dust-filled half shell rising above a large deep hole. The new Basa.

The Bloomfield Stadium is a short walk from Jaffa's souk, where the limestone buildings are filled with furniture stores and the kind of bars that cater to people who take 'Happy Hour' seriously. I took the steep hill up to the church, leaving messages for Rami Mansour every ten minutes. I had given up hope when Rami sent an SMS with the address of the stadium in Hebrew. When I pasted the text into Google it pointed to a street in

Petah Tikvah, but when I showed the text to the pharmacist
who sold me ibuprofen and sunscreen, she assured me I was
heading in the right direction. The stadium was another fifteen
minutes' walk along the main street. This is the surviving Arab
district of Jaffa, named Ajami. The road through it was also
called Ajami Street, and is now Yefet Street, after one of Noah's
sons. Someone in the Tel Aviv municipality thought 'Jaffa' and
'Yefet' had a similar kind of sound, and so renamed the main
road. It's the kind of kitschy Bible half-reference you can find
anywhere in Israel.

I continued to ask directions as I walked through Ajami, and
got the same answer at the barbershop and the falafel restaurant:
straight on. The road dropped towards a busy junction. At last, I
saw two pitches inside a floodlit bubble. Even in the evening,
the air remained sluggish and the traffic fumes seemed to fill
the space above the pitch. I followed a chain-link fence around
the first pitch, where a few small kids were wrapping up a game,
watched by their French-speaking mothers. The second pitch
was much busier. It had been divided in half to accommodate a
junior team playing attack versus defence, while the lower half
was being prepared for a training drill. Two young men in
tracksuits set out cones, carried by an older guy in the unofficial
uniform of Israel: baggy shorts, a loose T-shirt and a shaved
head. The pitches are owned by the municipal Tel Aviv–Yafo
council, and were built in 2003 with the help of a US charity,
the American Committee for Tel Aviv, under a dollar-for-dollar
matching scheme. I had expected to find a real stadium, but
there was no doubt I was in the right place. Two small sturdy
men were waiting for me at the kerb: Rami and his father David
Mansour. Rami's head was shaved, and his skin had a warm soft

glow. His father had white hair, brushed back off his face. He looked both weather-beaten and wind blown, the very image of a man who had lived his entire life in a port city.

Though Rami runs the day-to-day affairs of the club, it was soon clear that David kept a close eye on everything. When Rami said the club had 300 players on its books, David corrected him: there are 280 members split over nine teams; children, juniors, seniors and a women's team. The first team is semi-professional; everyone else, from the kit men to the junior coaches, is a volunteer. Even the club's accountant, 68-year-old Koko Kalalian, was helping out by carrying bibs and cones on to the pitch. Koko is a Jaffa-born Armenian and a one-time semi-professional footballer who was among the first non-Jews to play in Israel's top leagues.

Rami's young son was training with the under-twelve squad, the fourth generation of the Mansour family to play for the club, providing a thread of continuity over ninety-odd years. The boys on the glowing artificial turf reflected the demographics of Ajami, with Muslims and Christians and a handful of East Africans. Koko told me the club had a couple of Jewish kids, too, playing in one of the junior teams. It was 7 p.m. and the senior team were emerging on to the pitch. The first-choice goalkeeper was already working with his coach, a Jewish ex-professional in his fifties, again with a shaved head, bulky stomach, and legs that seemed pale and thin in comparison. Rami told me the goalkeeper broke his shoulder just before the start of the last season and missed every game. No, he had got that wrong. The keeper broke his elbow last season: he broke his shoulder four seasons ago. The last season ended with relegation from Liga Alef, the third tier of Israel's convoluted league system. Who knows, things might have been different if he had stayed fit. The club had to give up its old ground to save money after dropping down a level. The training pitch doubles as the home stadium. The chain-link fence runs so close to the touchline that spectators sit on the wrong side of the fence, which must give a chequered view of the game. Rami told me that Tel Aviv municipality had promised to build a second stand behind the goal, but he did not know when it would arrive.

The coach for the 2016–17 season was an ex-professional, Hanan Fadida, in his first year as a coach after retiring from the Premier League side Ashdod FC. After relegation, Fadida left. The team was now being coached by a sports teacher from a college in Kafr Qasim, an Israeli Palestinian city close to the border with the West Bank. It was the evening ahead of a league match against Tayibe, another Palestinian team. The coach gathered the players into a circle to talk strategy and team formation. When he began to speak, he switched to Hebrew, which caught me by surprise. Everyone was an Arab speaker. Hebrew is the language of law, politics and government services in Israel. I guess it must also be the language of Israeli football.

After practice, Rami offered me a lift back to the old town. He dropped me at the summit of Ajami, close to his great-grandfather's church. Father Salim Khoury Shaya's house is still the family home. When the state of Israel was declared in 1948, however, four of the priest's seven children were out of the country. Yosef Yekutieli had the job of requisitioning Palestinian homes, under a newly passed 'abandoned property' law. Yosef's office determined the home was four-tenths abandoned by comparing the number of family members against the number of its inhabitants on a specific date, 14 May 1948, the day Israel was created. This wasn't a simple land grab, but a careful inventory of property and people, legalistic and bureaucratic. Yosef's office ruled the Mansour family home was 40 per cent abandoned, which meant the state owned 40 per cent of the building. In 2016, the government demanded its equity at current market prices. David Mansour had to find two million shekels to buy out the government's share, or else the family would forfeit their home. The family took the case to court, but lost a series of appeals. In the end, they paid the money: the house is back in the family's name.

Yosef Yekutieli fades out of history after the creation of Israel, but his creation of the FA, the football leagues, the Sports Stadium Corporation and the Maccabiah Games are testament to his extraordinary impact, even before one considers his ruthless implementation of the Abandoned Property Law. Yosef's life is a testament to the power of men who can take meetings, push papers, write letters, construct proposals, cross-reference data, make lists and file accounts. It is possible, however, that Yosef's greatest impact lies outside of any of these fields: his son, Gideon Yekutieli, is the father of Israel's nuclear bomb.

Chapter Twenty-One:

Refugee Football

Jaffans fled their homes in every direction, south to the fishing villages of the Gaza Strip, north into Nazareth, or west to the hills of Jerusalem and Nablus. The late Palestinian artist Hasan Hourani recalled his father's answer when he asked why he had chosen Hebron, of all places. His father said that when they were escaping, they were only able to afford one donkey, so they loaded all of their furniture and valuables on its back, and set out walking.

'I understand, Dad. But why Hebron?'

'That's where the donkey died.'

The British surrendered the mandate for Palestine on 15 May 1948. The same day, the political leaders of the Yishuv declared an independent state of Israel, with Ben Gurion at the forefront. A civil war for Jerusalem had begun before the British abandoned the country, with the Palestinian forces led by Abd al-Qader al-Husseini, a forty-year-old journalist and politician of the al-Husseini family. Al-Husseini was killed in April, and his column was defeated before the departure of the British, but his defensive lines in Jerusalem were held by junior Arab officers of Jordan's Arab Legion, who responded to the Israeli declaration of independence by rushing to hold the Old City, leaving their British commanding officers in the position of backing their men or risking disobedience. These lines became the armistice lines of 1948, with barbed wires and tank traps marking a curving line around the Old City walls.

The initial flurry of fighting in May ended almost immediately with a ceasefire, which gave Ben Gurion the chance to reorganise his forces. The Haganah became the Israel Defence Force (IDF), under a more integrated and centralised command structure. The reformed IDF saw action in October in the Galilee, which they seized after defeating a newly formed Arab Liberation Army, a 6,000-strong force sponsored by Syria. In October, they fought the Egyptian army around Gaza where the two coastal cities of Gaza and Rafah had received the majority of the refugees from Jaffa. These actions ended with an armistice with Egypt in January 1949, which saw the creation of what would become known as the Gaza Strip, the most densely populated area in the world.

The IDF was the mechanised force of the new state and its role was to secure the borders. The Beitar/Irgun forces were used as irregular forces, employed within these borders to clear civilian Palestinian population centres. These forces were responsible for a series of civilian massacres that greatly exacerbated the refugee crisis.

The war made three-quarters of a million Palestinians homeless, leading to the creation of refugee camps across Palestine, as well as Jordan, Lebanon and Syria. The newly established United Nations, still meeting in London in 1948, passed the British 'mandate' over Palestine to Egypt, who would rule the Gaza Strip, and to Jordan, who got the West Bank. The story of football in Gaza and the West Bank shows how differently Egypt and Jordan reacted to gaining hundreds of thousands of Palestinian refugees.

The ruling Hashemite family of Jordan had a chequered history after commanding the victorious Arab forces in the First World War. Prince Feisal had hoped to be crowned King of Syria, but was forced out of Damascus in 1918 by the British and the French. The family subsequently lost Mecca in 1925 to a coalition led by the Saud family, and Iraq to a military coup in 1958. Jordan, ruled by Feisal's younger brother Abdullah, turned out to be the most viable of the Hashemite kingdoms. From the beginning, Abdullah treated Jerusalem warily, knowing it could prove a poisoned chalice. Throughout the 1950s and 1960s, Israel maintained a pressure-cooker environment, taking pot shots at moving vehicles, and conducting hundreds of incursions and cross-border raids into the West Bank. Hashemite rule was only possible with the consent of powerful tribal Bedouins, who are very different to the highly political, urban Palestinians. The Hashemites could not afford to see their relations with either the Bedouins or the Israelis destabilised by Palestinian political demands. As a consequence, they neglected Jerusalem, hoping to starve the city of its political and cultural life and move the centre of balance to their capital: Amman. Palestinian football in the West Bank went into decline. By the 1970s, however, Palestinian teams emerged in Jordan that carried the Palestinian political identity forward. As these Palestinian teams competed against Jordanian teams, football became a kind of theatre in which the anger and divisions in society were paraded and re-enacted.

Despite being wary of Jerusalem, however, the Hashemites hoped their status as the new Sharifs of Jerusalem would bring them the respect of other Arab leaders. Egypt sought power and influence another way, via revolutionary politics. When General Gamal Nasser came to power in the 1952 coup, he twisted Palestinian nationalism to reflect his own pan-Arab politics. Gaza was tightly controlled by the Egyptian security services, but Nasser hoped to conjure a picture of autonomy. Gaza became the home of a 'national' Palestinian football federation and, throughout the 1950s and 1960s, its officers applied to FIFA for membership – unsuccessfully. For two seasons, a Hungarian coach was paid to work with the Palestinian squad, and the team not only played friendlies against Egypt, but competed in the Arab Games that took place in Alexandria in 1953, Beirut in 1957, Casablanca in 1961 and Cairo in 1965.

In 1965, Palestine reached the quarter-finals of the Arab Games. The goalkeeper was Marwan Kanafani, the brother of Ghassan, one of the most famous Palestinian revolutionaries, comparable in many ways to Che Guevara. Ghassan Kanafani was already a celebrated novelist and playwright by the mid-1960s, but his day job was as the press spokesman for the Popular Front for the Liberation of Palestine, the Marxist group that became best known for hijacking aeroplanes. Ghassan was murdered at the age of thirty-six in 1972 by Israeli operatives who planted a large car bomb beneath his Austin 1100; the model my grandmother also drove in 1972. Kanafani's novels have a brilliant, intense readability, but when I think of him, it is the Austin's shiny walnut dashboard and pale leather seats that comes into focus.

Jordan never recognised the puppet regime in Gaza as the national government of the Palestinians. The Hashemites resented Nasser and his proxies stoking Palestinian nationalism. When the Jordanian King Abdullah was shot and killed in Jerusalem in 1951 by a Palestinian militant, Jordan blamed Egypt, which added to tensions and rivalries between the two states. Abdullah's seventeen-year-old grandson Hussein was picked as the new king. However, he was at boarding school in England. Jordan remained under the control of the British-led army, commanded by Colonel John Glubb, an officer with a solid military Anglo-Irish background. (Glubb named his oldest son after the Crusader king Godfrey, which gives some indication of how he saw his role in the city. His son changed his name to Faris, joined the Popular Front for the Liberation of Palestine [PFLP], and became a close friend of Ghassan Kanafani, which gives an indication of how he viewed his father's work, as well as an insight into Palestinian life in the 1960s.)

The policy of running down Palestinian institutions meant that West Bank teams were kept out of Jordan's leagues. Jerusalem's al-Araby entered a long period of decline, which it survived by drifting through a series of mergers with smaller and poorer teams. Ironically, at the same time, football in Jordan was run by Ibrahim Nusseibeh, who was appointed Minister for Sports in the mid-1950s. Nusseibeh picked Abdel Rahman al-Habbab to head the Jordan FA. Football in Jordan was now run by Palestinians, without any Palestinian teams actually being admitted to the top divisions.

Until the 1950s, Jordan's best teams were associated with minority communities; the Armenian Homentemen team and a Circassian team known as the Koban Club. The people described as 'Circassian' were soldiers, military slaves and mercenaries from the Caucasus. In practice, the Circassians tend to be Chechens, but the name Koban shows a romantic awareness of their ancient heritage: the Koban are a Bronze Age people. The Palestinian football star Jabra al-Zarqa signed for Koban in 1948 before moving to Damascus in 1950 to play for Al-Shorta (the police team, nicknamed 'Security of the Capital'). In the early 1950s, the Koban Club was Arabised by royal decree, and changed its name to Al-Ahli or 'the Nation'. The Hashemites also invested in another Amman team, Al-Faisaly, formed in 1932 and named in honour of Prince Feisal. The years from the late 1950s to the late 1970s brought an almost unbroken run of victories for Al-Faisaly, which remained unchallenged until Palestinian clubs managed to break into Jordanian football in the 1970s.

All of Jordan's Palestinian clubs are based inside refugee camps. For years, these teams played in the lower leagues. Of the three biggest, two are from Irbid, a city on the Syrian border: Al-Jalil, established in 1953, and Shabab al-Hussein, established in 1954. The Amman club, Al-Wehdat, was formed in 1956. *Falastin* newspaper relocated to Amman after 1967 and began to cover these new teams. The 1960s saw the rise of a Palestinian movement known as the Revolution, a generation of youthful left-wing writers and fighters. The revolutionaries asserted their independence from the Arab rulers that surrounded them. After

Jordan lost the West Bank in the war of 1967, this assertion of independence became literal, with the creation of a revolutionary state-within-a-state inside Jordan, which comprised armed militias, checkpoints and rudimentary ministries, as well as operations to collect 'taxes'. Jordan was unable to accept the presence of this radical, militarised mini-state, especially one engaged in cross-border raids with Israel. In 1973, in a conflict known as 'Black September', the Palestinian militias clashed with the mechanised Jordanian battalions. It did not end well. The Palestinian survivors moved on to Lebanon.

The football team most associated with the Revolution is Al-Wehdat. The team is based in south Amman, the poorest refugee community in the kingdom. In the late 1960s, Al-Wehdat began to be regarded as the national team of the Palestinians of Jordan, described in exactly those terms by the Palestinian leader Yasser Arafat. Al-Wehdat drew fans from Palestinians living across Jordan, not just the camp. The club won promotion from the second division in 1975, at a time when the wounds of Black September were still very raw. Five years later, in 1980, Al-Wehdat won its first league title.

The Amman derby between Al-Wehdat and Al-Faisaly is the defining match of the Jordanian sporting calendar. It is also the fixture most likely to see violence. Supporters of Al-Faisaly have a chant: 'One, two, three/Abu Hussein divorce her.' Abu Hussein is the familiar name of Abdullah II, the present King of Jordan, and his wife, Queen Rania, is a Palestinian woman. In riots in 2010, part of a stadium fence gave way, injuring somewhere between fifty and two hundred and fifty Al-Wehdat fans. In the attempt to escape from the chaos, fans broke out of the stadium where they were attacked by baton-wielding police. Despite the fury of the derby, Al-Wehdat long ago eclipsed its rival. By 2018, it was coached by Palestinian-Jordanian Jamal Mahmoud, who has also coached the Palestinian national team. In May 2018, Al-Wehdat took the league title by nine points over Al-Faisaly.

Chapter Twenty-Two:

Tayibe

On the Friday morning following practice, I returned to the Jaffa Orthodox team's pitch to meet Rami, David and Koko, and get a lift to the Tayibe fixture. I thought we would be travelling by bus, but the bus had been sold when the team was relegated. The players were taking their own cars. In Israel, Jewish and Palestinian citizens live in separate communities and very few cities have any kind of mixed populations. In consequence, the league teams are regarded as being either Jewish or Palestinian, defined by the town they represent even when the actual squads feature a mix of players. Tayibe, like Jaffa Orthodox, is a Palestinian team.

Tayibe lies close to the border between Israel and the West Bank, about twenty-five miles north of Jaffa, close to the West Bank city of Tulkarem. This area is the historical bread basket of Palestine and Tayibe is an agriculture city. In 1948, the area was surrounded by the army and a curfew prevented the villagers from getting to their fields. By 1949, after the armistice between Israel and Jordan was signed, the villagers found their own farmland had been seized under the absentee property law. It was now Israeli state land. The villages became gulags, controlled by checkpoints and curfews. The villagers went to work each day in fields they no longer owned. The military controls lasted for twenty years, governing where the locals could travel and what time they must be home at night.

A few days before I travelled to Tayibe, the Israeli football historian Amir Ben Porat had filled me in on the history of Palestinian football teams. The Palestine Football Association was renamed the Israel Football Association in 1948, and for its first decade the only non-Jewish club to play any league football was a short-lived Catholic team from Haifa. In the late 1950s, a handful of Islamic clubs tried to form their own league: 'The authorities shut them down,' Ben Porat told me. The Palestinian teams could not join the Israel FA leagues, nor form leagues of their own. But the biggest obstacle to football was Martial Law. Until 1967, anyone living in a non-Jewish city had to apply for military permits to leave their homes. Even if it was possible to join a league, the teams would never know in advance if they could make a fixture or return home before curfew.

The situation changed thanks to the rivalry between Hapoel and the Maccabi. The two sports associations were funded by the Israeli government, and the value of the grant depended on the number of member clubs each had. This gave the associations an incentive to sign Palestinian teams. Very quickly every Palestinian city, down to the smallest village, ended up with two clubs, one Hapoel and one Maccabi. Even Beitar joined in the racket, admitting a conservative Catholic Action club from Nazareth into their association. Membership of Israeli sports associations brought in a little funding, but the great thing for

Palestinians was that football was suddenly possible. Ben Porat said, 'For the Arab clubs, the advantage was that they could call someone to speak to the army when they needed to travel to a match. Having a Jewish friend that can speak to the District Commander, that makes all the difference.'

It shows the thirst for football that Israel went from having no Palestinian teams to dozens, and it happened almost overnight. The number continued to increase, as Martial Law was lifted in 1967 and Palestinians with Israeli citizenship began to enjoy more normal freedoms. There are now 90 Palestinian clubs out of the 221 in the Israeli leagues. This is extraordinary. Palestinians make up 20 per cent of Israel's population, but 40 per cent of the football leagues. Or, to put it another way, they are one in five of Israel's citizens, but two in five of its footballers. The enthusiasm for football didn't come from nowhere. Like David Mansour's Jaffa Orthodox team, there was a deep well of knowledge, and of talent. The local kids had always been playing and following football, with an expertise often carried by internal refugees from Jaffa and Haifa.

However, while they make up 40 per cent of the leagues, they chiefly play in the lower, non-professional leagues. It wasn't until 1996 that a team made it into the top division, and that team was Tayibe FC, the opponents of the Jaffa boys on the day I saw a match.

Ben Porat followed Tayibe FC throughout their top flight 1996–7 season. He believes Tayibe's success came at an opportune moment. Yitzhak Rabin, the Prime Minister who had guided Israel into the peace process of the early 1990s, was murdered in 1995. The election of Benjamin Netanyahu, in his first term as Prime Minister, saw the peace process go into a permanent freeze. These were dark times, and the story of a successful Arab team benefited Netanyahu because it appeared to show Israel was a meritocracy in which anyone could succeed and flourish.

The FA declared that the Tayibe stadium was unsuitable for first-class football. The rules state that a team unable to play at its own grounds must play at one over 25 km away, but Tayibe were given special permission to play some of their home games in Netanya, 20 km away. Ben Porat believes this was just one example of the ways in which Tayibe were given an easy ride. He is convinced nobody wanted Tayibe to fail, and the fact it dropped straight back down to the second division was due to mismanagement rather than political obstacles. As the season began to unravel, the club switched managers twice. The team only took fifteen points from thirty games, and ended the season with a goal difference of minus forty-seven.

Yet even if no one put fresh obstacles in Tayibe's way, they suffered, as the death of the player Waheeb Jabarra shows. Jabarra went into cardiac arrest during a game against Bnei Yehuda FC. This was a home game, but the Netanya stadium was unavailable. The match was played instead in Umm al-Fahm, an isolated Palestinian city in the north where Israel borders the West Bank. The police inquiry into the death highlighted the slow response and the delay as the team waited on the pitch for an ambulance to arrive. During the wait, Jabarra was treated by the medical teams of both clubs. He was eventually taken to a well-equipped hospital in the Jewish town of Afula, over half an hour away, in preference to the facilities in

Umm al-Fahm. The statistics on health care in Israel show that Jewish Israelis live five years longer than Palestinian Israelis, and the infant mortality rate is three times higher in Palestinian districts.

Tayibe went bankrupt following its sole season in the top flight. It went through a variety of name changes and mergers as it fell through the leagues. The current team is the survivor of these mergers. As we approached the city, we began to spot the cars of our team members and even the coach, all driving in the same direction. A number of Jaffa's players live in Kafr Qasim, another farming community on the West Bank–Israel border. Kafr Qasim is the site of a notorious 1956 massacre, on the eve of Israel's participation in the Suez War. The army brought curfew forward by a few hours, without telling the workers in the fields. When orders were given to shoot any Palestinians seen on the roads, forty-nine farmers were killed.

Kafr Qasim has its own football club, which plays in the league above Jaffa Orthodox. But the city's star team is its beach soccer side, known as Brothers of the Pepper (*Abna Filfili* in Arabic, *Bnei Falfala* in Hebrew). The team dominates Israeli's beach soccer league, which is some achievement considering Kafr Qasim is at least 15 miles from the nearest beach. The Jaffa captain also plays for the beach soccer team. His name is Amer Yatim, a dizzyingly upbeat guy with pale eyes and bright teeth, like a human strobe-light of conviviality. When he arrived at Tayibe's stadium, he greeted everyone with wild enthusiasm, his team, the opposing team, the staff, all of the fans. He made me feel as if I was failing as a human being, though I was simply being English.

Ouriel Daskal had told me that Tayibe has a grass pitch,

which is rare outside the Israeli premiership. It may be grass, but it is so lumpy and foamy that walking on it is like hiking on moorland. I wondered if the pitch might favour beach soccer stars. It would be impossible to play the ball along the ground. When the game started, Amer tried to beat every opponent by chipping the ball over their heads. The game was a slow affair. Most attempts at goal were volleys, taken at a distance. Amer's good humour eventually left him. When he shoved a Tayibe player in front of the referee, he was sent off. It was his second yellow card.

On the drive home, Rami and Koko analysed the 2–1 defeat. No one thought Amer's dismissal was unfair. I didn't want to admit I had paid less attention to the match than the countryside. The Tayibe stadium is higher than any other building in the city. I could see over the border into the West Bank, as far as the hills around Nablus. It was very hot in Jaffa, but it was far cooler in the hills.

Chapter Twenty-Three:

Sakhnin

In 1997, a year after my father-in-law died, his three sisters and his brother organised a family reunion in Bethlehem. We hired a bus and took a trip up to the Galilee, something that would be unimaginable today, a party of fifteen Palestinians on a day-trip from the West Bank. I suspect 1997 was the last year that it was possible. In retrospect, the peace process between the Israelis and Palestinians was already over.

Our trip took place in early summer at the end of the apricot season, as the figs were beginning to ripen and explode. The Galilee holds a lake, of course, where Leila and I had taken a holiday in the first year of our marriage, swimming in the cool fresh water and sunbathing in a garden owned by the Church of Scotland guesthouse. But the Galilee is also the name of the hilly region between the lake and Haifa on the coast. Much of this area, 75 square miles' worth, is known as the Misgav Block, run by the Misgav Regional Council. Though it covers such an enormous area, the Misgav Block is sparsely populated: it holds just thirty small neighbourhoods, and is home to fewer than twenty thousand people. As we drove through the winding hill-sides, we caught glimpses of red roofs in clusters among forests of pine trees. In contrast to these sparsely scattered communi-ties, the Palestinian town of Sakhnin packs 33,000 people into just two streets. Sakhnin is surrounded by the Misgav Block, but not part of it. It is run by its own city council but is subordinate to the Jewish-only regional council in a very clearly defined apartheid-style system. Sakhnin used to be an agricultural cen-tre but the irrigation system for the fields was turned off by the authorities in a drought in the late 1980s and never turned back on again. Sakhnin is famous now for two things: an annual event known as Land Day, and for football.

There is a memorial on the road into Sakhnin to com-memorate the six deaths in a protest on 30 March 1976. The protest marked a fresh round of land confiscations to extend the Misgav Block, a project the government openly called 'The Judaisiation of the Galilee'. The protesters were met with live fire. Aside from the six people killed, three men and three women, around a hundred were injured and many hundreds of people were arrested in protests that spread across Israel. The date became an annual protest day for the Palestinian citizens of Israel: Land Day. Back in 1997, Land Day was far more significant to Israeli Palestinians than to Palestinians in the West Bank and Gaza. I was not aware of it, at all. Though in truth there were many things I was unaware of in the first few years of my marriage, in the days of my Pollyanna-ish trust in the peace process. Land Day only became a day of protests for all Palestinians, both in Israel and occupied Palestine, around 2007. As I visited in March 2018, I was very aware the protests would begin at the end of the month.

Sakhnin is a small city in an isolated spot, but the football team is the only Palestinian club currently playing in the Israeli Premier League. The story of the Sons of Sakhnin United FC (*Ittihad Abna Sakhnin* in Arabic, *Ihud Bnei Sakhnin* in Hebrew) began in 1965 when a young politician and sportsman named Mazen Ghnaim signed up to the Hapoel association. The next year another group of players joined the Maccabi. Like a lot of towns, Sakhnin continued to have two teams playing in the lowest national leagues until the 1990s.

The change began when Hapoel and Maccabi began privatising the country's football clubs by selling the teams to entrepreneurs and individuals. In 1991, Mazen Ghnaim and another local, Mohammed Abu Yunis, proposed a merger and the two Sakhnin teams were bought and rolled into a single 'united' team. (The Arab word *Ittihad* or *Etihad* means 'unity' but in football is used to translate the ever-popular club name 'United'. There was some hilarity in Manchester when this was discovered, after Etihad Airlines bought the naming rights for Manchester City's stadium.) It seems improbable that the most successful Palestinian club in Israel would come from a town as small as Sakhnin, a city of 27,000 Muslims and 6,000 Christians. The route to success was slow but steady: Sakhnin reached Israel's second tier in 1997. At times the progress was marred by rivalry and violence. In 1999, two years after Tayibe dropped out of the top flight and while it was already in freefall, the two teams met in a game that ended with running street fights between Tayibe and Sakhnin fans. The greatest hostility Sakhnin faced, however, was from the Israeli police. The police chief of the Misgav Block ensured it was impossible for Sakhnin to reach the top division.

As Sakhnin climbed through the divisions, the Misgav police chief, Inspector Guy Reif, began imposing fresh restrictions on Sakhnin and their supporters, closing games to the public or delaying starts. Once Sakhnin reached the second division, he banned the team from using the home ground, claiming that its position made it too difficult to police. The club was forced to hire temporary grounds in Haifa, losing out financially as well as losing the traditional home-side advantage. The situation only changed when Reif was sacked for gross misconduct, on another issue. This happened shortly after the politician and ex-general Ariel Sharon made an explosive march around the al-Aqsa compound in 2002. Sharon's march was a deliberate replay of the 1929 demonstration by Beitar boys that kicked off the 1929 riots. Sharon was in the midst of a political campaign, and wanted to declare that the compound belonged to Israel, just as his forebears had once chanted 'The Wall is ours'. Sharon's march was illegal under Israeli law, but the Labour government dithered over enforcing the ban, unwilling to concede there may be areas in Jerusalem that an Israeli general ought not to visit. He entered the narrow gate at the head of a thousand-strong force of policemen, a display designed with a flair for the violent spectacle that characterised all of the late general's actions. On the TV news, the visit played as a military invasion. The pictures are credited with sparking the Second Intifada, a confrontation between Palestinian and Israeli forces. It is often forgotten that the first protests began inside Israel, where Israel's own Palestinian citizens were incensed by the stunt. In the days immediately following, twelve Israeli citizens (and a thirteenth person, a boy from Gaza who was visiting relatives) were shot dead by police. Five of the dead came from Sakhnin.

The investigation into the deaths in Sakhnin revealed that Inspector Reif had confronted protesters with just a junior officer at his side, and with no plans for back-up. Alarmed by the scale of the protests, Reif pulled his gun and began to fire at the crowd. He is known to have killed one youth. How many other deaths were Reif's direct responsibility is still unknown. The police shot dead one child who was sitting at a road junction wearing the T-shirt of a charity that promoted Jewish–Arab coexistence. It would be unthinkable for Israeli police to fire at a protest by Jewish citizens, but lethal force is regularly used as a first resort against non-Jewish citizens. The internal investigation into Reif's conduct found only minor operational defects and Reif was not charged. A public outcry led to Reif's suspension and an external investigation, the Or Inquiry. This did lead to charges, but only indirectly. What changed everything was the increasingly unstable behaviour of Inspector Reif.

At the Or Inquiry, Reif had claimed secret intelligence that Sakhnin was at the centre of an armed terrorist conspiracy. His testimony went poorly, and Reif left the courtroom convinced no one had believed him. He returned to his old police station, armed with his service pistol, though he had been told to surrender the weapon. Standing in the street, he began firing at the building. Reif is a thickset man who wears his hair in a military buzzcut. He tends towards bluster in interviews, perhaps to disguise the fact that he is prone to panic. The shots at the police station were reported to have been a madcap attempt to give weight to his story of a terrorist conspiracy: Reif was said to have hoped to blame terrorists lurking in the hills. Reif's officers ran out to the street and were reported have found their hapless chief in a state of distress, begging them to ignore the shots and 'forget' they had seen him. The prosecutors noted what was termed circumstantial evidence of his escapade but chose not to press charges, stating there were no eye witnesses to the actual shooting nor any physical evidence it took place. Instead, Reif was fired on the advice of the Or Inquiry.

Reif's successor overturned the ban on games at Sakhnin's stadium. Results improved dramatically and in 2003 Sakhnin won promotion to the Premier League, alongside Ahi Nazareth. Sakhnin borrowed some players, signed Brazilian Gabriel Lima from a Bulgarian side, and hired an experienced new manager, Eyal Lahman. An Israeli Jew, Lahman was not yet forty, but had been managing teams for twenty years, ever since his playing career ended in serious injury as a teenager.

Once again, Sakhnin had to find a new stadium. This time it was the Israeli FA who decided that Sakhnin's home ground was unsuitable for top-flight football. Given their poverty and lack of facilities, the club was widely predicted to drop back to the lower division. In fact, it was Ahi Nazareth who were relegated. Sakhnin turned into a tight, organised and physically intimidating team.

In their first season, the team won the Israel Cup: one of the more remarkable events in Israeli football. The hero of the 2003–4 season was Abbas Suan, a home-grown midfield player and club talisman. Lahman's tactics were a version of Israel's 'Jerry Bunker' game, drilling Sakhnin into a defensive side that made them difficult to beat. Suan's toughness and tenacity breathed life into the dour strategy. Everyone describes Suan as the one player who will simply never give up: he is always looking for a way to win. Games that might easily have been draws kept turning in Sakhnin's favour. On the way to the Cup final, Sakhnin twice ended matches with penalty shootouts, and Sakhnin players kept their nerves to win. Both times, Suan set the tone by taking the first strike.

When Sakhnin faced FC Ashdod, a player named Haim Revivo, a famous footballer of his day, led a pitch invasion and abused Lahman of being a traitor for 'working for Arabs'. After the event, club chairman Mazen Ghnaim thought it wise to organise a reconciliation meeting. Lahman refused to participate, saying: 'What? They insult me one day and apologise the next?'

The team was also helped by an extraordinary run of perform-ances from Hapoel Haifa, who were then a second-division side. Hapoel Haifa had been declared bankrupt three years previously and were only being kept alive by the administrators. But as the cup run that year proved, the club had turned a corner. On the way to the final, Hapoel Haifa took out three of the most dangerous top-flight teams. Sakhnin and Hapoel Haifa met in the final at the Ramat Gan stadium, near Tel Aviv. Haifa scored in the forty-first minute, taking a one-goal lead into half time. It was only in the sixty-first minute that Sakhnin equalised thanks to Avi Danan, one of the Jewish players in the side. Sakhnin nosed ahead three minutes later with a goal from the 23-year-old Lior Asulin, another Jewish Israeli on loan from second-division Maccabi Herzliya. There was a tense ten minutes when Haifa might have equalised, but then came a third goal from Gabriel Lima, who was having a career-best season. Asulin put the game beyond all Haifa's hopes with a penalty in the eighty-eighth minute: the game was over.

It was a phenomenally popular win, in what was another depressing year. I was living in Bethlehem in the West Bank, and it was bleak. The Intifada had been crushed with tanks and aeroplanes. There were soldiers on the street in front of our house; the curfews lasted for weeks. The situation in Israel was nothing like this, but everything was swathed in mistrust and uncertainty. Ariel Sharon had bulldozed his way through to become the Prime Minister of Israel, but had fallen out with his own party and was now in the process of forming a new coalition around a platform that declared Israel could draw its own borders unilaterally, and so end all its territorial disputes with Palestine. How he hoped to bypass negotiations and yet reach an international agreement, no one would ever know: Sharon fell into a coma in January 2006 and never woke.

In some ways, the situation in 2004 was similar to the year that Tayibe won promotion. The future looked dark, but the story of a winning Arab team seemed to promise something else: that Israel might one day become a happy country, a country at ease with itself.

All the Hebrew-language newspapers congratulated Sakhnin, often in Arabic, while opinion pieces spoke about a new dawn. The chairman, Mazen Ghnaim, had often spoken of his desire to create a 'Rainbow Team' and this took on a prophetic aura as the goodwill flowed. Israel's President, Shimon Peres, saw the victory as historic. He speculated that it would change Israel for ever. Ronnie Bar-On, a Likud MP, praised Sakhnin as an Israeli team winning an Israeli victory, while also noting they were from an Arab town. Sakhnin was a team with a Jewish manager, and had won the Cup with goals from two Jews and a Brazilian Catholic. Yet, as Bar-On's comments inadvertently made clear, this was the 'Arab' sector. Israel is a multifaith and multi-ethnic society and it always will be, but it was only in the margins, in towns like Sakhnin, that it was possible to see the outline of an Israel that reflected this reality.

Suan became the face of victory. He was called up to the national team. Suan had once complained that Sakhnin was poor because no Israeli businesses would back the team. Sakhnin could not win the sponsorship that would help them move up a gear. Now Suan landed a personal contract to advertise the national lottery. As a member of the Israeli squad, he played in Israel's colours, the same colours as a Jewish prayer shawl, and was loved and feted by almost all Israelis, even forgiven when he stayed silent during the 'Hatikvah' anthem. Suan is still remembered as a hero for scoring a decisive late equaliser in Ireland in 2006 that kept Israel in the running for a place in the World Cup.

Yet despite the tide of goodwill that flowed their way, Sakhnin has never become a club for all Israelis. It might represent universal values of openness and inclusivity, but it is in a double-bind. Only a Palestinian club could represent the real make-up of Israel, which means it will simultaneously remain stuck in an 'Arab' ghetto. To liberal Israelis, the idea of a society at ease with its minorities is attractive yet scary: it opens the doors to a different state, one that belongs, at best, to a peaceful multicultural future, and at worse to a fractured state that no longer offers anything to Jews. Ten years after the 2004 Cup win, the football writer Shaul Adar travelled to Sakhnin to watch their home game against visitors Be'er Sheva. His lasting impression was of the Arab Bedouins who had travelled from Be'er Sheva not to support 'their' local team but to see Sakhnin. Adar reported a Jewish fan as saying that Sakhnin had sacrificed their opportunity to be the team of all Israel because they had become 'political'. Sakhnin fans wave the Palestinian national flag. (This was illegal in Israel until recently. It may still attract fines from the Israel Football Association, who regard the flag as a provocation: a political demonstration.) Fans also hold up images of Handala: a Palestinian cartoon figure who is part Peanuts and part symbol of resistance. These displays by the fans fuel suspicions that every move towards coexistence is a cover for an Arab takeover.

At the end of the 2014–15 season, Ran Kadoch, the Sakhnin goalkeeper who was born in the West Bank settlement of Ma'al Adumim, posted an image on his Facebook page. The photograph showed six Sakhnin players celebrating a goal: four were on their knees in a Muslim prayer, one was making the Christian sign of the cross, and Kadoch was saying a Jewish prayer. To Kadoch, at least, this is what a normal Israeli team looks like.

Chapter Twenty-Four:

La Familia

The year Sakhnin won the Israel Cup, fans of Beitar Jerusalem posted a black-framed advert in a Jerusalem newspaper declaring that Israeli football had died. In the next weeks, these fans created a new 'Ultras' faction that they named 'La Familia', using the cod-Italian of Hollywood Mafia films to honour the Italian roots of all Ultras, the right-wing, borderline criminal gangs that feed off the hardcore supporters on the football terraces. In Israel, however, the name La Familia also looked back to 'The Fighting Family', a term used in the immediate post-war period by the veterans of Lehi, Irgun and Beitar to show they were comrades and always would be. By taking the name La Familia, the Beitar fans were indulging in fantasies inspired by the *Godfather* films, but they were also showing they knew their history. Of course they did: the story of Lehi and the Irgun is on the national curriculum, and tours of the museum are part of their national service duty.

La Familia's Ultras are patriots for a city they believe is scorned by Israel's elites. They have embraced the anger and resentment of the Beitar story, which at heart is a story that the Jewish homeland is under greater threat from appeasement by fellow Jews than from Arabs. Many of the original members of Beitar Jerusalem were still in an African detention camp in 1948 when Ben Gurion declared independence. When they finally got back, they discovered that Ben Gurion was negotiating an armistice with Jordan via the United Nations that placed the Old City of Jerusalem outside of Israel's borders. In September 1948, the last remnants of the Stern Gang tried to derail the peace talks by murdering the UN negotiator, Folke Bernadotte. It did not work. Ben Gurion completed the negotiations and Israel's borders were set, with only the city's western suburbs in Israeli hands. To Beitar, it was just one of the most blatant betrayals by a Jew in a series of betrayals. Yosef Yekutieli had sold out the fighting spirit of the Maccabi to win the approval of FIFA; Yitzhak Rabin sold out Judea and Samaria to appease the Palestinian Liberation Organisation (PLO); even their hero Ariel Sharon went bad in the end and tried to establish borders smaller than the whole of historic Palestine.

In the 1950s, Beitar Jerusalem continued to play at the YMCA stadium. They were a second division team, in an aging Christian stadium, but this was the only football in Jerusalem and the games represented a cheap form of entertainment to new immigrant families from Morocco, Iraq and Syria. These immigrants are the 'Second Israel', so called because they arrived after the creation of the state. They brought their own unhappy stories of being driven from their homes in Baghdad or Damascus by revolutions and sectarian hatred. In Israel, they found new complaints. The prejudice they experienced from European Jews seemed to amount to a form of racial discrimination. The

Mizrahim – the Jews of the Maghreb and the Middle East – were blocked from rising through society, in part because they were forced to live in cities far away from the coastal hub of Israeli life. They were literally dumped on the fringes of the country in transit camps, before being moved to poorly built towns with inferior schools and health services. The desert city of Be'er Sheva is one such city but for much of Israel's life, Jerusalem, too, was a fringe city. Iraqi and Moroccan immigrants lived in vertiginous housing projects, with poor transport links, roofs that leaked in the wet winter months and windows that rattled in the high winds blowing off the desert. Ben Gurion's Mapai (which evolved into the Israeli Labour Party) received the blame for treating the Second Israel as commodities who could be packed off to populate the hard-to-reach cities. In their resentment, the Mizrahim gravitated towards the opposition party, first to Begin's Herut (the successor to Beitar) and then to Likud (the successor to Herut). The Mizrahim in Jerusalem not only supported the Beitar team, they absorbed the Beitar politics.

You do not have to step far off the tourist trail to discover Jerusalem is a damaged and ugly city. There is a professional class that works in government and higher education but, beyond this elite, the city is composed of just three communities, all of whom loathe each other. It is the home of the country's largest community of Mizrahi Jews. It also has the highest proportion of ultra-Orthodox Jews. Finally, Jerusalem is the largest Palestinian city with the Old City and East Jerusalem still an overcrowded, Arabic-speaking dilapidated metropolis. Taken together – Mizrahim, Haredim and Falastin – these are the three largest minorities in Israel, and by a wide margin the poorest of Israel's communities, all concentrated in one city.

Jerusalem is built upon poverty, divisions and military installations. Yet Jerusalem is also Israel's 'Eternal Capital', as the slogan runs; it is supposed to be a beautiful and holy city. If Jerusalem is essential to Jewish nationalism, then the fans of Beitar are perhaps right to believe that only their presence keeps the dream of all Israel alive. After all, 70 per cent of Israelis live on the Mediterranean coast, and rarely visit Jerusalem. As long as Israelis with money and education live by the beach, the self-image of Beitar fans as the real Jewish nationalists is reinforced.

The Mizrahim imported a love of football from the countries they had left behind. Hapoel Be'er Sheva began life in a desert transit camp outside the city while they waited for their new homes to be awarded. The club was briefly suspended from the leagues in the early 1950s because the city was deemed inaccessible by the other clubs. After an up-and-down career over half a century, Be'er Sheva has enjoyed a winning decade under the direction of tech entrepreneur Alona Barkat (who is also the sister-in-law of Nir Barkat, the current Mayor of Jerusalem).

Beitar Jerusalem outgrew the second division in 1968, the year after Israeli forces captured the Old City and the West Bank. It was a quick lesson in how extra resources and money pumped into the capital could benefit the city, the team, its fans and Jerusalemites in general. Over the years, however, Beitar has had a myriad of financial problems. There have even been attempts to relegate the club for disciplinary and financial infractions. But Beitar always escaped sanctions, because it was owned by the Likud party, and its board included politicians such as Ehud Olmert, who would become the Mayor of Jerusalem (and later succeeded Ariel Sharon when the Prime Minister fell into his coma).

Beitar's first trophy came in June 1976 with a 2–1 victory over Maccabi Tel Aviv in the Israel Cup. That September, they followed this up by claiming the Super Cup, the summer contest between the league champions and the cup winners. These back-to-back victories were seen as augurs for the rise of Likud, and the party duly won the May 1977 elections.

The move from the YMCA to the current 'Teddy Stadium' in 1991 was a long time in the planning. The YMCA stadium was sold to developers before a new stadium was built. Beitar was forced to play two seasons at Jaffa's Bloomfield Stadium, deep inside the enemy world of socialists and Arabs.

Teddy Stadium, named after one-time Jerusalem Mayor Teddy Kollek, is built over the remains of a Palestinian village named Malha, three miles outside of Jerusalem. The villagers made new homes on a steep hillside in Bethlehem, after being forced out of Malha by Irgun irregulars in July 1948. For Israelis, the Malha site has a different significance: it marks a new phase in the expulsion of football and other leisure activities from downtown Jerusalem by religious Jews.

Beitar got off to a strong start in the new stadium. As the country moved rightwards in the years following the murder of Prime Minister Yitzhak Rabin, Beitar showed its knack for capturing the national spirit. Control of the team had fallen into the hands of a Jerusalem impresario named Moshe Dadash. Yet the club was still connected to its parent political party, Likud, which gave figures such as Olmert and Reuven Rivlin (the current President of Israel) a say in the club's management. It was only in 1999 that the club became a limited company and finally severed the formal relationship with the parent political association. A piece of land used as training facilities was sold to raise money during the privatisation process, and this money somehow ended up in the pocket of Moshe Dashad, who claimed it as a repaid debt owed to him by the club. This small piece of land and the profits from its sale played a significant part in the corruption charges against the Prime Minister Ehud Olmert. As always in Israel, it is difficult to separate politics from real-estate deals. Olmert is the highest-ranking Israeli official to be jailed for corruption.

Shaul Adar is a long-time fan of Beitar Jerusalem, and believes the team of 1999–2000 might have been Israel's break-out side, in the way that Bayern Munich, Manchester United or Barça manage to transcend their cities and appeal to a world audience. Teddy Stadium was easily the best stadium in the country in those days. Adar found Beitar's style of play thrilling, while Teddy Stadium even had a sparkle of celebrity, although the celebrities were Likud politicians. Adar dates the souring of Beitar to the appearance of the banner 'Forever Pure' on La Familia's East Stand, which ensured that racism became the defining feature of the club. But it is not as though the club was not defined by racism before the sign went up. To be 'forever' pure you have to be pure already. If La Familia were guilty of anything, it was commercialising racism: they turned club policy into the shout-line on the poster.

Chapter Twenty-Five:

The First Signings

In the early 1950s, Bulgarian families arriving from post-war Europe were housed in Jaffa's old town, in homes deemed 'abandoned' by Yosef Yekutieli's department. The immigrants founded their own Bulgarian team, named Maccabi Jaffa. In 1960, Maccabi Jaffa became the first Jewish side to sign a non-Jewish player, Boghos Ghougassian, the star striker of Jaffa's Homenetmen Club. This was still in the days before non-Jewish sides could play in the FA leagues, and Ghougassian seized the opportunity to play professional football.

Today, football is often cited as the one area of public life in Israel with something like a level playing field, and this is thanks to Ghougassian and Maccabi Jaffa. Almost all Israeli clubs field mixed squads of Israeli Jews, Israeli Palestinians and foreign signings. All except one: Beitar Jerusalem. This is the meaning of the boast 'Forever Pure', the one team 'unsullied' by Palestinian players.

In 1972, Boghos was joined at Maccabi Jaffa by Koko Kalalian, who was a promising midfielder. By this time, other clubs were willing to consider non-Jewish players and in 1972 Hapoel Tel Aviv signed the sixteen-year-old Rifaat 'Jimmy' Turk, another Jaffa boy. For a long time, Jimmy Turk was the most famous Palestinian footballer in Israel. He made his full team debut for Hapoel Tel Aviv at eighteen in 1974. In 1976 he became Israel's first non-Jewish international.

Jimmy Turk is still a much-loved figure as a sportsman but also as a politician. He ran for the Tel Aviv council in 1998 as a member of the Meretz, an Israeli party that sprang from an older Marxist faction. In 2003, Turk served a term as the city's Deputy Mayor. In his footballing and political career, Turk has represented the 'red' side of Tel Aviv, the socialist politics of a city that proudly regards itself as Israel's most progressive and liberal. My friends Eitan and Tamar live on the block beside Tel Aviv's City Hall where Turk once had his offices, a tree-lined boulevard with a central cycle lane and whizzing electric bikes. The square in front of City Hall is named Rabin Square to commemorate the Prime Minister who was murdered for his peace deal with the PLO. The Walter Gropius-style Bauhaus housing blocks that surround the square benefit from UNESCO World Heritage status as a direct result of the peace process.

Rabin Square is the traditional centre for political demonstrations in Israel. This is where you see protests in support of social issues or peace initiatives. Tel Aviv is a unique city, but it is also the city that turned out to celebrate the release of Simcha Hinkis from prison in 1935. The period when Tel Aviv hoped to become a multicultural and multi-ethnic city can be mapped to the period that coincides with Jimmy Turk's career, from his signing to Hapoel Tel Aviv, to his term as Deputy Mayor. It is difficult to imagine another Palestinian following in Turk's footsteps. The Deputy Mayor in 2018 was Arnon Giladi, who was elected on a promise to erase Jaffa's Arab character by building new Jewish-only developments in the city, and ran a campaign stating, 'It's Us or Them: A Hebrew City or an Islamic State of Jaffa'. Giladi's enthusiasm for real-estate deals has brought its own problems. In December 2017, he was arrested as part of the investigation into corruption, bribery and money laundering that surrounds the Likud politician and lawyer David Bitan and the property developer Dror Glazer. The case known as Lahav 433 is still ongoing, and Giladi remains under suspicion of accepting bribes from Glazer.

Outside of Tel Aviv, the liberal period was over long before Sakhnin won the 2004 Israel Cup. Beitar Jerusalem was on the skids, which allowed La Familia to give shape and direction to a club that was losing its vitality on the pitch. In 2005, the club declared bankruptcy, and La Familia became the main conduit between the club's hierarchy and the fans. The club's new owner, the Russian-Israeli businessman Arkady Gaydamak, recognised La Familia as the official supporters' club. The Israeli football writer Uri Levy reports that Gaydamak used his personal assistant as the go-between with La Familia, donating money, covering the costs of banners, and even providing premises inside the stadium, replete with the latest film and media entertainment equipment (the stadium is owned by the city, not by the club). The financial fragility of the club gave La Familia its power, as they could mobilise fans to support the team, sell tickets and organise travel to away games. Surprisingly, though, Gaydamak had begun his tenure at Beitar by donating $400,000 to Sakhnin, who were facing their own financial problems. The donation was part of an attempt to bring

Sakhnin's star Abbas Suan to Beitar Jerusalem. The deal was all but done when La Familia orchestrated violent protests. Gaydamak blinked first, and stepped back from the deal with Suan. Gaydamak had his own reasons for appeasing La Familia: he hoped their backing would help him win elections to become Mayor of Jerusalem. In the end, Gaydamak was humiliated: his party won zero seats in the city government. When they had the ear of the most senior politicians in the country, Rivlin and Olmert, why would La Familia back a newcomer like Gaydamak? Gaydamak's welcome of La Familia did nothing for his ambitions. All it did was legitimise La Familia's racism, and create a safe space for even more extreme groups in Teddy Stadium, notably Lehava (an anti-Christian and anti-Muslim party) and Kahane Chai (a banned Jewish terrorist organisation).

As recently as the 1990s, Beitar had fielded two Muslim foreign signings, a Tajik and an Albanian. The year before Gaydamak took over, the Nigerian player Ndala Ibrahim was driven out of the team by physical violence, after playing just four matches. The African-born player Toto Tamuz, raised in Israel by Jews and a practising Jew, had a four-year career with Beitar in 2006–10, but was so regularly humiliated and insulted that the club was fined and sanctioned with a points deduction. La Familia responded by setting fire to the Israel Football Association offices and daubing them with graffiti. Each time a senior figure within Beitar Jerusalem expresses the least interest in coexistence, La Familia has demanded that a player or board member speak to them in private and hear their views. In every instance, the private meeting has ended with the club backing down with a press statement declaring respect for the clubs' tradition – the 'tradition' that Arab and Muslim players are not welcome. Even the

Argentinian manager Ossie Ardiles, who briefly coached the team in 2006 and almost returned in 2014, has said: 'The Teddy is a special place and I don't know if an Arab player can play with this level of animosity from our own supporters. Yes, of course, I would prefer this feeling didn't exist, but it does.' In an interview with Shaul Adar, a spokesman for the club stated the aim was to adopt a 'gradual approach' and bring La Familia towards a more liberal understanding, which ignores the fact that a chief entertainment of La Familia is to attack liberals.

The most infamous story of the Gaydamak era was his decision to bring in two Chechen players. La Familia responded once more with arson, burning down the Beitar Jerusalem offices. The club's trophy room went up in flames, destroying the history of the club. When one of the players, Zaur Sadaev, scored a goal for Beitar against Maccabi Netanya there was a mass walk-out of 100 Beitar fans.

Malha is also home to a shopping mall, the best and largest in the Jerusalem district. Both stadium and mall are visible from the vineyards at the edge of Bethlehem. Jerusalem is off-limits to Palestinians from the West Bank. However, at Christmas, the army issues permits that allow Bethlehem's Christians to attend mass at the Holy Sepulchre cathedral. Of course, everyone uses the permits to go shopping at Malha Mall: a culture shock when the mall suddenly fills with Arabs spending money, dancing around the mall, and asking each other what Aunty wants in her stocking. The rest of the year, the only Palestinians shoppers would see are the cleaners, shelf stackers and trolley parkers; the very bottom of the heap in what is already a poor city. On Monday 19 March, 2012, Beitar fans launched an attack on these mall workers.

The attacks came after Beitar had played a home game against Bnei Yehuda FC, another team associated with Israel's Mizrahim, and coached at the time by one of Beitar's most popular old players, Yossi Abukasis. There was no animosity at the game. But the match was an early kick-off, and when Beitar beat Bnei Yehuda 2–1, the young fans were hungry. They had rushed to the game from their colleges or work, and now they streamed into the Malha Mall food hall. Video shows the fans dancing on tables, throwing food and chanting. The chanting is ugly. All Beitar chants have the same theme, and that night the chants were 'Death to Arabs' and 'Mohammed is dead'. A group of Palestinian women were eating with their children and were spat at and insulted. Cleaning staff intervened and the Beitar kids backed off, but returned in greater numbers. There were now 300 Beitar fans in the food hall, and they attacked the handful of Palestinian cleaners in force. An incident had turned into a riot, with witnesses saying workers were physically hurled at windows, individuals beaten by several twenty-strong mobs, while more fans rampaged through the mall. The security team were outnumbered. The police were called, but took forty minutes to arrive. The police restored calm, eventually, and at 10.30 p. m. the mall was cleared and the doors locked.

The story only appeared in Israel's newspapers five days later, after the CCTV footage was leaked to the press. When *Haaretz* newspaper discovered the story, it led with the extraordinary fact that no arrests had been made. The police explained that this was because there had been no complaints. The police also released their own CCTV footage, which showed the cleaners who had come to the aid of the original family swinging mops at the hooligans. The clip had been edited to look as though the riot was the result of provocation. It was only as the story grew that arrests were made.

La Familia and Beitar continue to be pampered and indulged by all the key Israeli authorities: the police, the Israel Football Association and by Israel's political class. Everyone agrees that there are issues with the supporters of all teams in football, in every country, and these generalisations allow La Familia to hide in plain sight. The songs and banners are compared to Sakhnin, for instance, with their Palestinian flags and pictures of Handala, suggesting there is a symmetry between Beitar and rival teams. This ignores that La Familia regards itself primarily as a fighting force. In 2016, for instance, the police raided the homes of fifty-one members of La Familia, uncovering large quantities of weapons and explosives: twenty stun grenades, nineteen homemade bombs, two pounds of explosives and more. The police declared the focus was organised crime, however, and the arrestees were drug dealers. The parent organisation uniting the criminals was La Familia, yet it was unscathed by the investigations, and the FA imposed no penalties on Beitar.

This atmosphere of tolerance and forgiveness is effectively a penalty on other teams. For two weeks before every fixture with Beitar, for instance, Sakhnin's management must negotiate with the police in Jerusalem, who meet the buses of the team and supporters 20 miles outside of the city. The convoy is escorted 20 miles to the stadium and back to the quarantine zone. There is no sightseeing, no visits to cousins in Jerusalem, no prayers at Jerusalem's church or mosque. Even home games are affected. Sakhnin's stadium was built with a grant from Qatar, which enrages some Israelis who regard the Gulf state as hostile, yet the stadium meets Premier League standards. Nevertheless, the police often insist fixtures against Beitar are staged elsewhere, or behind closed doors, as they were throughout the 2017–18 season. The situation only benefits Beitar because all rivalry enhances their reputation as the one 'pure' team. They are the outsiders, despite being the team of the government.

Playing against Sakhnin is in many ways the most important fixture of Beitar's season: there is no point being virulently racist without a target. From Bethlehem, you can sometimes hear the noise of the spectators rising above Teddy Stadium. It is clear it is not just the East Stand and La Familia singing the anti-Arab chant, 'Burn their villages', nor songs praising the murderer of Yitzhak Rabin. Of course, there have been campaigns to see Beitar Jerusalem punished for creating an environment so tolerant of violence and hatred, including a petition headed by Jimmy Turk. The kind of measures that would be effective are well-known and have worked in other countries: stadium bans for abusive fans, court orders to prevent them travelling, signing in at a local police station during away fixtures. None of this has happened, in part because the finances of Beitar Jerusalem are such a mess that pushing too hard, whether through club fines or restrictions on fans, could see the whole club fold. Gaydamak lost a fortune and risked his sanity keeping the club afloat.

The owner in the spring of 2018 was Eli Tabib, who made his money in Miami property. Before taking control of Beitar in 2013, Tabib spent a year as owner of Hapoel Tel Aviv, which ended when he was charged with assaulting a child. His bid to run Beitar Jerusalem was waved through after he agreed to assume the club's debts. Two years later, he was found guilty of the assault and the FA banned him from the day-to-day running of Beitar. The ban was ignored, according to the newspapers. I was assured by an Israeli sports journalist that when the games are televised, Tabib can be seen giving commands from the stands. There have been two attempts on Tabib's life by Israeli gangsters, fuelling speculation that his business affairs may be even murkier than the average Miami real-estate mogul.

The annual Land Day on 30 March 2018 kicked off with the first in a series of weekly protests at the no-man's-land around the Gaza Strip. The protests were met with live fire. Casualties mounted up in the weeks leading up to 15 May, Nakba (or 'Catastrophe') Day, the day that commemorates the forced clearing of Palestine's towns and villages and the creation of the huge Palestinian refugee crisis. At the beginning of that week in May, US President Donald Trump announced that he would recognise Jerusalem as the capital of Israel, ignoring previous US government policy, and the Geneva Accords prohibition on recognising land annexed by force. The embassy plaque was unveiled by two evangelical preachers, bringing history full circle to the days of the Jews' Society and their prayers for biblical-style destruction.

The move by Trump was welcomed by most Israelis. Yet Eli Tabib's decision to rename his club 'Beitar Trump Jerusalem' still caught everyone by surprise. A lot of what passes for political debate in Israel is about the wind-up: throwing out explosive little 'jokes' instead of dialogue. It's the style of a radio shock-jock or, of course, a football fan. Yet even knowing that the name change is a wind-up, the change makes sense: Trump *literally* speaks the language of Beitar and Israel's right.

He is the trolls' trollster. The change was never likely to stick: Beitar's name and insignia is so loaded with Jewish symbolism that the insertion of a German family name into the middle would be unlikely to fly for long. Indeed, Tabib followed up the name change by declaring he was looking to offload the club.

The 2017–18 season was dismal for Beitar, though Tabib claimed he was leaving the club on a high. The club were always second best to the high-flying Be'er Sheva. In the Israel Cup final, Beitar lost to the perennial under-achievers, Hapoel Haifa, in what may be another example of the good luck brought by Tamar Keenan's performances in the play *We Are the Champions*. Perhaps the team should change its name to Hapoel Tamar Haifa.

A tech entrepreneur, Moshe Hogeg, bought Beitar in the summer of 2018 and declared the new season would begin with a Sakhnin game played in front of spectators. He spoke to Sakhnin's chairman, Mohammed Abu Yunis, and assured him that religion and ethnicity would no longer play a role in Beitar Jerusalem's team selection. But his predecessor Gaydamak had also said that, and quickly backtracked. Before the game began, a gang of thirty blackshirted Beitar fans attacked a fan identified as an Arab, with no police charges or arrests made.

There is no pressing reason to change Beitar Jerusalem, because the behaviour of La Familia has proven to be a positive in Israel. At the end of January 2018, Israel's sports ministry released a video of Beitar fans chanting 'Burn their villages'. In the short film, the Sports Minister, Miriam 'Miri' Regev, stands among the fans, looking toothsome and youthful while La Familia bounce and chant around her. Before entering parliament, Regev was the Deputy Spokesperson for the Israeli Army at the rank of colonel. Even with a background in PR, she saw no problem in releasing the video and no one in her ministry even thought to cut away before the familiar chant began.

Chapter Twenty-Six:

The New Palestinian FA

Yosef Yekutieli had dreamed and schemed a Palestine Football Association into existence in 1928, and though the organisation he founded was renamed the Israel Football Association with the creation of the state of Israel, the peace process allowed a new 'Palestinian Football Association' to emerge like Rip Van Winkle stretching and creaking back into life from a sixty-year sleep. The new Palestinian FA was one of the rewards of the Oslo Accords in the early 1990s, and while it was a fiction that the body was a revival of the old one, Palestinians at last had representation at FIFA. The Palestinian FA is responsible for the leagues in the West Bank and Gaza, and for running the national team. The historian John Sugden was at the 1998 FIFA congress when the vote was taken to admit Palestine and he recalls the explosion of jubilation. At the centre of the celebrations was the politician Jibril Rajoub, punching the air and hugging the team. In the late 1990s, Jibril Rajoub was number two in the Preventative Security Service, the secret police of the Palestinian Authority. It is a reflection of how important FIFA had become that one of Palestine's smartest political operators was there, on the scene, lobbying and cajoling for the votes to go his way. FIFA was the first international body to recognise Palestine as a state.

Jibril Rajoub is Mr Football in Palestine, one of the key players behind the FIFA bid and the current President of the Palestinian Football Association. Although he is all but synonymous with the FA, he was not closely involved in the sport in 1998. His journey through football over the past decade has been an exercise in political rehabilitation, which goes to show the potential of soccer in Palestinian politics.

Jibril (which is the Arabic version of 'Gabriel') was born in Hebron in 1953. He was a youth leader in the West Bank in the 1980s when my late father-in-law, Anton Sansour, was Vice President of Bethlehem University. Anton and Jibril would have to meet regularly to negotiate student issues, which ranged from strikes and protests to disputes about grades, and contacts with the Israeli Army over imprisoned students. Jibril was repeatedly arrested, and learned to speak Hebrew in prison, where he also met his long-time Chief-of-Staff, Omar Abu Hashia. During the First Intifada, Jibril was bundled from prison into exile. He settled in the city of Tunis, which had become the headquarters of the PLO following the US-brokered deal to ship the organisation out of Beirut in 1982. When the Oslo Accords brought the PLO leadership back to Palestine in 1994, Jibril Rajoub returned, too, as an advisor to PLO Chairman Yasser Arafat.

The Oslo Accords created the idea of two states, Israel and Palestine, on the footprint of historic Palestine. To all intents and purposes, the Oslo Accords dissolved the PLO as the representative of the Palestinian people, replaced by the Palestinian Authority (PA). Jibril was a crucial part of PA President Arafat's team, not simply because he was an intelligent political operator, but also because he bridged the communities and generations. Jibril had grown up under Israeli occupation, when all the senior leadership had been living on the run as refugees since 1948. President Arafat needed Jibril's experience and contacts on the ground in Palestine, and in Israel for that matter. Jibril was made head of the West Bank secret police with the rank of colonel, promoted to brigadier-general in 2003 after he was named National Security Advisor. The intelligence service he and Omar Abu Hashia created employed several thousand men from the generation that had come of age during the first 1980s Intifada. Much of their work revolved around containing Hamas, the conservative rivals to Arafat's pragmatic and secular Fatah party. Jibril's forces targeted Hamas members, who in turn complained of arbitrary arrests and even torture in custody. The hopes of peace soon soured: Prime Minister Yitzhak Rabin was dead, and Israel's settlement programme actually sped up during the Oslo years.

Jibril's security force had always maintained close links with the Israeli military. In the years following Rabin's murder, many Palestinians began to see this closeness as a form of collaboration: why worry about Israel's security when there is no peace process to protect? Jibril had already earned the enmity of Hamas supporters, but he now risked losing his own base. After Ariel Sharon swept to power in 2001, Jibril also found himself targeted by Israel. Four months after Prime Minister Sharon's victory, Jibril's family home was shelled by Israeli forces. This drew a rare rebuke from the US Ambassador to Israel, Martin

Indyk, who asked why Sharon was 'hitting' the man who could prevent violence: 'Maybe the strategy is to encourage them to act against their own people but I don't imagine there is an example in history where such a strategy has succeeded.' Sharon's hope of imposing a solution on the Palestinians began with the re-invasion of all major Palestinian cities. He first attempted this in October 2001, in the chaos following terror attacks on the US a month earlier, but this was forestalled after US intervention. He undertook a second, successful invasion over the Easter weekend in 2002, but if Sharon ever had a workable plan after the invasion, he took it to his grave.

Yasser Arafat's death and Ariel Sharon's long-term coma occurred within fourteen months of each other, both apparently as the result of hospital procedures. This has left conspiracy theorists seeking to turn the fatal illnesses of two elderly and unhealthy men into mysteries. (The men were also born eighteen months apart, Sharon in 1928 and Arafat in 1929.) The new PA President, Mahmoud Abbas, sacked Jibril Rajoub. This was a huge demotion, but it gave Jibril a chance to reshape his political destiny. This was how he moved into sport, becoming head of the Palestinian Football Association, the Palestine Olympic Committee, and even the scouts.

I had arranged to meet Jibril on Monday 12 March, 2018, at the national stadium he had built in al-Ram. This is a small town between Ramallah and Jerusalem; in effect, Jibril put the stadium as close to Jerusalem as he could get. Al-Ram is separated from the city's municipal borders by a two-lane highway, divided down its central reservation by Israel's huge wall. I was visiting alone. Leila and I no longer lived together, and when I planned my trip, it occurred to me I did not necessarily have to base myself in Bethlehem. This is why I had an Airbnb in Israel; this was a research trip, and living in Tel Aviv offered all the slick convenience of the crueller side of the Israeli–Palestinian divide. I crossed into the West Bank on Sunday night, entering Ramallah in the ominous greenish glow of a world lit by Israeli Army floodlights. The bus dropped me close to al-Manara Square and I walked through the evening city. It was a shopping night and the streets were full of families strolling together. I passed the ice-cream shop, famous for its bubble-gum flavoured scoops, and walked up the hill to my hotel. The Hotel Casablanca is the kind of place that might have seen better days, though I can't imagine when they might have been. I seemed to be the lone guest.

Ramallah is the centre of government, as well as industries such as banking and insurance, but this wealthier, international Ramallah is based in the suburban hills above the city centre. The downtown area is overcrowded, fumy and noisy. My favourite restaurants of five years ago had become down-at-heel and depressing, but I found a friendly grill place. It was even showing an Atlético Madrid game. I ate too well and slept better, waking in a mood that made the hotel seem warmer, though still empty. At 10 a.m. I was in the Café de la Paix behind city hall, waiting for a lift from Susan Shalabi, the director of the Palestinian Football Association's international department.

Susan Shalabi is a fast-moving and sporty-looking woman in her forties, though the impression of speed might be down to her diet of caffeine and vape smoke. When I asked if she had ever been a footballer, she proudly told me she had been a teenage basketball champion. Jibril recruited Susan from the foreign ministry when he took over the Palestinian FA in 2008.

In the car on the drive to the stadium, Susan tells me about the problems the teams faced in former years. Travelling between Palestinian cities had become so difficult that matches were often postponed. When they did take place, the record-keeping was so poor that Palestine was in danger of being thrown out of FIFA. The clubs had no interest in any system that allowed for promotion and relegation, and the top flight operated as a closed shop to prevent change. There were even worse problems lower down the leagues. In 2003, a team from a Hebron youth league was discovered to be an underground Hamas cell. Six players were either caught or killed carrying out terrorist bombings. It was a replay of Beitar Jerusalem in the 1930s and 1940s: young men were planning attacks without leaving any communication trail, while counting on team spirit to protect each other.

The West Bank Premier League has sponsorship and glitz, and in the Jerusalem club Hilal al-Quds it has that most modern of football phenomena, a faded club revived by an ambitious and wealthy owner. Hilal al-Quds (meaning the Crescent Moon of the Holy City) was founded in 1972 and after a long period of decline recovered its glory days under Dr Bassem Abu Aseb, the founder of a chain of private medical centres. Abu Aseb bought the best players from other teams in the league and, in 2018, Hilal became the first West Bank club to win the double: the West Bank league and the knockout cup. Hilal play at the national stadium in al-Ram, because Israel makes it impossible to stage Palestinian matches inside Jerusalem.

In the season I visited, Hilal's main rivals were Shabab al-Khalil, founded in 1943. It is the oldest club in the West Bank, and the only team that can trace its history back to the Palestine Sports Federation. The city of Hebron (*al-Khalil*, or 'The Beloved' in Arabic) dominates football in the West Bank, with six Premier League teams playing in or around the city. Hebron is a large city, and the business capital of the West Bank with an import–export trade that has given the city an outward-looking mindset: looking outward to China, mostly. Hebron's great advantage is having two decent stadiums, located in densely populated urban centres, which means the fans can actually get to matches. As a result, clubs in Hebron have the most devoted and best-informed supporters in the West Bank.

The resurgent team in the 2019 season is Markaz Balata or Balata Youth Club from the refugee camp in Nablus. While Nablus is the largest city in the West Bank, it has never taken to football, a sport that was carried to the city by refugees from Jaffa. The camp's club was founded in 1954, but its pedigree is arguably older even than Shabab al-Khalil's, extending back to the 1920s and the days when Jaffa's Islamic Sports Club was playing in the Basa stadium.

Susan's home city of Tulkarem has two teams, with Markaz Tulkarem representing the refugee-camp team, and Thaqafi Tulkarem the town. The rivalry has led to street fights, the West Bank's only example of fan violence. Finally, in the 2018 season, the league had two teams from Bethlehem. Al-Khader, or 'The Green' (the name of a mythic chivalric knight who is identified with St George), was founded in 1967, after the end of Jordanian rule and before Israel's colonisation of the West Bank. It plays in one of the better stadiums, built with Portuguese aid money in 2007 at the edge of Bethlehem. The wall and military check-points are just metres from the terraces.

Al-Khader emerged in the decade from 1967, now remembered as a second golden age of football, when a spirit of

revolution and national pride gripped Palestine. Despite its pedigree and stadium, al-Khader feels distant from the life of
Bethlehem, and has failed to find a large fanbase. The stadium
is fuller during the annual cabbage festival than it is during football matches. Al-Khader finished bottom of the league in 2018
and, alongside one of the Hebron teams, lost its place in the
Premiership. The promoted teams, al-Bireh and al-Mukaber,
from Ramallah and Jerusalem, both play in the national stadium at al-Ram.

Wadi al-Nes is the miracle of the West Bank Premier League.
Where most teams express a 1970s optimism, Wadi al-Nes was
created in the 1980s in a vulnerable spot surrounded by Jewish
settlements. The team was founded by a local named Youssef
Abu Hammad, and built around his oldest sons to give them a
reason to stay in the town. The current team features Hammad's
younger sons by his second wife, and includes some of the very
best players in the country. Khader Yousef Abu Hammad was a
forward for the national team for many years, while his brother,
the tall Tawfiq Ali Abu Hammad, has played as the national
goalkeeper.

The Gaza Premier League is very much poorer than the
West Bank, though many fans see Gaza as the real home of
Palestinian football. The sport was carried south by the
refugees from Jaffa after 1948. All of Gaza's stadiums are inside
densely populated areas, and the local clubs have strong
support. The oldest is Shabab Rafah, the club of the Egyptian
border town, which was founded in 1953. Gaza has been under
strict lockdown since 2007, when Hamas ousted Fatah in a
short civil war. Since then, Gaza City has seen its stadium
twice destroyed by Israeli aerial bombardments, in 2006 and

2012, the second time killing four teenage players in a bombardment that brought over a hundred deaths. The destruction of the stadium saw a petition by fifty-two footballers including Eden Hazard, Papiss Cissé and Demba Ba demanding sanctions against Israel. The lockdown makes life difficult for Gazan players signed to teams outside of Palestine, though the proximity to Egypt means that many of Gaza's most talented footballers have been signed by Egyptian clubs. Gaza's isolation causes problems when players have to join the international squad, but inside Gaza the league continues. Despite Hamas control, the leagues are administered by Rajoub's Palestinian FA. The Palestine Cup has been resurrected: the winners of the West Bank and Gaza leagues meet over two legs in Gaza City and at the al-Ram stadium to win the revived trophy.

The sportswriter Bassil Mikdadi, the authority on modern-day Palestinian football, notes that all the national side's captains have come from the strip: defender Saeb Jendeya, who was captain for twelve years; Ramzi Saleh, a goalkeeper who has played for both Cairo's Al Ahly and Port Said's Al Masry club; and the powerful centre back Abdelatif Bahdari, who plays for Cairo's El Gaish.

It is easy to catch football on TV, or even on phones and laptops as matches are broadcast online, previously on Facebook and now on the Livestream platform. Football is once again part of the fabric of national life. Membership of FIFA also helps the Palestinian FA appeal Israeli restrictions. Under FIFA rules, Israel has a responsibility to allow Palestinian players to make training sessions and travel to tournaments. The Palestinian FA appeals decisions, liaises with the Israeli military and keeps track of infringements, using FIFA as leverage. Captain Saeb Jendeya was once prevented from leaving Gaza to join the national team because he was asked the name of the hotel where the Palestine team were booked to stay, and he could not say. An Olympic footballer, Mahmoud Sarsak, was arrested in 2012 and held for three years without charge, even going on hunger strike for three months. Sarsak's campaign brought support from the International Federation of Professional Footballers (FIFPro), and UEFA. Sarsak eventually won his release, and though he no longer plays football he campaigns for the rights of footballers. The rising star of the national team, the 23-year-old striker Mahmoud Wadi, was trapped in the strip in 2017. When the Rafah crossing into the Sinai opened briefly at the tail end of August 2017, Wadi was one of the few to get out. He had a stellar season at his club Al-Ahli in Jordan before signing to Egypt's Al Masry in 2018.

Susan welcomed me to the Palestinian FA headquarters and al-Ram stadium with a tour. The stands are filled with blue and yellow seats. The artificial turf had been peeled back to reveal large concrete paving slabs. The season was paused for the international break, and a team of contractors were working on a solution to a persistent sewage problem. Israel has no sewage plant in Jerusalem, so the city's shit drains into the Kidron Stream where it is carried to the tourist beaches and spas of the Dead Sea. In the winter rains, however, the sewers that lead to the Kidron Stream cannot handle the sudden increase in water. Israel has found a workaround by using larger-diameter sewage pipes while restricting the size of Palestine's pipes. This ensures the back-up flows into the West Bank, away from the Israeli homes in the city.

The al-Ram stadium is not only awash with shit, it has often been targeted directly by the Israeli military. In February 2014, two teenage players were ambushed by Israeli soldiers as they left a training session and shot multiple times in the legs and feet, ending the careers of both. Israeli soldiers fire gas grenades into stadiums during games: matches have been abandoned and players hospitalised at al-Ram, in Hebron and at al-Khader, the most recent in January 2019. The pattern of gas attacks suggests a deliberate strategy, but even if it is not military policy, the incidents highlight the power of young Israeli soldiers on checkpoint duty where assaults, sexual abuses and thefts are a daily occurrence.

The real achievement of the Jibril Rajoub era is perhaps the resurgence of international football. Up to 2015, only three international matches had been staged inside Palestine. The chant 'Football is more noble than war' was first heard in the newly built al-Ram stadium. Membership of FIFA and playing regular football in the West Asian Football Federation has rapidly improved Palestinian football, as the team's rise through the world rankings shows. When I visited, Palestine had just overhauled Israel in the international rankings.

In the early years of FIFA it was so difficult for players to get to training sessions that the Palestinian FA recruited players from the diaspora with foreign passports, who could train abroad and could guarantee to make matches. These players were often unknown in Palestine, including Chilean professionals and American college amateurs. This has changed. International tournaments attract TV audiences as big as those for Barça matches, and footballers are national figures. Not just the male players, either. When the national women's captain Honey

Thaljieh ended her career, she won an internship in the Geneva headquarters. She now has a high-flying career as FIFA's communications director.

Jibril has been good news for Palestinian football, but no one is in any doubt that football is a political vehicle for an ambitious man. President Abbas is in his eighties and on the weekend I visited Ramallah, the city was filled with the latest rumours about his health. He was said to have undergone surgery in America, or maybe Paris. The details were vague, but the rumours swirled. Abbas has no obvious successor, but Jibril Rajoub is often mentioned as a leading candidate. When Susan introduced me to Omar Abu Hashia and members of his team, I asked about Abbas's successor and no one was shy in declaring that Jibril would make a great president. The problem may be that he has waited too long. In the ten years he has been at the Palestinian FA, Palestinian politics under Mahmoud Abbas have sunk into such a stasis, Jibril may have missed his moment.

There is worse news, however. When I arrived in al-Ram, I was only beginning to become aware that Palestinian football was on the verge of crisis – and one entirely of Jibril's own making. He had made a rare misstep, and it may yet end his political ambitions.

Chapter Twenty-Seven:

Jibril

Jibril Rajoub's office appears to be two large rooms, imperfectly knocked together to leave half as a living room and the other a work space, where the large desk is flanked by a Palestinian flag and the flag of the Palestinian Football Association. The room is modest, with just a few touches of low-end glitz, such as the lampshades and a shiny plastic coffee pot. The walls are decorated with photographs, mostly photographs of Jibril Rajoub. He stands to greet me cordially but coolly, lifting a hand to point to his sofa. Palestinians are the warmest of hosts, but Rajoub is not at all warm. He is a square-shouldered man, neatly balding, slow-speaking. He introduces himself by his military rank, General Jibril Rajoub. As an ice-breaker, I ask if he grew up playing football and he tells me, of course, and points to a framed picture on the wall.

'I'm playing there.'

The picture is a press stunt: Rajoub is dressed in a football strip, looking out of place and out of breath as he attempts to control a ball. He has the kind of wit I associate with tough guys:

he dares you to contradict. When I laugh, he simply shrugs. It is notable that his team is happy around him, though. Susan jokes easily, while he stands slightly apart. His demeanour is so relaxed, it hovers just above sleepiness.

Jibril Rajoub has been head of football for a decade. He notes that before his tenure, no season had actually ended. It is a colourful rather than accurate precis, but he doesn't expect to be taken 100 per cent literally. The rumours of President Abbas's operation prompt me to ask Rajoub if he would ever stand for president. He leaves such a long pause before answering that I can hear the whirr of the air-conditioning.

'No, I will stay at the Football Association *for ever*,' he says, at last, in a tone so low and so laconic you feel there must be a hint of a smile.

The great issue, on that day in March 2018, was not Mahmoud Abbas's health: it was the coach of the national squad. Three months earlier, Jibril Rajoub had sacked the long-term coach Abdel Nasser Barakat and replaced him with a Bolivian named Julio César Baldivieso. It was an immensely unpopular move. Palestinian sports fans were so angry there was a growing campaign on social media with the hashtag *#GoAwayJulio*. Thanks to Barakat, Palestine was on the verge of qualifying to reach the tournament of the AFC Asian Cup. In the process, Barakat's team had overhauled Israel in FIFA's international rankings. Barakat was the most successful coach in Palestine's history, but he represented much more: a humble man who had made real sacrifices to follow his passion for football. Barakat had worked in construction, taking two jobs and passing up the chance of other careers because they would take him away from football. At heart, Jibril's decision to remove Barakat just seemed unfair. Why not stick with Barakat through to the Asian Cup finals in Qatar in January 2019, when he had done the hard work of getting the team to the edge of the qualifiers?

The new coach Baldivieso had asked for time to work with the team, ahead of three friendlies and the final Asian Cup qualifying match. Jibril had agreed, and brought forward the national break by thirty days so the players could meet the coach at a special training camp. This was why the contractors were tearing up the artificial turf of the al-Ram stadium: there was suddenly time to do essential work that had been waiting until the end of the season. The contractors were alone in being happy. The West Bank Premier League was winning fans and building confidence after years in the doldrums and the decision to shut it down for a month damaged the sense of goodwill and killed the competition's momentum. Worse, it did not even make sense. So many members of the national squad now played football outside of Palestine, in Sweden, Chile, Egypt and the States, they were not going to be at Baldivieso's training camp anyway. The camp was not even in Palestine, but Saudi Arabia. This was because Baldivieso's appointment was a gift of Saudi's most powerful football administrator, Turki Al-Sheikh, the Chairman of its General Sports Authority, and President of the Islamic Solidarity Sports Federation.

When I spoke to Omar Abu Hashia about the appointment of Baldivieso, he insisted there was no deal with Saudi Arabia, even though the details of Al-Sheikh's involvement were already widely known. Susan argued that Barakat's new job within the national set-up was a promotion: he had been made the director of football. This was one way of glossing a decision that neither Barakat nor the players had wanted. Yet there was no reason to doubt the wisdom of hiring Baldivieso. The Bolivian had far more experience, both national and international, even if the most eye-catching item on his CV was his 2009 decision to play a twelve-year-old in a professional football match. The twelve-year-old player was his own son.

A lot of the resentment came because of the way the appointment was made. The Kingdom of Saudi Arabia has a habit of meddling in the affairs of other nations, which is a source of scorn and resentment in Palestine. Relations had worsened since the Saudi team had refused to play its qualifier with Palestine at the stadium in al-Ram, forcing a relocation to Amman. In Palestine, this was regarded either as a slur or as gamesmanship; and either way it was not yet forgiven. In addition, there was a wider sense of alarm over the ascension of Saudi's new ruler, Crown Prince Mohammed bin Salman. The 33-year-old is close to President Donald Trump's senior advisor and son-in-law Jared Kushner, which had raised the possibility that the Saudis would apply political pressure on Palestine, on behalf of either America or Israel. In this fraught climate, it was difficult to read Al-Sheikh's gift: was it meddling? Or was it an olive branch? After all, there was reason to hope that Baldivieso could strengthen the Palestinian side. And the offer had come with a pot of cash. Al-Sheikh was not only paying Baldivieso's wages, he was topping up the gesture with a gift of a million dollars.

When I spoke to Jibril Rajoub about the appointment, he only stated that he had every confidence in Baldivieso. But I doubted it. There were already rumours that Jibril would not give Baldivieso much time to prove his worth. Maybe just a couple of matches.

This proved true. Baldivieso was preparing for the three friendlies, against Bahrain, Kuwait and Iraq, interrupted by the final qualifying match for the Asian Cup against Oman, one of the weaker teams in the tournament. Palestine registered a nil–nil draw against Bahrain on 22 March 2018. The game was screened on YouTube with a single fixed camera at a distance that made the ball invisible on my screen. As I watched, I was never sure if the vague and disjointed performance I was seeing was a kind of optical illusion. Could Palestine really be as bad as all that? In the early days of the national team, Palestine's games could be relentlessly dour. The team has gained finesse over twenty years, yet the defensive resilience had remained, led by a series of extraordinary goalkeepers. Bassil Mikdadi claims the goalkeeper is the archetypal Palestinian footballer: the last-ditch defender. The goalkeeper has often been the captain, the best player, and the first player to be bought by a foreign team. This is the spirit that has given Palestine's national team the nickname, *Fida'i*, Arabic for 'commandoes', but also the term for a daring, self-sacrificing fighter. Mikdadi said, 'even when Palestine is overmatched, they will fight for every inch of the pitch'. This just wasn't happening in the Bahrain match.

Word came that Jibril Rajoub had warned Baldivieso he had better win the qualifier against Oman on 27 March. Perhaps Baldivieso was rattled, because Palestine lost two goals to nil. Sure enough, Baldivieso was sacked. He had overseen just two games. Jibril, however, chose not to simply reinstate Barakat. Perhaps his pride forbade it. Instead, he promoted Barakat's ex-assistant, an Algerian named Noureddine Ould Ali.

*

Twenty years ago, in 1998, FIFA's recognition of Palestine was regarded as a considerable diplomatic achievement. It was fiercely opposed by Israel. The historian John Sugden was in the room when the news was announced because he was researching a book on the outgoing President João Havelange, who had run FIFA since 1974. Havelange beat the incumbent, the Englishman Stanley Rous, after Rous had alienated members from the developing world by his support of apartheid-era South Africa. This was a time when protesters were regularly told it was important to resist boycotts and 'keep politics out of sport'. In Sugden's view, Havelange's progressive attitude towards racism and apartheid was born out of his political calculations rather than ideals. He needed votes. Throughout his tenure, he continued to bring in nations from the developing world, and secured their loyalty with deals that brought money into their football associations. Looking back on his quarter century in charge of FIFA, Havelange stated that his greatest achievement was taking an organisation with $25 in the kitty, and leaving it with $25 million.

On Sugden's account, Jibril picked an opportune moment to press Palestine's candidacy. Havelange was standing down, and needed votes to swing behind his chosen successor, Sepp Blatter. In 1998, Jibril may well have been lobbying on behalf of Blatter at the same time as campaigning for Palestine's membership. Sugden argues that Blatter super-charged Havelange's model, effectively turning FIFA into a criminal organisation. Blatter's reign saw FIFA officials charged with racketeering offences in the States. The indictments ultimately led Blatter to step down. In December 2015 he was banned from FIFA for eight years, reduced to six years on appeal.

FIFA parades under a banner of international friendship between nations, a post-colonial version of the old Victorian ideal that every sportsman is a friendship ambassador. This is an idea that Palestinians can buy into. They want to compete, as proclaimed in the terrace chant, because 'Football is more noble than war.' But membership of FIFA is also about agreeing to set rules, under international law. Susan is the Palestinian FA's international director. She is responsible for ensuring Palestinian clubs follow the law on international signings, for instance, whether from Chile and other Latin American countries, or from Israel. In 2014, the Israeli FA handed a ninety-nine-year ban to Attaf Abu Bilal, a Bedouin Arab, who was discovered to be playing for teams in both Israel and Palestine without clearing the paperwork (the ban has since been lifted). Both Palestine and Israel must comply with FIFA's rulebook, which has allowed Palestine to open a new political front, because so much of Israel's behaviour is illegal under international laws adopted by FIFA.

Jibril threw his energies into campaigning against clubs based in Jewish settlements, such as Ironi Ariel, the team of the vast Ariel settlement. FIFA forbids member states from giving room to teams based outside their national borders. The UN has ruled the Jewish settlements breach the Geneva Convention. FIFA's bye-laws insist that member states abide by UN rulings, and goes even further by insisting members should actively promote international law.

Jibril has consistently raised the stakes against Israel. When FIFA under Sepp Blatter refused to rule on the Ariel issue, Jibril sought a vote of the entire FIFA membership. The vote could have seen the Israeli FA suspended from FIFA. The prospect of one state forcing out another so alarmed Blatter, he adopted delaying tactics to prevent the issue being debated. After Blatter was ousted and replaced by Gianni Infantino, this ruse was regarded as too subtle. Infantino personally declared that FIFA was never going to rule on Israel's settlements. Israel appeared to have won an indefinite stay of execution, by presidential fiat. Jibril again refused to admit defeat by taking the issue to the Court of Arbitration in Sport in Lausanne. When I met Jibril, he and his team had returned from the CAS hearing just two days earlier. Susan was full of hope. FIFA's lawyer had claimed the offending clubs were not an issue because the teams were too minor and the quality of football too low. The British jurist Philippe Sands had questioned their sense of scale; wondering at what point an infraction becomes visible. The panel drew the parallel with Russia, where teams from the annexed territory in the Ukraine had tried to play in the Russian leagues, before Russia thought better of it. Nevertheless, the CAS ruled that President Infantino was acting within his rights: he could set the agenda of his own organisation.

Had Jibril pursued the issue too far? There was a suspicion that he was playing to his own base inside Palestine. Mikdadi was unimpressed: 'The football association spent over a year trying to achieve the very unlikely – getting Israel kicked out of FIFA. OK, there's an argument to be made for kicking out Israel. But the FA President has to focus on initiatives that are realistic, and improve the footballing ecosystem in Palestine.' Mikdadi listed some of the problems, from substandard training facilities to the treatment of professionals, with clubs often failing to pay their players on time.

In the summer of 2018, Israel were to play Argentina in a friendly in the 30,000-seater Sami Ofer stadium in Haifa. As the date rolled around, President Trump made his decision to recognise Jerusalem as Israel's capital. Israel's sports minister Miri Regev responded by demanding that Israel's FA move the game to the Teddy Stadium, explicitly declaring that the match should be hosted in the capital. The protests at the Gaza fence were becoming bloodier by the week, and there was momentum behind calls for Argentina to boycott the game entirely. Jibril Rajoub declared that if Argentina played in Jerusalem, Palestinians should burn the captain Lionel Messi's shirt in the streets outside. In the event, moving the game from Haifa was a step too far for the Argentine FA, who chose to cancel the game outright. If Miri Regev's intervention had led to the match being pulled, it was Jibril's remarks that received all the attention. Jibril's words were interpreted as a threat against a player and, in September 2018, FIFA handed Jibril a twelve-month ban for inciting hatred and violence. It was a warning that Jibril's attempts to drag FIFA into politics were not going to be tolerated under Infantino.

Back in March of that year, I asked if I could have my picture taken with Jibril Rajoub. We stood between the two flags by his desk. Susan took the picture. Looking at it, I am surprised that Jibril is shorter than me: he seems larger in the flesh. The banner of the football association incorporates a black and white football, its design reflecting the pattern of the Palestinian keffiyeh – so familiar as the headdress worn by Yasser Arafat – which also features in the design. As Susan later tells me, the idea that sport and politics do not mix is ridiculous. 'It's like a child repeating, I am not afraid, I am not afraid, I am not afraid. If you keep repeating something, it's not because you believe it, but because you want to convince yourself it is true.' FIFA resists any attempt to politicise football, while insisting that football is a medium for spreading international understanding and peace. It is as though peace and understanding are not political goals: they are the *best* political goals.

Chapter Twenty-Eight:

The Grass Ceiling

In 2010, I watched the South African World Cup in Bethlehem at a café close to Rachel's Tomb, where the games were projected onto the Israeli wall that surrounds the city. What began as a dark joke became a fun way to enjoy the football. We sat on the terrace, eating shwarma sandwiches and drinking cold bottles of Taybeh beer, while the sound of *vuvuzelas* buzzed in the speakers above our head. In the midst of World Cup fever, when even a *vuvuzela* can seem musical, it is possible to buy in to the dream of sport and international fellowship. It was a particularly happy time because Max, my brother-in-law, was getting married. The guests had come from around the world. As we gathered to watch Ronaldo and Portugal, an American cousin asked a Russian uncle, 'Who's the team in white?'

'Is *Demokraticheskaya Respublika Korea.*'

'The Democratic team? So, that's South Korea?'

'*Nyet.* Is North.'

(The score was 7–0 to Portugal.)

*

South Africa is the great success story, the hope that goodwill can overcome racism, violence and oppression. But for all the World Cup-inspired optimism the situation in Bethlehem was dire. There is nothing as relentlessly shitty as a military occupation. The whole business of the army is to remind you that resistance is futile, and remind you of it over and over again. The wall had utterly destroyed a pretty corner of Bethlehem. It snaked down the main road and wrapped around the tiny chapel, Rachel's Tomb, like a hand reaching through a letterbox to steal a neighbour's purse. The district ended up divided in two, meaning that people living on opposite sides of the street faced a mile-long trek to visit each other's homes. All that was visible of the chapel I remembered from visits to Bethlehem in the 1990s was the dome of its roof, seen from the top of surrounding buildings, behind the 18-foot graffiti-covered wall. There are watchtowers, and yards of sandbags and that peculiar camouflage netting that swathes military installations. I could see the whipping antennas of military jeeps and catch glimpses of young soldiers carrying guns.

Somebody might say, sure, but Rachel's Tomb had to be prised out of Bethlehem to ensure the safety of Jewish pilgrims. But how has such an argument become normalised? The craziest, the most violent solution, benefiting one community at the expense of every other, is passed off as reasonable? What do we imagine racism and apartheid are, if this is not race-based apartheid? The chapel is a local landmark, deep within Bethlehem, and it only has history and meaning because of its location. The chapel was built in the later Roman Empire, in the Christian era, and dedicated to a Jewish matriarch. The chapel adjoins what is now a Muslim cemetery. By long established custom, the chapel has become a place of prayer by local mothers, of all faiths, who were looking for help with conception, pregnancy and childbirth, and any other comfort that a matriarchal saint might supply. Now this is all gone. The last time I visited, in 2010, I arrived in the midst of an all-male Jewish ultra-Orthodox prayer group. The chapel was out of bounds to women.

In those days, football had less to do with hope, for me, than escape. I loved a lot about living in Bethlehem, but life was unbelievably tense. The Oslo Accords had been intended to kick-start a transition towards two states. The death of the Oslo process has led to the opposite, a single state in which 8.8 million Israeli citizens enjoy rights and protections that are denied to another 4.5 million non-citizen captives. The citizens and non-citizens live right alongside each other, entirely separate yet intimately intertwined, often no more than the width of a wall apart. It is a desperate political situation. If there is no chance of ever seeing two states, Israel and Palestine, sharing this space, what is the future like?

It may seem odd, but football may provide a kind of answer. Among the 8.8 million citizens of Israel, more than two million are non-Jews, and the vast majority of these identify as Palestinians. The Palestinian community forms a large minority, one in five of the population, and an even larger slice of Israel's footballing world. More than 40 per cent of Israel's football clubs are owned and run by Palestinian Israelis, making it the national sport so far as Israel's Palestinian citizens are concerned. Maybe its popularity is down to cost: football is so cheap. All you need is a soccer ball and something to represent the goalposts. Israel's Palestinian towns do not enjoy the same facilities as Jewish cities – the sports halls, the tracks, the swimming pools – so the low entry costs for football are a big attraction. The politician Ahmad Tibi, who represents Tayibe in the Israeli parliament, has argued that the popularity of soccer is a symptom of poverty. But this ignores the fact that sport has always carried a prestige among Palestinians. As far back as 1908, the first teams were drawn from the Palestinian elite, and soccer has retained its standing both as a sport and as a way of shaping a political identity.

I talked to Amir Ben Porat, over a coffee in a north Tel Aviv mall, about his year following Tayibe in the 1996–7 season. He told me about the admiration shown towards footballers by the Tayibe community, adding that it was reciprocal: 'the players work hard to earn trust as role models'. The reverence for football crosses all the social divides of religion and class among Palestinians. Many notable political leaders have also been accomplished football players, from Izzat Tannous to Ismail Haniyeh, who is the current leader of Hamas in Gaza, and is said to have once been a formidable midfielder for the Islamic University of Gaza. As I write this, Ahmed Tibi and Mazen Ghnaim, the founder of Sakhnin's team, are in the process of creating an alliance to contest the upcoming Israeli elections. Football gave Ghnaim his start in politics, and many see him as the most powerful and pragmatic of Palestinian politicians in Israel, having cannily eschewed parliament to focus instead on creating a nationwide alliance of local mayors.

Football enjoys nothing like this level of respectability among Israel's Jews. Ouriel Daskal tells me the way Jewish Israelis speak of football players mirrors the way they talk about Arabs. Footballers are seen as stupid, as childish, and easily tempted into a fast life of loose morals. This contrasts with basketball players, who are regarded as smart. Why, I wonder? Ouriel shrugs. 'Basketball is the game of the Ashkenazi community, and football is the sport of Arabs and Mizrahim.' I was taken aback to discover that Israelis see football as the sport of the Middle East. After all, the game is a European invention. Israeli clubs play in UEFA tournaments alongside the great European club sides. Yet among Ashkenazi Jews with a Russian heritage, football is often simply one game among others. For the Mizrahim, in contrast, it is the only sport that matters. The 2018 season ended with Hapoel Be'er Sheva and Beitar Jerusalem, the two big teams of the Second Israel, taking the top two spots in the Premier League.

Most Palestinian Israelis play their football in the glamour-free lower divisions of the FA leagues with only Sakhnin, Lydda (Lod) and Nazareth competing as professional teams. Although these clubs are regarded as Arab teams, their squads are mixed. All contain Christian, Muslim and Jewish players as well as backroom staff. The same is true of Jewish sides: almost all include Palestinian Israeli players in their squads – all except Beitar, of course. This is why football is often cited as the one corner in Israel where you can find something like meritocracy and equality. Football is a level playing field, as both Daskal and Ben Porat tell me. Ouriel says that Jewish Israelis simply never meet Palestinians – unless they play football. It is the one industry where Jewish professionals grow up with Palestinian friends and colleagues, where they visit Palestinian homes socially, and attend parties and celebrations.

The only other industry that reflects the actual make-up of modern-day Israel is its pharmacies: 35 per cent of high-street pharmacists are Palestinian. The counters at big chains, like Super Pharm, are often run by young Palestinians. In part, this is because the chains pay wages towards the lower end of the scale, but also because they provide a place where recent graduates can get through their initial probation year. The idea of a country where only footballers and pharmacists mix as equals sounds like a scenario dreamed up by Mark E. Smith, late singer of the Fall, who had a considerable interest in both. But there is a straightforward reason for the number of Palestinian pharmacists. The Oslo Accords were a three-way deal that included Jordan. As part of the trust-building process, a deal was struck to allow Israelis to continue their higher education in Jordan. Israel's Palestinian minority had always found it difficult to win places at Israel's universities. When they started applying to Jordanian universities, the pharmacy degrees proved the most popular draw.

When I booked my Airbnb apartment, I marked the date of the Maccabi Tel Aviv home game against Maccabi Petah Tikvah in my notebook, with three hand-drawn asterisks beside it. The game isn't the most glamorous fixture, not even of the Israeli Premier League calendar. Now that it was the tail end of the season and there was nothing left to play for, I didn't expect excitement. Yet in my mind, at least, the match had assumed historical importance. It is the oldest surviving competitive fixture in Israel, or in Palestine for that matter, dating back to the first days of the Palm Court. A further reason to see the match: Rami Mansour was going. Rami, his father and Koko Kalalian are die-hard Maccabi Tel Aviv fans. When I confessed

I was surprised, Rami laughed: 'Yes. Most people like the Reds.' Meaning most Palestinians support Hapoel Tel Aviv. Rami had the most guileless reasons for supporting Maccabi Tel Aviv: the team played better football.

Eating lunch with Ouriel Daskal in the Minzar Bar, he mentioned he could get me a ticket: it wasn't a problem. He called a friend in the Maccabi Tel Aviv press office and that was that. He did wonder why I had chosen this match. He knew all about my book but didn't see why that was a good enough reason to sit through an actual match. He warned me it would be terrible.

The press officer said my ticket would be waiting at the hospitality office on the north side of Netanya stadium. Netanya? This was supposed to be a home match. I knew the Bloomfield Stadium was being rebuilt, but had somehow forgotten this meant the match had been moved. I faced a journey to the beach city 20 miles north of Tel Aviv. Kick-off was not until 9 p.m., which was far too late. This was the same day as my meeting with Jibril Rajoub, however, so perhaps the late kick-off was not such bad news. The journey from Ramallah, across Israel to the coast was hell. The worst part of the journey was not even the army checkpoint between the West Bank and Israel, but getting through rush hour in Jerusalem. It took almost ninety minutes to move out of Jerusalem central bus station, 100 yards to the first junction. It was another three hours by road to reach Netanya. We arrived at Netanya's bus station with just fifteen minutes to spare, but I was still nowhere near the out-of-town stadium, built as part of a shopping mall development.

A guy working the phone accessory stall suggested I take a service taxi from the rank across the road. A team of minibuses run on a loop around the city, picking up and dropping off passengers at street corners. The drivers chat to each other in Russian with their phones on speaker, swapping passengers out of their own mysterious sense of efficiency. Outside of Moscow, Netanya is the most Russian city I have ever visited (though when I looked at the figures, I discovered that the Ariel settlement in the West Bank is even more Russian). After being swapped between taxis at the southern tip of the beach highway, I reached a parking lot across from the stadium. It had taken more than five hours to cover less than sixty miles and I had missed kick-off. The noise of the crowd rang around the high pale walls. My ticket was waiting at the north end of the stadium, and I was at its south-west corner. I set off running. The stadium seemed to be rocking: it felt like a much bigger night than I'd expected, but I couldn't work out which of the two stands held the Tel Aviv supporters. I found a VIP entrance, where a Russian bouncer allowed me to speak to a woman with a checklist. A list that did not contain my name. I told her that I was a writer. I even mimed holding a pen, hoping that she did not think I was asking for the dinner cheque.

'A journalist? No,' she told me. 'This door is only for VIPs.'

The same bouncer suggested I needed Door N. I continued running. The stands were filled with fierce drumming. I had almost done a complete circuit when I reached Door N, only to be told the press entrance was back the way I had come. I had completed a full circuit when there was a huge roar, the unmistakable sound of a goal celebration. I ran holding my phone ahead of me to try to get a live match report, but could not work out what I was missing. I found a man at the door to the press box dispensing wristbands to journalists, but I didn't have my ticket and he didn't have a list. I needed to find a box office.

I kept running.

The first box office was closed. The second was open but had no list of journalists. I wished I had simply bought a ticket, as I should have done in the first place. But the man behind the glass told me not to worry, pointing across a paved terrace to a black and silver kiosk.

'Try the press office.'

A press office!

The kiosk was just twenty yards away. Even better, it had my ticket, though Ouriel's contact had spelled my name wrong: Nick Blakman. The envelope also contained two tickets for Nigel Hasselbaink, the Dutch footballer who was playing for the Israeli side Kiryat Shmona that season. I decided to hand Hasseilbank's tickets back to the press officer, in case he turned up late.

I started running again.

My ticket was coloured silver, which was one rank higher than a normal ticket. This gave me access to an area sealed off from the general public by a low velvet rope, and allowed me to buy burgers and mass-produced simit rings from a counter without a queue. I began to wonder if Israeli football was less a level playing field than a place where the old hierarchies of Jew and Arab had been replaced by new distinctions of celebrity and privilege. I had missed a meal, so I gratefully bought a simit ring and a Coke.

Inside the stadium, the real misery began. At the time Maccabi Tel Aviv was coached by Jordi Cruyff, the son of Johann Cruyff, the creative genius behind possession-based football. Jordi Cruyff arrived at Maccabi Tel Aviv in 2012 as the director of football and the team immediately enjoyed three years of success with European managers. Success had faltered over the last few seasons. Cruyff's decision to appoint himself as coach in June 2017 had not improved the squad. The game I saw was dreadful. It was disjointed, cautious and clumsy: the worst of every world. Because I had missed the build-up, I had not seen the team sheet. I missed more of the match as I tried to read the names of the starting line-up on my phone. As I scrolled down through the match report I discovered Maccabi Tel Aviv had an English player named Nick Blackman: he had scored for Maccabi Tel Aviv in the fifth minute but the goal had been disallowed for offside.

Nick Blackman? It occurred to me, it may not have been my name misspelled on the tickets waiting at the box office.

The two best-known players on the team sheets were Yossi Benayoun, Tel Aviv's 37-year-old midfielder, and Tal Ben Haim, Petah Tikvah's 35-year-old defender. The pair had spent a decade in the English premiership. In this match, Ben Haim was an unused substitute; Benayoun was on the pitch but he looked slow. I was surprised both were still in the game, at an age when other athletes had retired. I sent a couple of SMS messages to Rami, wanting his opinion, as well as angling for a lift back to Tel Aviv. Although Maccabi Tel Aviv scored twice in the first half, I could not imagine Rami, David and Koko were enjoying the game. Tel Aviv were poor, but lucky that Petah Tikvah were even more awful, despite the cheering and drumming of their enthusiastic fans. I had heard Petah Tikvah had signed the Haifa-born forward Fadi Zidan, winner of the West Bank league in 2015 with Hebron's Ahli al-Khalil. His name wasn't on the team sheet. They did have one other Palestinian player in their twenty-seven-man squad, and he was on the bench: Muhammad Sarsour, another unused substitute. I could not see a Palestinian name in Maccabi Tel Aviv's line-up, but it took me a little more checking before I confirmed that the club did not have a single Palestinian in the entire squad. The number of Palestinians at the club had declined year-on-year under the Canadian owner Mitchell Goldhar, who bought Maccabi Tel Aviv in 2009. There was a policy of actively seeking Jewish players from other countries, such as Nick Blackman, Brazil's Daniel Tenenbaum and the American Aaron Schoenfeld. And there was also a policy of not even hiring Palestinians, or so it was fair to deduce.

In a national league where the quality is so low, it seems bizarre that neither team could find more athletic, faster players from the community who make up 40 per cent of the leagues. Palestinians are keeping the grassroots going, and doing it for love, with no prospect of payment. They are building thriving clubs, speaking Hebrew, and supporting the big Israeli teams. Yet the level playing field clearly only goes so far. A grass ceiling?

I left before the end. The stadium was quieter now, but still full of sighs and oohs that stayed with me until I climbed aboard a taxi. In a hundred years, would this be the best future under Jewish Israeli rule: a country that was proud of its history, but was equally content to be second-rate, if that was the price for excluding a huge section of the population?

Sources and Notes

This is an informal history in what is still the new field of football studies, and I have adopted an informal approach to the notes, though I hope rigorous enough to answer questions on sources and research. I received enormous help and personal kindness from Issam Khalidi and Amir Ben Porat, the fathers of this field. I also received warm help from the football-writing community. I am especially grateful to Bassil Mikdadi of Football Palestine and Uri Levy of BabaGol. I owe a great debt to Jonathan Wilson for connecting me to the sports writer Ouriel Daskal, who in turn introduced me to so many other contacts. I am also grateful to John Sugden, Professor of Sociology of Sport at Brighton University.

I also owe thanks to the families of the significant figures in the football history of Israel and Palestine, especially to Edna Kohen, daughter of Yosef Yekutieli, and to Amon and Daniel Yekutieli, his grandsons, who put me in touch with their Aunt Edna.

Thanks also to Hazem Nusseibeh, the nephew of Ibrahim Nusseibeh. I am also grateful to Bashar Nusseibeh, Ibrahim's great-nephew.

I received nothing but kindness and enormous assistance from everyone at the Jaffa Orthodox football team, and especially David Mansour, his son Rami Mansour and, of course, Koko Kalalian.

I want to thank Dolly Namour and the staff of St George's School, Jerusalem.

I had enormous help from Susan Shalabi, director of the Palestinian FA's international department.

I am not sure if the press officer of Maccabi Tel Aviv should get thanks or apologies after I accidentally took Nick Blackman's tickets.

I owe a huge debt to my editor Andreas Campomar, a great sports writer in his own right; to my agent Matthew Hamilton, for guiding this project; and to Alessandra Bastalgi for her sympathetic suggestions. I am very grateful to my copy-editor Howard Watson; to my legal reader Meryl Evans (who picked up mistakes far beyond the legal sphere); and to Claire Chesser at Constable who guided me through the final stages of delivering this book.

Chapter One

The story of Hakoah Vienna is well-covered in Bowman's history of the team (see Bibliography). The visit to Palestine by Hakoah is covered by Issam Khalidi in his history of football in Palestine, and his study of sports coverage in *Falastin* newspaper, 'The Coverage of Sports News in *Filastin* 1911–1948'. Issa al-Issa wrote about his relations with Sir Herbert

Samuel in his unpublished memoirs, 'Memories of the Past'. *Haaretz* journalist Arie Livnat also wrote about the story, 11 January 2011.

Chapter Two

Issam Khalidi's history of Palestinian football includes immensely valuable research into the FIFA archives. He generously shared research material, and this book would not exist without him.

The Auspicious Reordering is well covered in Roberto Mazza's book, an antidote to the 'orientalist' histories that portray the Ottoman Empire as an empire in terminal decline almost from the beginning.

Edward Said hated football, and his memoirs speak of the pain of being bad at sport with a 'jock' father.

Chapter Three

David Tidhar's monumental who's who of the Yishuv, *Encyclopedia of the Founders and Builders of Israel,* contains 6,000 entries. Tidhar probably knew each one personally. But it is his references to the small circle of friends who grew up with him in Jaffa, and laid the foundations for sport in Israel, that proved so helpful to this book. Tidhar is an exaggerator, perhaps even a liar, but he is also unbiddable: his perspective is his own. This is what makes his accounts so valuable. He was the overseer of the encyclopaedia and a contributor. The pen portraits of his childhood circle are vivid, and I have proceeded on the assumption that he wrote them. They provide an insight into the perspective of a Jaffa boy who grew up before the First World War. Almost all Israeli historians write political histories from a perspective formed from the 1920s onwards. They lose the strangeness of the Bnei Moshe era, and the perspective of Tidhar's generation: the colonialism, the religious eccentricity. David Tidhar shows the crossover between Yosef Yekutieli's Maccabi and Menachem Arber's Beitar, both of which share a common heritage in a tradition originated by a Christian: Zvi Orloff/Nishri.

Goldschmidt's school is covered in Kaufman's essay, 'Shimshon Poalei Zion'.

Chapter Four

Tidhar often uses the term 'rabbi' to apply to the elders of Bnei Moshe, such as Yehezkel Danin. There is a clear transition from a time when lay elders are the religious authority, to the employment of Rabbi Kook when the Yishuv takes on more of the trappings of the mainstream Ashkenazi Jewish faith.

The first Russian Jewish pilgrims are described by Mark Twain in 1867: '[Tiberias] is one of the four cities of the Israelites [the others being Hebron, Jerusalem and Safed] . . . and is to them what Mecca is to the Mohammedan and Jerusalem is to the Christian'. Talmudic rabbis in Tiberias were venerated like saints, and the tombs became pilgrimage sites. From Twain, we learn that Jerusalem was of far less religious interest. In the Talmudic tradition, the term 'Zion' is an analogue of heaven, a paradise located beyond time where justice prevails. What changes over the next fifty years is that Jewish nationalists adopt an evangelical Christian perspective and begin to identify the supernatural Zion with the actual city of Jerusalem. Moreover, they begin to see their newly coined Christian-inflected faith as a more original or foundational religion than that offered by the Talmudic rabbis – this perspective comes from Bnei Moshe.

The War of the Languages is threaded through David Tidhar's encyclopaedia, under the entries of individual activists.

Chapter Five

The naval conflicts of the 1914–18 war are well covered by Robert Massie's *Castles of Steel*.

Tidhar wrote about the 1915 football match in his memoirs, *In the Service of the Motherland (1912–1960)*.

The account of Armenian refugees is taken from Yair Auron's book on the Armenian genocide.

Tidhar claims responsibility for several murders. The most convincing is the killing of Governor Hasan Bey's aide Aref el-Arsan, recounted by Tidhar in 1961. The story is covered in Nachman Ben Yehuda's *Political Assassinations by Jews*.

Tidhar supplies most of the information on Yekutieli's wartime experiences.

Izzat Tannous wrote about his own experiences in his memoirs, *The Palestinians*.

Chapter Six

Ronald Storrs writes about the old school sports field in his memoirs.

The role of Cairo's Al Ahly in both the Egyptian revolution of 1919 and the Arab Spring has received a lot of attention recently, but James M. Dorsey covers it all well in his tour de force, *The Turbulent World of Middle East Soccer*.

Roberto Mazza's account of the 1920 riots in *Jerusalem: From the Ottomans to the British* rests on the contemporary accounts provided to the French and to the British inquiry. Vladimir Jabotinsky's later version, published posthumously, provided a platform for his claim to be the leader of an original Haganah (a 'Jewish Legion'), distinct from the Histadrut force. My emphasis on the role of the Maccabi boys is drawn from Tidhar, and based on the fact that young Jewish rioters were lifelong members of Orloff/Nishri's various classes and groups. Snipers at Jaffa Gate would know the spot was a potential flashpoint: the first Palestinian demonstration against the Balfour Agreement in 1918 took place there.

Yosef Yekutieli wrote a memoir focusing particularly on his life with the Maccabi in 1971. My knowledge of this book is second-hand, taken from the Israeli sports historians listed in the Bibliography. Yekutieli also wrote letters, in a variety of European languages, which are preserved in Ramat Gan and online. He also wrote a short piece on football in Palestine for the FIFA yearbook in 1931. Information on Yekutieli's early life comes from Tidhar.

Chapter Seven

The Haycraft Report into the Jaffa riots is widely available online. The use of air power as a tool of colonial policing was Winston Churchill's idea. See Omissi, *Air Power and Colonial Control*. The aim was to reduce troop numbers by using air power.

Issa al-Issa's account of his meeting with Sir Herbert Samuel is drawn from his memoirs (al-Issa's unpublished memoirs are widely quoted in monographs and articles; see Tamari, 'Issa al Issa's Unorthodox Orthodoxy'), and from Khalaf, '*Falastin* versus the British Mandate and Zionism (1921–1931)'.

Khalidi tells the story of the scouts in 'Palestine Sports and Scouts'. Any visitor to Palestine would be astonished by the role the scouts still play as the marching bands of the local social and sporting clubs.

Chapter Eight

The account of the meeting between Mond and Yekutieli is constructed from accounts in contemporary newspapers, Yekutieli's 1971 memoir and David Tidhar's biographical notes on Caspi.

Walter Rothschild's papers are held in the Library and Archives of the Natural History Museum, to which he donated his own vast collection. His best-known work, A Monograph of the Genus Casuarius, was written with W. P. Pycraft, one of the palaeoarchaeologists taken in by the Piltdown Man hoax. Among the Germans sponsored by Rothschild, Theodor Eimer is the best known: a neo-Lamarckian polemicist who is responsible for the term 'orthogenesis': the idea that evolution progresses along determined pathways so that biological creatures are authors of their destiny.

Also see Max Nordau's Degeneration. Nordau's work frequently blends racial physiognomy with a critique of culture. It is derived from the popular version of Nietzsche, a debt even more apparent in the earlier Conventional Lies of our Civilisation (1883, in English 1886) and Malady of the Century (1887).

The scandal of the Palestine Potash Company is recounted in Jacob Norris.

Chapter Nine

The quotes from Filastin appear in Khalidi's paper, 'The Coverage of Sports News in Filastin 1911–1948'.

The violence of games between the Maccabi and the British is recounted in Kaufman and Galily, 'The Early Development of Hebrew Football'. Kaufman and Galily are also a major source for the rivalry between Hapoel and Maccabi. See also Kaufman, 'Maccabi versus Hapoel'.

Chapter Ten

Khalidi provides an account of Ibrahim Nusseibeh's club in his history *One Hundred Years*, but I was also fortunate to have help from Hazem Nusseibeh, a one-time Palestine tennis champion and later a Jordanian minister, diplomat and senator.

Accounts of the first Tel Aviv derby are preserved in contemporary newspapers, and appear in Kauffman and Galily, 'Reading Sports in Palestine'. The class and ethnic conflict between the Maccabi and Hapoel is also covered in Ben Porat, *Between Class and Nation*.

Chapter Eleven

David Tidhar has enjoyed a rediscovery in recent years. See Dalia Karepl, *Haaretz*, 15 October 2016.

For an account of the Hebron riots see Benny Morris, *Righteous Victims*, and Hillel Cohen, *Year Zero of the Arab–Israeli Conflict 1929*.

Tidhar's ill-fated Egyptian tour is covered in Harif and Galily, 'Sport and Politics in Palestine, 1918–48'.

A 2001 interview with Amnon Harlap by Uri Zimri and Batya Or for the Sports and Physical Education Archive is preserved by the Wingate Institute and available online.

Another interview was conducted for *Ma'ariv* newspaper; see notes for Chapter Thirteen, below.

Chapter Twelve

Khalidi, *One Hundred Years*, is the main source for Palestinian football history.

Khalidi's account of the PSF sports festival appears in his paper 'Coverage of Sports News in *Al-Difa'* 1934–1948'. *Al-Difa'* was the newspaper for the Nashashibi party, though it later developed its own line. The *al-Difa'* campaign for sports pitches and stadiums took place in protest at the work of Yekutieli's Sports Stadium Corporation, which was building a new stadium for the Maccabiah and also building in the Galilee.

Chapter Thirteen

Amnon Harlap gave his interview to Ron Amikam, *Ma'ariv*, 17 September 2001.

The poem by Alexander Penn appeared in *Davar*. Penn was literary editor of the newspaper and wrote poems on contemporary events.

Chapter Fourteen

The story of Simcha Hinkis is covered in Hillel Cohen.

Amnon Harlap information comes from the interviews for the Wingate Institute and *Ma'ariv*.

Chapter Fifteen

The early history of Beitar is covered in Reznick, 'Betar'.

Jabotinsky's nom-de-guerre 'Ze'ev' (Wolf) derives from his 1910 essay occasioned by the lynching of African-Americans following the victory of boxer Jack Johnson over Jim Jeffries. Jabotinsky used a quote from Thomas Hobbes as the title of his essay, 'Homo Homini Lupus' (Man is a Wolf to Man). The essay argues that men are naturally chaotic violent creatures and need strong ties both to restrain and to bind them.

Jabotinsky's romantic *Samson* novel was optioned by Cecil B. DeMille for his film, *Samson and Delilah* (1949). DeMille postponed the film until after the war, by which time Jabotinsky had died. Jabotinsky continues to be lauded as a political prophet. But his voluminous writings are no longer well-known, or even in print, in English or in Hebrew (he often wrote in Russian). He was prolific, and new work continues to be discovered, yet it is impossible to construct any consistent ideology. His romantic novels were popular with Beitar members; certainly, Menachem Begin was a fan. But the ideology of revisionist activists in Palestine in the 1930s bears the far greater influence of Ahimeir, Stern, Mileikowsky, etc.

Facsimiles of *Doar Hayom*, edited by Abba Ahimeir, are available from the National Library of Israel and online. Mileikowsky (Netanyahu) also wrote and edited the Beitar newsletter.

Chapter Sixteen

The story of the PSF is recounted in Khalidi, *One Hundred Years of Football*. The letter from Nachum Chet to Colonel Kisch is also quoted here.

Morris and Hillel both write on the period of Beitar's terror campaign and Black Sunday.

The Irgun Museum booklet provides no details of the film. I took no notes at the time so I hope I recall the look of the printing press correctly. The interaction between master and apprentice is indelibly fixed in my memory.

SOURCES AND NOTES

Chapter Seventeen

Footage of the Australian tour can be seen on YouTube and accounts can be read online at the *Palestine Post*, and in 'Palestine Soccer Team', *Sydney Morning Herald* (27 June 1939), p. 15.

Chapter Eighteen

A version of the story of the Anders army and the mass defections appears in Menachem Begin's memoir, *White Nights*.

For the wartime leagues, see Kaufman, 'Shimshon Poalei Zion', also Sorek, 'The Sports Column as a Site of Palestinian Nationalism in the 1940s'.

Chapter Nineteen

Accounts of the revived Palestine Sports Federation are in Khalidi, *One Hundred Years*.

Begin gives an account of the King David hotel bombing in *The Revolt*. His argument revolves around the idea that there was time to evacuate, and that the British falsified the records by claiming there was no warning at all. The British, however, never claimed to have had no warning. The claim is that the warning was not received in time by anyone capable of acting on it. See Clarke, *By Blood and Fire* (the title is a reference to Jabotinsky's 'Beitar Anthem').

Harold Wilson's memoirs of the 1948 decision are in his book *Chariot of Israel*, itself a campily biblical name that reflects the attitude of the day.

Chapter Twenty

The story of the home of Father Salim Shaya and the way it was held to ransom is recounted by Or Kashti in *Haaretz* (26 May

2016). The account was confirmed by Rami Mansour. I asked how the affair ended and he told me, 'We paid.'

Gideon Yekutieli was outed as the father of the Israeli nuclear programme in Avner Cohen, *Israel and the Bomb*.

Chapter Twenty-One

The population of Jaffa is taken from Itamar Radai, 'Jaffa, 1948: The Fall of a City', *Journal of Israeli History*, vol. 30, no. 1 (2011).

The story of Nasser hiring a Hungarian coach for the Palestinian team is touched upon in Khalidi, *One Hundred Years*.

The Jordanian police attack on Al-Wehdat fans is discussed by Mikdadi, 'Wehdat-Faisaly Fallout', Football Palestine (13 December 2010).

Chapter Twenty-Two

The result of Ben Porat following Tayibe during their year in the top flight is his essay: 'Cui Bono: Arabs, Football and State'.

For an account of the Kafr Qasim massacre, see Robinson, 'Kafr Qasim Local Struggle, National Struggle'.

Chapter Twenty-Three

Shihade uses football to study the policing of Palestinian communities. See Shihade, *Not Just a Soccer Game*.

The abandonment of what seemed like an open-and-shut case against Reif is recounted by Baruch Kra in *Haaretz* (3 June 2002). The report of the Or Inquiry is available online.

Sakhnin's victory in the Israel Cup is recounted by Kessel and Klochendler in *Goals for Galilee*.

There were several documentaries made about Sakhnin and these were analysed in turn by Bernstein and Mandelzis, 'Bnei Sakhnin through the Documentary Looking Glass'.

For another account of Sakhnin, this time as a team that undermines Israeli identity, see Adar, 'The Complicated Symbol'.

Chapter Twenty-Four

Beitar Jerusalem attracts endless analysis. Adar, in 'For Richer for Poorer', blames Beitar's problems on disenfranchisement and poverty. There is no analysis of Beitar's longer history of racism and terrorism. These are considered in Levy and Median, 'Beitar Jerusalem'.

For the police raids against Beitar that recovered explosives and weapons, see Peter Beaumont, *Guardian* (26 July 2016).

The best insight into Beitar Jerusalem is perhaps *Forever Pure*, a film by director Maya Zinshtein (2017). The film-makers follow Gaydamak's attempt to sign Chechen Muslim players.

The Malha food-hall riot was eventually reported by Oz Rosenberg, *Haaretz* (23 March 2012). See also Eeta Prince-Gibson, *Jewish Telegraphic Agency* (9 April 2012).

An account of the violence at the first Beitar vs Sakhnin match of the season was written by Ran Shimoni, 'When an Arab Fan is Beaten by Israelis Under Beitar Jerusalem's Nose', *Haaretz* (27 September 2018).

An account of Miri Regev's video was written by Michael Schaeffer Omer-Man, +972 *Magazine* (23 January 2018).

Chapter Twenty-Five

Maccabi Jaffa went bankrupt, and the team merged with several other teams. Jaffa Orthodox is in a direct lineage with Maccabi

Jaffa, as a result of these mergers. A new Maccabi Jaffa has been revived recently but it plays in Tel Aviv, not Jaffa.

The charges against Arnon Giladi were reported by Eli Senyor, *YnetNews* (2 February 2018).

The unveiling of the embassy plaque by two US preachers was covered by David Smith, *Guardian* (15 May 2018).

The Gaza protest fatalities on the day of the Jerusalem plaque unveiling numbered fifty-two, see *Guardian* (22 May 2018). This is an ongoing crisis as I write in February 2019 but the figures just to 13 August 2018 are staggering: 155 dead, 17,259 injured, including 4,348 struck by live fire, 68 amputations, 5,000 dunams of farmland destroyed by firebombing.

Chapter Twenty-Six

The treatment of Rajoub in Israel is complicated. See Yair Galily, 'From Terror to Public Diplomacy'. Although Israel signed up to FIFA, a rules-based association, any political moves taken against the Israel FA are routinely described as new forms of warfare ('political war') or terrorism ('political terror'). See also, Ber, Yarch and Galily, 'The Sporting Arena as a Public Diplomacy Battlefield'. Prejudices and ambivalences towards football, Arabs and Palestinian politicians are heightened because of FIFA's wealth and undoubted corruption.

The destruction of Gaza's stadiums is covered in an uncredited article for CNN (7 December 2012). Also Scott McIntyre, 'Remembering the Dead', SBS Australia (26 September 2014).

Chapter Twenty-Seven

The saga of Baldivieso was covered in almost identical ways by both the Israeli BabaGol website and Football Palestine websites. See Uri Levy, 'A Palestinian Turmoil', BabaGol (8 April 2018).

Bassil Mikdadi, 'Baldivieso Crumbled Under Pressure', Football Palestine (27 April 2018).

For the drawn-out campaign by Rajoub against Israel, see Keir Radnedge, 'Demand for Israel to be Expelled is Back on the Agenda', World Soccer (17 January 2017).

Chapter Twenty-Eight

After the Oslo Accords, many sports programmes, such as the Peres Center for Peace, sprang up to support peace initiatives. The backing of FIFA means there is money to run programmes and research their effects. See Litvak-Hirsch, Galily and Leitner, 'Evaluating Conflict Mitigation and Health Improvement through Soccer'.

Amir Ben-Porat originated football studies in Israel. His research underpins much of my work, but the conversation reported here was in a café in a north Tel Aviv mall.

The role of pharmacy degrees has been extensively covered in the press and academic papers. The Israeli sketch comedy show, *Eretz Nehederet*, made a Palestinian pharmacist, Salma, a regular returning character. Of course, she was played by a Jewish woman, Liat Har Lev, in an example of race-based caricatures and appropriation that few Israelis seem to register as offensive.

The decline in the numbers of Palestinian players for Maccabi Tel Aviv since the Goldhar/Cruyff takeover has been highlighted by Rami Younis, +972 *Magazine* (27 April 2016).

Selected Bibliography

Adar, Shaul, 'The Complicated Symbol', *Blizzard*, no. 17 (2015).

——, 'For Richer for Poorer: How Nationalism Has Shaped the Rise and Fall of Beitar Jerusalem', *Blizzard*, no. 3 (2011).

Auron, Yair, *The Banality of Indifference: Zionism and the Armenian Genocide* (New Jersey: Transaction, 2000).

Begin, Menachem, *The Revolt: Inside Story of the Irgun* (London: Allen, 1951).

——, *White Nights: The Story of a Prisoner in Russia* (New York: Crime Club Doubleday, 1977).

Ben Israel, Talia, 'The Integration of Physical Education into the Curriculum of Israel's Pre-State Education System', in Amir Ben Porat and Yair Galily (eds), *Sport, Politics and Society in the Land of Israel* (London: Routledge, 2009).

Ben Porat, Amir, *Between Class and Nation: The Formation of the Jewish Working Class in the Period between Israel's Statehood* (Connecticut: Praeger, 1986).

——, 'Cui Bono? Arabs, Football and State', *Soccer & Society*, vol. 17, no. 4 (2016).

——, 'From Community to Commodity: The Commodification of Football in Israel', *Soccer & Society*, vol. 13, no. 3 (2012).

——, 'The Usual Suspect: A History of Football Violence in the State of Israel', *Sport in History*, vol. 36, no. 1 (2016).

——, 'Who Are We? My Club? My People? My State? The Dilemma of the Arab Soccer Fan in Israel', *International Review for the Sociology of Sport*, vol. 49, no. 2 (2012).

Ben Yehuda, Nachman, *Political Assassinations by Jews: A Rhetorical Device for Justice* (New York: New York Press, 1992).

Ber, Reut, Moran Yarch and Yair Galily, 'The Sporting Arena as a Public Diplomacy Battlefield: The Palestinian Attempt to Suspend Israel from FIFA', *Journal of Communication*, vol. 23, no. 2 (2017).

Bernstein, Alina and Lea Mandelzis, 'Bnei Sakhnin through the Documentary Looking Glass: Telling the Story of Arab Football in a Jewish State', *Sport in Society*, vol. 12, no. 8 (2009).

Bowman, William D., 'Hakoah Vienna and the International Nature of Interwar Austrian Sports', *Central European History*, no. 44 (2011).

Cohen, Avner, *Israel and the Bomb* (New York: Columbia University Press, 1998).

Cohen, Hillel, *Year Zero of the Arab–Israeli Conflict 1929* (Waltham: Brandeis University, 2015).

Clarke, Thurston, *By Blood and Fire: The Attack on the King David Hotel* (New York: Putnam, 1981).

Dorsey, James M., 'Asian Football: A Cesspool of Government Interference, Struggles for Power, Corruption and Greed', *International Journal of the History of Sport*, vol. 32, no. 8 (2015).

——, 'Gulf Autocrats and Sports Corruption: A Marriage Made in Heaven', *Sport in Society*, vol. 21, no. 5 (2018).

——, *The Turbulent World of Middle East Soccer* (London: Hurst, 2016).

Galily, Yair, 'From Terror to Public Diplomacy: Jibril Rajoub and the Palestinian Authorities Uses of Sport in Fragmentary Israeli–Palestinian Conflict', *Middle Eastern Studies*, no. 54 (2018).

——, 'Sport, Politics and Society in Israel: The First Fifty-five Years', in Amir Ben Porat and Yair Galily (eds), *Sport, Politics and Society in the Land of Israel* (London: Routledge, 2009).

Harif, Haggai, 'Israeli Sport in the Transition from a Mandatory Community to a Sovereign State: Trends of Continuity and Change', in Amir Ben Porat and Yair Galily (eds), *Sport, Politics and Society in the Land of Israel* (London: Routledge, 2009).

Harif, Haggai and Yair Galily, 'Sport and Politics in Palestine, 1918–48: Football as a Mirror Reflecting the Relations between Jews and Britons, *Soccer & Society*, vol. 4, no. 1 (2003).

Hughes, Matthew, 'Terror in the Galilee: British–Jewish Collaboration and the Special Night Squads in Palestine during the Arab Revolt 1938–39', *Journal of Imperial and Commonwealth History*, vol. 43, no. 4 (2015).

Jabotinsky, Vladimir, 'Homo Homini Lupus' (1910), trans. Yisrael Medad (Tel Aviv: The Jabotinsky Institute), available online at http://en.jabotinsky.org.

——, *The Iron Wall* (1923), available online at http://en.jabotinsky.org.

——, *Samson: The Nazarite* (London: M. Secker, 1930).

Kaufman, Haim, 'Maccabi versus Hapoel: The Political Divide that Developed in Sports in Eretz Israel, 1926–1935', in Amir Ben Porat and Yair Galily (eds), *Sport, Politics and Society in the Land of Israel* (London: Routledge, 2009).

——, 'Shimshon Poalei Zion: The Unseen Sports Association', written for the Wingate Institute, published online by Mako.co.il (September 2009).

Kaufman, Haim and Yair Galily, 'The Early Development of Hebrew Football in Eretz Israel, 1910–1928, *Soccer & Society*, vol. 9, no. 1 (2008).

——, 'Reading Sports in Palestine: The Early Days of Sport Reports in the Hebrew Mandatory Press', in Amir Ben Porat and Yair Galily (eds), *Sport, Politics and Society in the Land of Israel* (London: Routledge, 2009).

Kessel, Jerrold and Pierre Klochendler, *Goals for Galilee: The Triumphs and Traumas of the Sons of Sakhnin, Israel's Arab Football Club* (London: JR Books, 2010).

Khalaf, Noha Tadris, '*Falastin* versus the British Mandate and Zionism (1921–1931): Between a Rock and a Hard Place, *Journal of Palestine Studies*, no. 45 (2011).

Khalidi, Issam, 'Coverage of Arab Sports in *Palestine Bulletin* and *Palestine Post* 1925–1948' (History of Palestine Sport, 2017), online at http://www.hpalestinesports.net.

——, 'Coverage of Sports News in *Al-Difa*' 1934–1948' (History of Palestine Sport, 2016), online at http://www.hpalestinesports.net.

——, 'Coverage of Sports News in *Filastin*', in Alon K. Raab and Issam Khalidi (eds), *Soccer in the Middle East* (London: Routledge, 2013).

——, *One Hundred Years of Football in Palestine* (Amman: Dar al Shouk, 2013).

——, 'Palestine Sports and Scouts: Factional Politics and the Maccabiad in the 1930s', *Jerusalem Quarterly*, no. 63 (2015).

Khalidi, Issam and Alon. K. Raab, 'Palestine and the Olympics', *International Journal of the History of Sport*, vol. 34, no. 13 (2017).

Kremnitzer, Mordechai and Amir Fuchs, *Ze'ev Jabotinsky on Democracy, Equality and Individual Rights* (Tel Aviv: Israel Democracy Institute, 2013).

Levy, Uri and Yossi Median, 'Beitar Jerusalem: The History Behind the Chechen Affair', *Futbolgrad* (25 February 2016).

Litvak-Hirsch, Tal, Yair Galily and Michael Leitner, 'Evaluating Conflict Mitigation and Health Improvement through Soccer: A Two Year Study of Mifalot's "United Soccer for Peace" Program', *Soccer & Society*, vol. 17, no. 2 (2016).

McCarthy, Justin, *The Population of Palestine: Population Statistics of the Late Ottoman Period and the Mandate* (New York: Columbia University Press. 1990).

Massie, Robert, *Castles of Steel: Germany and the Winning of the Great War at Sea* (London: Vintage, 2007)

Mazza, Roberto, *Jerusalem: From the Ottomans to the British* (London: I. B. Tauris, 2009).

Montague, James, *When Friday Comes: Football in the War Zone* (London: Mainstream, 2008).

Morris, Benny, *Righteous Victims: A History of the Zionist–Arab Conflict, 1881–1998* (New York: Knopf, 1999).

Nordau, Max, *Degeneration* (London: Heinemann, 1895).

Norris, Jacob, *Land of Progress: Palestine in the Age of Colonial Development 1905–1948* (Oxford: Oxford University Press, 2013).

Omissi, David E., *Air Power and Colonial Control: The Royal Air Force, 1919–1939* (Manchester: Manchester University Press, 1990).

Raab, Alon K., 'The Universe is Shaped Like a Football: Football and Revolution', *International Journal of the History of Sport*, vol. 31, no. 7 (2014).

Reznick, Shlomo, 'Betar: Sport and Politics in a Segmented Society', in Amir Ben Porat and Yair Galily (eds), *Sport, Politics and Society in the Land of Israel* (London: Routledge, 2009).

Robinson, Shira, 'Kafr Qasim Local Struggle, National Struggle: Palestinian Responses to the Kafr Qasim Massacre and Its Aftermath, 1956–66', *International Journal of Middle East Studies*, vol. 35, no. 3 (2003).

Said, Edward, *Out of Place: A Memoir* (London: Granta, 2000).

Shihade, Magid, *Not Just a Soccer Game: Colonialism and Conflict among Palestinians in Israel* (New York: Syracuse University Press, 2011).

Sorek, Tamir, *Arab Soccer in a Jewish State: The Integrative Enclave* (Cambridge: Cambridge University Press, 2010).

——, 'The Sports Column as a Site of Palestinian Nationalism in the 1940s', in Amir Ben Porat and Yair Galily (eds), *Sport, Politics and Society in the Land of Israel* (London: Routledge, 2009).

Storrs, Ronald, *The Memoirs of Sir Ronald Storrs* (New York: G. P. Putnam's Sons, 1937).

Sugden, John and Alan Tomlinson, *Football, Corruption and Lies* (London: Routledge, 2016).

Tamir, Ilan and Alina Bernstein, 'Do They Even Know the National Anthem? Minorities in Service of the Flag – Israeli Arabs in the National Football Team', *Soccer & Society*, vol. 15, nos 5–6 (2015).

Tamir, Ilan and Yair Gailily, 'When the Private Sphere Hides from the Public Sphere: The Power Struggle Between Israeli National Identity and Football Fandom', *International Review for the Sociology of Sport*, vol. 52, no. 2 (2017).

Tamari, Salim, 'Issa al Issa's Unorthodox Orthodoxy: Banned in Jerusalem, Permitted in Jaffa', *Jerusalem Quarterly*, no. 59 (2014).

Tannous, Izzat, *The Palestinians: Eyewitness History of Palestine under British Mandate: The Origins of the Palestinian–Israeli Conflict* (New York: IGT Company, 1988).

Tidhar, David, *Encyclopedia of the Founders and Builders of Israel* (Touro College Library: New York, 2019), http://www.tidhar.tourolib.org.

——, *In the Service of the Motherland (1912–1960): Memories, Images, Certificates and Photographs* (Tel Aviv: Yedidim, 1961, in Hebrew).

Twain, Mark, *The Innocents Abroad* (London: Collins, 1954).

Wilson, Harold, *The Chariot of Israel: Britain, America and the State of Israel* (New York: Norton, 1982).

Zinshtein, Maya, *Forever Pure* (film, 2017).

Index

Judea 58, 202

KAA (Belgian team) 118
Kafr Qasim FC 175, 188, 189
Kahane Chai (Jewish terrorist organisation) 210
Kalalian, Koko 174, 185, 207, 245, 249
Kanafani family 180–1
Keenan, Tamar 86–7, 208, 216
Kemal, Mustafa (Atatürk) 53–4
Kenya 164
Kfar Eldad, Bethlehem 160
Khalidi, Issam 23, 138
King David Hotel, Jerusalem 139, 165–6
Kiryat Shmona FC 248
Kisch, Colonel Frederick 81, 98, 102, 111, 138, 139, 153
Kishinev, Moldova 33
Koban Club 182
Kohen, Edna 39, 40
Konya 68
Kook, Rabbi Avraham 32, 44–6, 104, 132, 151
Krakow 77
Ku Klux Klan 142, 146
Kuwait 234

La Familia 201–2, 206, 209–11, 213, 214, 216
Labour government (British) 167
Labour government (Israeli) 194
Labour Party (British) 167–8
Labour Party (Israeli) 13, 60
Lahav 433 case 209
Lahman, Eyal 196, 197
Land Day 192, 215
'Land of Israel' (Biblical concept) 35
'Land of Israel' FC 93, 106–7
Latrun 164
Latvia 102–3
Lazio 130
Lazio's naval academy, Italy 103
Lebanese Football Association 137, 163
Lebanon 27, 42, 110, 136, 137, 163, 179, 183
Lebanon Football Association 117
Lehava party 210
Leila 191, 221–2
Levant 52
Levente clubs 60
Liberal Party 72
Libya 28
Liga Alef 174
Likud party 13, 203, 204, 205, 206, 209
Lima, Gabriel 196, 197
Lloyd George, David 72
Łódź 78

Luxembourg 167
Lwów (Lviv) 77
Lydda 81
Lydda (Lod) FC 82, 244

Ma'al Adumim 200
Maccabi Avshalom Petah Tikvah 118
Maccabi Haifa 94, 112, 156, 157, 158
Maccabi Hasmonean Jerusalem 119
Maccabi Herzliya 197
Maccabi Jaffa 207
Maccabi Jerusalem 48, 112, 136
Maccabi library, Ramat Gan 101
Maccabi Nes Tziona 81, 112
Maccabi Netanya 211
Maccabi Nordia junior FC 78, 85
Maccabi organisation 4, 5, 38, 43, 48, 66–7, 72, 74, 76–8, 81–2, 88, 89, 92–4, 95–6, 100, 103, 106–8, 112, 116, 117–18, 119–21, 123–4, 126, 135, 139, 148–50, 153–4, 186, 193, 202
Maccabi Petah Tikvah FC (later Avshalom Petah Tikvah) 67, 112, 125, 245, 249
 see also Avshalom Petah Tikvah
Maccabi Petah Tikvah sports club 48, 66, 67
Maccabi Rishon LeZion 48, 67, 155
Maccabi stadium 125
Maccabi Tel Aviv FC 4–8, 10, 11–13, 15, 48, 53, 56, 60–2, 64, 81, 83, 84, 94, 95, 112, 116, 118–19, 126, 128, 135, 136, 148–50, 156–8, 172, 205, 245–50
Maccabi Union 48, 70
Maccabi World Congress 84, 84–5
Maccabi World Union 74, 124
Maccabi youth team 80
Maccabiah Games 115–16, 121, 124, 176
Magen Shimson tournament 81, 98
Malha 205, 211
Manchester City 17, 18, 19
Mansour, David 171, 173–4, 176, 185, 187, 190, 245, 249
Mansour, Rami 171, 172, 173–5, 185, 190, 245–6, 249
Mansour family 176
Mapai party 77, 167–8, 203
Markaz Balata (Balata Youth Club) 224
Markaz Tulkarem 224
Martial Law 186–7
May Day riots 1921 65–6, 72
Mecca 179
Megiddo, battle of 57
Melbourne 150
Melchett Cup 153
Meretz 208